LONDON BUS HANDB

Nicholas King

Capital Transport

Nineteenth edition 1998
ISBN 185414 199 6

Published by
Capital Transport Publishing, Harrow Weald

Printed by
CS Graphics, Singapore

Contents

Introduction and Review of 1997

This book gives details at December 1997 of the bus fleets of operators who hold LT contract services. It covers the former LBL fleets, other operators who provide contracted services for London Transport, and the major sight-seeing fleets.

Developments during 1997 have included the introduction of low-floor Dennis Darts in many of the fleets as routes are upgraded. In some cases these new vehicles have replaced older double-deckers, and in others they have enabled the withdrawal of minibuses and midibuses. Orders have been placed for 100 low-floor double-deckers to be delivered to MTL London and Stagecoach East London from 1999, accompanied by the appearance of prototype vehicles at the Coach and Bus Show in October 1997. LT has also released outline details of its 'concept decker', a low-floor double-deck design incorporating features which it hopes may be adopted for future build for London.

Meanwhile, orthodox new double-deckers have also appeared in several fleets, chiefly Volvo Olympians but also including Dennis Arrows and DAFs. Within these arrivals, the new 'Pyoneer' design of East Lancs has made its début. A number of Optare Excel single-deckers have also entered service. During the year, the Dennis Dart (in both standard and low-floor forms) has become the most prolific vehicle in the London fleets, overtaking the MCW Metrobus which had previously held this distinction. Other new types to appear in London have been the Mercedes-Benz Vario and the Beaver 2 body design from Plaxton.

The process of fleet modernisation has led to an increasing trickle of MCW Metrobuses and Leyland Titans leaving the former LBL fleets. Notable amongst these is the cascading of Titans from Stagecoach East London and Selkent to provincial members of the group. Earlier Dennis Darts have started to leave some of the fleets, alongside MCW Metroriders and Optare StarRiders, both of which types have become somewhat rarer during the year. By contrast, the remaining Routemasters have survived virtually unscathed, and indeed London Central have commenced a programme to fit 38 of their RMs with Scania engines – a remarkable process for vehicles which are nearer forty than thirty years old, and still substantially in original condition. Only the impending conversion of route 139 to low-floor single-deckers, scheduled for February 1998, shows any instance whereby standard Routemasters will be taken out of service, in this case from MTL London.

On the debit side, full-size single-deckers seem to have fallen out of favour; London General sold their thirteen Volvo B10Bs to City of Oxford during the spring, whereby the 'Clapham Omnibus' marketing identity of route 88 disappeared, and Metroline have delicensed their complete fleet of 31 Dennis Lances.

Several operators have joined a programme funded by LT to expand the use of low emission fuels in London. To promote this use of green energy, a number of Routemasters have received appropriate super-rear advertisements. Super-rear advertisements have also proliferated as a means of major advertising which does not infringe LT's requirement that vehicles on routes in the central area must carry a livery of at least 80% red. Most of these displays incorporate contravision treatment of the window areas.

A notable new arrival on the scene of LT routes has been Harris Bus, who have taken over routes 108, 128, 129 and 150. For these routes, a striking new livery of blue and green has been introduced. Capital Citybus have expanded their portfolio with the acquisition of routes 91 and N91 from MTL London. One vehicle introduced on these routes incorporated full rear destination displays, the first time that this feature has been seen on rear-engined vehicles in London. Armchair gained a significant stake in the Ealing area with contract gains in May. Epsom Buses gained routes 413 and S1 from London General during the autumn of 1997 as a result of continued staff shortages with the incumbent operator. Limebourne have taken over routes 42, 156 and C3. Nostalgiabus have gained contracts for school journeys on 127, 156 and 613 and started new commercial route 306 over part of the 406. Maidstone & District took over most weekday workings on the 402 from Kentish Bus in June 1997.

The CentreWest group was sold to FirstBus in March 1997, and their logo now appears on vehicles. In November 1997 a change of name to FirstGroup was announced. Metroline Holdings was floated on the Stock Exchange in June 1997. The London United group was purchased by Transdev in July 1997. Most of the Docklands Transit operation was sold to Stagecoach Holdings on 22nd July 1997, coming under the control of Stagecoach East London until fully-absorbed on 11th October 1997, by which time new Dennis Darts had arrived to oust older minibuses.

The Cowie Group have rationalised many of their operations between constituent operators, including a substantial reduction in Londonlinks and steps towards the transfer of Kentish Bus work in Central London to other members of the group. Part of this process has involved exchanges of routes with Stagecoach Selkent. Further such exchanges will affect Leaside, Grey-Green and County in the coming months. On 6th November 1997 Cowie Group shareholders approved a change of title to Arriva Passenger Services.

There has been some rationalisation of work between CentreWest and London Buslines, leading to the departure of double-deckers from the latter fleet. CentreWest have also started to withdraw many of their Mercedes-Benz (MA class) and Renault midibuses, cascading them to other FirstBus operators, and this process is expected to gain momentum with the arrival of further Darts, including 41 to be bodied by Marshalls of Cambridge.

In October 1997 the private hire fleet of Leaside was transferred to County at their new Edmonton base.

London Transport Buses has disposed of the reserve fleet of 30 RMs. Some went to former LBL subsidiaries, either for further service or for spares, but most were sold to dealers. Three RMLs were retrieved from Sovereign following reductions in route 13, and have been reassigned to MTL London. LTB own a low-floor Dennis Dart (DLP1) which is on extended evaluation by CentreWest, and a low-floor Volvo (VWL1) which is in use by London General. LTB also own 43 RMLs leased to London Sovereign and South London.

In the London United group, Westlink have purchased 21 new Volvo Olympians for route 57, and six Optare Excels for an increased requirement on route 371. These represent a significant upgrading of what has until now been essentially a low-cost operation.

Metrobus, in addition to gaining route 64, acquired the business of East Surrey; this has continued as a separate subsidiary, and is not therefore included in this book. Metrobus South Coast was also established in East Sussex following the collapse of Leisurelink, Newhaven.

Following a review of operations, MTL London closed down their SightseerS operation in August 1997, disposing of most of the coaches which had been acquired from R&I Tours in October 1995 and absorbed into the main fleet in June 1996. MTL London and Cowie also co-operated in a rationalisation of services along the corridor between Enfield and Waltham Cross in April 1997, involving revisions to their LT and commercial routes.

Above right: Route branding of the 140 was one of the first London United developments following the company's purchase by Transdev. *Capital Transport*

Right: The Dennis Dart continues to be a popular choice in London. This one, ordered by Docklands Transit, is a recent delivery to Stagecoach East London. *Colin Lloyd*

South London discarded the distinctive livery for buses on route 159; the relevant Routemasters now carry normal red livery, though with yellow relief. Yellow relief was also extended to Leaside buses on route 38, coupled with marketing logos introduced when the contract was regained during the summer of 1997. South London have also gained route TL1, which replaces the Connex South Central rail service from West Croydon to Wimbledon while this is incorporated within the new Croydon Tramlink system.

In addition to taking over Docklands Transit, Stagecoach East London gained the London City Airport service from D&J when the latter ceased operation on 1st April 1997. Several Mobility Bus routes have changed hands. Beneficiaries have been Crystals and Thorpe's, the latter leading to the departure of Javelin Coaches from the LT contract list.

Within the sightseeing fleets, Big Bus have continued to add pre-used Fleetlines to stock. London Pride have continued to favour MCW Metrobuses and Metroliners, as well as gaining some redundant Leyland Titans, and have ordered ten liquid petroleum gas engines for fitting into Metroliners. They also introduced all-night sightseeing services in July and August 1997. London Coaches acquired the sightseeing work of Blue Triangle in March 1997, and have since discarded some of their Routemasters, although the ERM class of extended vehicles survives intact for the moment.

LT contract awards for 1998 include routes 211 and C1 to Travel West Midlands, who will trade as Travel London from June 1998; Optare Solo low-floor midibuses will be introduced on the C1. The negotiated net cost arrangements that have applied to previously untendered 'red bus' routes since 1993 will, by 2001, all be placed on a formally-tendered basis. From April 1997, most contracts have been issued on a Tendered Net Cost basis, under which the operator retains any revenue in excess of the price agreed with LT for the contract. Other ex-LBL routes meanwhile operate on a Tendered Gross Cost basis, where LT retain the revenue and the contract price is intended to cover the operator's costs.

The author gratefully acknowledges the assistance of many of the operators included in this book. Particular help has been given by Colin Lloyd, David Stewart, and officers of LOTS and the PSV Circle.

December 1997   NICHOLAS KING

Above right: Epsom Buses entered London Transport work during 1997, being responsible for three contracted routes at the end of the year. This new Mercedes minibus is seen at Sutton. *D. Heath*

Right: From February 1998 the SR class, an important part of the minibus boom of the mid-eighties, is expected to have been reduced in normal service to routes P5, P12, P13 and P14. The new London Central livery is carried by SR52. *Malc McDonald*

ARMCHAIR

Armchair Passenger Transport Co Ltd, Armchair House, Commerce Way, Brentford, TW8 8LZ

Armchair Passenger Transport gained LT tendered routes 260 from June 1990 and 65 from January 1991. These followed their original foray into bus operation with other routes which have since ceased. The company was also successful in gaining tendered work from both Royal Berkshire and Surrey County Councils.

Further LT routes to be won were the 117 from August 1996 and 190 from December 1996, both of which required the purchase of new buses. These took the form of new Dennis Darts with Plaxton bodywork, which carry a revised livery with white roof and black window surround and skirts. Routes E2 and E8 were gained from May 1997 and required a further 25 Dennis Dart SLFs with Plaxton Pointer bodywork. New Volvo Olympians are on order for 1998 to replace older double-deck stock. Route 237 has now also been awarded, though the 260 has been lost.

Current LT routes operated are 65, 177, 190, 260, 371 (school trips), E2, E8. H16 is also operated commercially. The fleet carries orange and white livery, and is housed at Commerce Way, Brentford.

Below: On 24th May 1997 the contract for route E2 (Brentford to Greenford) passed from CentreWest to Armchair, who introduced new 10metre low-floor Dennis Darts with Plaxton Pointer bodywork. P682RWU was photographed in Ruislip Road East later that month. *Colin Brown*

Right: Armchair's contract for route 65 was renewed from 28th June 1997. Leyland Olympian H559GKX, one of seventeen vehicles dating from 1991 with Leyland bodywork, had just arrived from the south at Cromwell Road, Kingston in August 1997. *Colin Brown*

BIG BUS

The Big Bus Company, Waterside Way, London SW17 7AB

Big Bus was the trading name adopted by Maybury's of London in June 1991 for their sightseeing tours. Operations expanded rapidly, and in April 1996 the present limited company was formed. A mixed fleet of vehicles has been operated, including a number of interesting front-engined buses, although the bulk of the present fleet is made up of ex-London Fleetlines.

The fleet is painted maroon and cream and is housed at Waterside Way.

When new in 1977, OJD247R was the first of the final order for 400 Leyland Fleetlines placed by London Transport. Twenty years later, it is in the fleet of Big Bus, with whom it is seen crossing the southern side of Trafalgar Square. Bodywork is by MCW. *Stephen Madden*

A number of Fleetlines in the Big Bus fleet show the now-fashionable half-roofing of the upper deck, which offers some protection during inclement weather. OJD390R passes along Whitehall during May 1997. *Stephen Madden*

A few of the front-entrance Routemasters supplied new to Northern General in the mid-1960s have made their way to London in later life. FPT588C joined Big Bus in 1992 after a period of use by Blue Triangle, Rainham. *Stephen Madden*

CAPITAL CITYBUS

Capital Citybus Ltd, Chequers Lane, Dagenham, Essex, RM9 6QD

Ensignbus gained LT route 145 (Dagenham to Redbridge Station) from 21st June 1986. This was to be the start of a major operation of tendered bus services. Frontrunner Buses (South East), a division of the privatised East Midland Motor Services, began LT route 248 (Cranham to Romford) from 24th September 1988. Many more routes were acquired by both companies until on 30th June 1989 Frontrunner's operations were purchased by Ensignbus from Stagecoach, who had taken over the East Midland group. The Ensignbus business, including the Dagenham depot, was then sold to the CNT group of Hong Kong on 29th December 1990. A new yellow livery was introduced, featuring Chinese characters in the fleetname. As a result of gaining further LT contracts, a new depot was opened at Northumberland Park in Tottenham. The company remained under CNT control for five years until it was bought by a management-led team on 21st December 1995. A revised fleetname started appearing on vehicles following the breaking of ties with its former owner. As well as the large number of LT contract services, the company also runs routes for Essex and Hertfordshire County Councils and commercial routes in the Thurrock area of Essex. LT routes currently operated are 67, 91, 97, 97A, 123, 153, 158, 165, 179, 212, 215, 236, 248, 252, 257, 296, 299, 318, 365, 369, 396, 511, 616, 645, 646, 650, 651, 670, 678, D5, D6, W6, W10, ELX, N91 and school journeys on routes 20 and 307. Other routes operated are 89, 173 (Essex County Council) and commercial routes 323, 324, 348, 349, 510, 512, 648.

Most of the fleet carries a livery of yellow with red relief, though some now have 80% red livery with yellow relief, and is based in depots in Dagenham (Chequers Lane), Northumberland Park (Marsh Lane) and Hackney (Waterden Road).

Below: Capital Citybus invested in four Optare Excel 35-seaters in 1996 for the 396 route between Illford and King George Hospital. These vehicles are represented in this view by No.702, at Gants Hill. *Gerald Mead*

Right: The newest double-deckers for Capital Citybus are Dennis Arrows carrying dual-door Pyoneer bodywork by East Lancs, delivered in the summer of 1997. *Colin Brown*

Facing page: As new vehicles continue to enter the Capital Citybus fleet, so the proportion of second-hand vehicles diminishes. No.112 is an MCW Metrobus of 1980 acquired from Derby, and was found on school route 645 at Woodford Wells in September 1997. Many schools services have been renumbered into this series, once the prerogative of trolleybus routes, as the opportunity has arisen. *Mike Harris*

In 1992/3, Capital Citybus received ten Olympians with Northern Counties bodywork, all of which were registered with 888 numbers reflecting the initials of the directors at that time. No.162 has one of the last Leyland-produced chassis, and bodywork of the original Palatine style. *Tony Wilson*

The last of the ten new Olympians of 1992/3, No.168, photographed at Ilford High Road, has a Volvo chassis and Northern Counties Palatine 2 bodywork. *Russell Upcraft*

Left: Despite its popularity elsewhere in London, the Dennis Dart is represented at present by just two vehicles with Capital Citybus. No.669, with Wadham Stringer bodywork of Portsdown style, arrived in 1995 following four years' service with a Kentish operator. This view shows it at Romford Market in July 1997. *Colin Brown*

Below: Capital Citybus acquired three Volvo B6 machines of 1994 from Flightparks, Gatwick in 1996. The Northern Counties Paladin bodywork seats the surprisingly low number of 31 passengers, because of the large luggage rack which can be seen on the off-side. No.684 makes its way along Cranbrook Road, Ilford. *Mike Harris*

Right: In 1996, seven Dennis Dominators with East Lancs bodywork were acquired from Leicester, where they had been rather prematurely withdrawn after only seven years' service. The single-piece front blind of No.342 contributes to a somewhat angular appearance at Western Road, Romford in May 1996. *Mike Harris*

Left: A batch of 23 all-Leyland Olympians was delivered in 1991, many of them taking over routes which had been forfeited by London Forest. No.136 stands at Woodford Wells on its way to Walthamstow in September 1997. Capital Citybus only operate school trips on route 20, the main service being in the hands of Grey-Green. *Mike Harris*

Right: Several vehicles were painted in East London Line livery for Underground service between Aldgate and New Cross. No.404, a Dennis Arrow with Northern Counties Palatine 2 bodywork new in 1996, was standing at Mansell Street in May 1997. *Mike Harris*

Left: The winning of the contract for route 91 from January 1997 imposed a requirement for vehicles in 80% red livery. Despite this, No.236, a Volvo Olympian with Alexander (Belfast) bodywork, manages to retain much of its Capital Citybus individuality at Kings Cross in May 1997. *Mike Harris*

Above: Some of the older vehicles in the fleet have since started to receive red-based livery to improve flexibility of allocation. Dennis Dominator 274, with Northern Counties Palatine bodywork, was the last of a batch of 24 vehicles delivered in 1990/1, and was caught at Euston Bus Station in March 1997. *Mike Harris*

CAPITAL LOGISTICS

Capital Logistics Ltd, Heathrow Coach Centre, Sipson Road, West Drayton, UB7 0HN

Capital Logistics operate a large fleet of coaches on external and internal contract services at both Heathrow and Gatwick Airports, with a few Dennis Darts employed on airport car park duties. The fleetname was altered from Capital Coaches in October 1997 following the purchase of Whyte's Coaches.

The firm entered tendered bus work in August 1993 with the acquisition of LT route H26, initially using four Mercedes-Benz minibuses. Later in 1993, these were superseded by new wheelchair-accessible Mercedes-Benz minibuses with Plaxton Beaver bodies. In November 1996, the company was successful in retaining the route upon re-tendering. Route U3 will be taken up early in 1998.

Fleet livery is white and yellow, and vehicles are kept at Sipson Road and at Eastern Perimeter Road, Heathrow.

Capital Coaches retained the contract for wheelchair-accessible route H26 in November 1996. Five Mercedes-Benz vehicles with Plaxton Beaver 18-seat body-work provide the backbone of the service, as demonstrated by L206ULX at Hatton Cross Station in August 1997. *Stephen Madden*

CENTREWEST

CentreWest London Buses Ltd, Macmillan House, Paddington Station, London W2 1TY

CentreWest was purchased from London Buses by a management-led team on 2nd September 1994, taking 507 vehicles. Apart from 30 full-size vehicles, all of the single-deckers were midibuses, CentreWest having made the greatest strides of the LBL subsidiaries in converting routes to this format.

In December 1995 CentreWest took over a number of LT contract routes in the Orpington area, re-opening the former Kentish Bus depot at Swanley for the purpose before occupying a new site at St Mary Cray in March 1996. In March 1996, the holding company of CentreWest also purchased the Bee Line and London Buslines companies, and some interchange of vehicles has since taken place between the fleets, particularly to improve the age profile of the acquired operations. On 26th March 1997 the CentreWest group was sold to FirstBus (renamed to FirstGroup in November 1997), whose logo is now appearing on vehicles.

The fleet operates from garages at Acton Tram Depot, Alperton, Greenford, Orpington, Uxbridge and Westbourne Park. Driver-training vehicles are allocated to various garages as required. Traditional London livery of red with white relief and grey skirt is still carried by the majority of the fleet, although many are receiving yellow relief and losing the grey skirt. Gold fleetnames cover local marketing names which include Gold Arrow, Orpington Buses, Ealing Buses, Uxbridge Buses and Challenger.

For route 222, CentreWest received fourteen of the low-floor Dennis Lances with Wright bodywork which were purchased by London Buses in 1993/4. LLW13, with Uxbridge Buses branding, cuts a fine figure in the latest version of livery at Bath Road, Hounslow in August 1997. *Colin Brown*

Left: To resource re-awarded contracts in the Ealing area from May 1997, CentreWest purchased 41 10metre low-floor Dennis Darts with Marshall Capital bodywork. DM123 stands at West Ealing in July 1997. Like many vehicles in the fleet, it shows CentreWest's ISO9001 quality accreditation, as seen just behind the front wheelarch. *Colin Brown*

Above: In September 1997 all but one of London Buslines' remaining double-deckers moved to CentreWest. LA24, a Leyland Olympian of 1993 with Alexander bodywork, had been freshly-repainted when encountered at Golders Green mid-month. *Colin Brown*

The busy 207 route remains in the hands of standard Metrobuses. M285, at West Ealing in July 1997, shows by its garage code that it is based at Acton Tram depot. *Colin Brown*

Twelve Volvo Olympians with Northern Counties Palatine 2 bodies were introduced at Orpington at the end of November 1995 when route 61 was gained. The network there is marketed as Orpington Buses. V8 loads in Bromley High Street during September 1997. *Colin Brown*

The 607 route was taken over by 15 further Volvo Olympians with Northern Counties Palatine 2 bodywork during the summer of 1996. They carry distinctive white relief on the upper-deck panels, as shown by V54 at Hanwell Broadway in September 1997. *Colin Brown*

23 Trafalgar Square
Oxford Street
Paddington Stn

LIVERPOOL STREET

FirstBus

RMC 1510

123

510 CLT

Facing page:
Carrying FirstBus
symbols, RML2667
approaches
Bayswater Road
from Marble Arch in
September 1997.
The route informa-
tion above the
lower-deck windows
applies to both
routes 7 and 23 on
which the type is
used from
Westbourne Park
garage; note also
the duty number on
a white card in the
cab window.
Stephen Madden

Left: RMC1510 has
been treated to a
full repaint in current
CentreWest livery. It
still appears in ser-
vice on fine (and
sometimes not so
fine) days, and is
seen at Marble Arch
in August 1997.
Laurie Rufus

Above: CentreWest have been staunch supporters of Wright bodywork on Dennis Dart chassis. DW164, one of the batch supplied to London Buses in 1993, was caught on layover at Golders Green in September 1997. The pod on the roof houses the radio aerial. *Colin Brown*

Left: The registration of Leyland Lynx LX10, transferred from a Routemaster, conceals its origins with Merthyr Tydfil in 1987. Still with the now-superseded fleetname style, it takes up custom at Bath Road, Heathrow in September 1997. *Colin Brown*

Right: New route A10 was introduced in August 1996 with British Airports Authority support to link Heathrow with nearby business areas. L6, a Dennis Dart SLF with Plaxton Pointer bodywork, was one of seven vehicles purchased for the service (one has since gone to London Buslines). This view at Stockley Park Estate shortly after the route started shows the distinctive livery. *Russell Upcraft*

Above: Two Mercedes-Benz Vario midi-buses with Marshall bodywork which arrived during the summer of 1997 were added to the MM class. MM25 pulls away at Mount Vernon Hospital in July 1997 working Hertfordshire County Council contract route R1, their usual haunt.
Russell Upcraft

Seven Mercedes-Benz 811D midibuses with Marshall C16 bodywork were delivered at the end of 1995 for Orpington Bus routes, followed by a further three in the spring of 1996. MM8 heads south in Bromley High Street in September 1996.
Russell Upcraft

The six remaining Leyland National 2s, all with Volvo engines, have all been converted as driver-training buses and painted in a special livery for the purpose. LS444, lacking foglights, was caught at Ealing in August 1997. *Geoff Rixon*

Nine of the ten Bristol LHs which remain with CentreWest are also used as driver-training buses. BL81 was passing through Ealing in September 1997. The Eastern Coach Works body was built to 7ft 6in width. *Russell Upcraft*

COUNTY BUS

County Bus and Coach Co Ltd, Bus Garage, Harlow, Essex, CM20 1YD

London Country North East was privatised to the AJS Group from April 1988. County Bus and Coach Ltd was established in January 1989 as the eastern part with its head office in Harlow. The Company was sold to the Lynton Travel Group in July 1991 and re-sold in October 1994 to West Midlands Travel. In February 1996 the Company was sold again, this time to Cowie Group plc (now Arriva Passenger Services).

The County name is not carried on vehicles. Instead, the trading names of Town Link, Lea Valley and Thameside are used for Harlow, Ware and Grays respectively. Since becoming part of the Cowie Group, the company has invested heavily in fleet modernisation resulting in many new vehicles, especially Dennis Darts, joining the fleet.

LT routes operated are 256, 346, 444, W14, W15, W16. Other routes operated with LT agreement are 310, 310A, 311, 327, 363, 370, 373, 500, 502, 505, 517. The network is completed by commercial routes in Essex and Hertfordshire. Most of the north-east London Mobility Bus network is also operated.

The fleet carries cream and green livery, and the London Transport contract vehicles are based at Edmonton (Lea Valley Trading Estate) and Debden (Longston Road). The full fleet is covered in the London Country Bus Handbook.

The bulk of County's London Transport work is undertaken with Plaxton bodied Darts such as this recently delivered example at High Barnet on a 'garage journey' of route 34. *Nick Malony*

Lea Valley mobility bus services are also in the hands of County Bus. MBT713 is one of four Iveco Turbo Daily vehicles with Marshall bodywork purchased in 1994, and was found working the Saturday service to the Isle of Dogs at Bakers Arms, Leyton. *Mike Harris*

CRYSTALS

CJ Springham, 127 Dartford Road, Dartford, Kent, DA1 3EN

Starting life as a taxi firm in 1970, Crystals bought their first minibus in 1972. The company was one of the first operators of LT tendered routes when route 146 was taken over in August 1985. Although the contract was retained in 1988, it was not renewed in 1993. The Company has since been successful in obtaining many Mobility Bus routes in both south-east London and west London, and routes R2 and R7 in the Orpington area.

LT routes operated are R2, R7 and Mobility Bus routes 851–58, 861–70, 931–37, 970–73. Vehicles on the bus routes carry a new livery of turquoise, whilst those on Mobility Bus routes are in red with yellow relief. Vehicles are kept at Dartford (Dartford Road).

Below: Of the seven Mercedes-Benz minibuses with in-house conversions purchased by Crystals in 1995 for LT routes, four are 29-seaters on 811D chassis. N604JGP stops to accept custom in Orpington in September 1996. *Malc McDonald*

Facing Page: In February 1997 Crystals gained the contract for various mobility bus routes in south east London. P347HKU, a Mercedes-Benz 711D with Crystals body conversion, runs along Kentish Road, Bromley in September 1997. *Mike Harris*

EPSOM BUSES

H R Richmond Ltd, Blenheim Road, Longmead Estate, Epsom, Surrey, KT19 9AF

Epsom Buses is the trading name for local bus work undertaken by Epsom Coaches, founded in 1920 by Mr H R Richmond. Bus work started on 3rd April 1986 when the Mole Valley route between Hampton Court and Richmond was taken over, and seven routes were gained on contract from Surrey County Council at deregulation in October 1986. Subsequently there have been several adjustments to the network. Routes 413 and S1 were taken over from London General during the autumn of 1997, and new route S4 has been introduced.
   Fleet livery for buses is cream with maroon relief

L894NAV, a Mercedes-Benz 709D with Marshall C19 bodywork, was purchased by Epsom Buses in 1993. This view of September 1997 shows it at Epsom Downs on commercial route S7 operating into Sutton. *Gerald Mead*

In October 1997 Epsom Buses took over route S1 from London General at short notice. H682YGO was one of four Optare MetroRiders to change hands with the service, and was seen at Belmont in the second half of the month. *Richard Godfrey*

GREY-GREEN

Grey Green Ltd, 53 Stamford Hill, London, N16 5TD

The George Ewer Group of coach companies was taken over by the Cowie Group in 1981, the latter's initial move into bus and coach operation, now renamed Arriva Passenger Services. The first gain in LT tendered operations was the acquisition of route 173 between Stratford and Becontree Heath for which former South Yorkshire Fleetlines were bought. These were painted into an orange, white and brown livery. The now familiar grey and green livery was introduced in 1989. Further LT route gains have progressed since, the major coup being the acquisition of route 24 (Hampstead Heath to Pimlico) in November 1988. This was the first of many central London routes lost by the former LT Buses companies to other operators.

During 1997, new low-floor buses are being purchased for recently retained contract routes 20 and 167 in east London.

LT routes operated are 20, 24, 66, 103, 125, 141, 167, 168, 173, 210, 275, 673, and school journeys on W13. Most of the fleet is painted in grey and green with orange relief; a few buses carry all-over red. The fleet is housed at Barking (Ripple Road) and Stamford Hill (High Road).

During 1997 Grey-Green re-equipped route 20 with new low-floor 10metre Dennis Darts carrying Alexander ALX200 bodywork. No.966 poses at Woodford Wells in September 1997. The size of the driver's instrument panel is particularly evident in this shot. *Mike Harris*

Grey-Green ordered three batches of Volvo Citybuses with Alexander bodywork in the late 1980s. No.150 was from the last batch of ten, delivered in 1990, which had single-door bodywork, and was seen at Barkingside in August 1997.
Richard Godfrey

In 1992, nine Volvo chassis of 1985 were rebodied by East Lancs as double-deckers to their EL2000 design. No.164 stands alongside redevelopment at Wood Green in September 1997.
Capital Transport

The first of the modern generation of Scania double-deckers for Grey-Green, No.159 carries Northern Counties Palatine bodywork, and was new in 1994. The introduction of newer vehicles on route 24 has enabled older Volvos to be cascaded elsewhere, though the replacements offer eight fewer seats than their predecessors.
Capital Transport

Thirteen Volvo single-deckers were bodied by East Lancs in 1990 for Grey-Green. No.914 threads its way through Highgate Village in April 1997 on route 210, an example of a route on which physical constraints (overhanging trees at Ken Wood) preclude double-deckers. *Tony Wilson*

Dennis Darts arrived with Grey-Green in 1993, when eight were purchased with ubiquitous Plaxton Pointer bodywork. No.937 passes King George Hospital, Goodmayes in April 1997. *Colin Brown*

HARRIS BUS

Harris Bus Company Ltd, Parker House, Manor Road, West Thurrock, Essex, RM16 1EH

Harris Bus was set up as a separate company from the associated Frank Harris (Coaches) in September 1986 in preparation for bus work following deregulation. In addition to local services which now include operations to and from the Lakeside shopping centre, Harris Bus gained LT route 108 from 19th April 1997, following this with 128, 129, 150 in October 1997 and 132 and 180 from 1998.

Vehicles carry a livery of blue and green and are housed at Crayford and West Thurrock.

Below: Harris Bus have invested in a total of 15 Optare Excels, eleven being needed for LT route 108. P331NHJ, a 33-seater new in 1997, demonstrates the striking Lewisham Link livery at Blackheath Village in May 1997. *Malc McDonald*

Right: The new Harris Bus colours are even more striking when applied to double-deckers, such as P341ROO, one of 22 Volvo Olympians with East Lancs Pyoneer bodywork new in 1997. One of thirteen with dual-door bodywork, it was caught at Ilford Lane in July 1997. *Mike Harris*

Six DAF
DB250
double-
deckers
with
Northern
Counties
bodywork
have joined
the Harris
Bus fleet.
P318KTW,
new in
1996, was
in use on
route 150,
under Ilford
Link brand-
ing, at Ilford
High Road.
Mike Harris

KENTISH BUS

Kentish Bus & Coach Company Ltd, Invicta House, Armstrong Road, Maidstone, Kent, ME15 6TY

Kentish Bus & Coach was re-named from London Country South East on 27th April 1987, and purchased the Proudmutual Group, later part of British Bus. British Bus was itself bought out by the Cowie Group in June 1996. There was at first considerable success in obtaining London Transport contracts, though some recent results have been less favourable, and this element of work has reduced. From 1st January 1995 some of the London operations were transferred to the newly formed Londonlinks company, and the rest being cascaded to the Cowie partners and Selkent from the summer of 1997. This process is expected to be completed in January 1998. The Kent-based fleet was renumbered into a common series with M&D in November 1997.

The main livery is green and yellow, replacing the former primrose yellow with maroon relief, though this is retained for London-based operations and on some vehicles based in Kent. Vehicles are based at Cambridge Heath, Dartford, Dunton Green and Northfleet. Those at Cambridge Heath are used exclusively on LT work, those at other garages on a mixture of LT, commercial and Kent County Council work.

One of sixteen Leyland Lynxes (some of which have subsequently moved elsewhere in the Invictaway group) acquired from Boro'line Maidstone in 1992, Kentish Bus No.410 (now 3063) carries the new livery for Kent-based operations in this view at Sidcup in August 1997. *Laurie Rufus*

Facing page: 1996 saw the arrival of ten mid-life Volvo Citybuses with East Lancs high-capacity bodywork from North Western with Kentish Bus and Londonlinks. The former took six, of which No.702 was seen in Woolwich in June 1997. It has since been renumbered 7702. *Colin Brown*

Left: The older Kentish Bus livery, which was still officially regarded as standard for London operations, is carried by 561 (now 5561), one of eight Volvo Olympians with Northern Counties Palatine 2 bodywork delivered in 1994. This shot was taken in Bexleyheath in July 1997. *Laurie Rufus*

Facing page: Thirteen Volvo Citybuses of 1989 with Northern Counties bodywork were transferred from Londonlinks to Kentish Bus in 1996 and 1997, chiefly to reflect revised working arrangements. No.642 is seen at Welling in September 1997. *Peter Plummer*

Above left: During the early 1990s, East Lancs rebuilt Leyland Nationals for many operators, the resultant "new" vehicle being marketed as the Greenway. Kentish Bus were one of the operators to invest heavily in this concept. No.345, in Woolwich during July 1997, conceals its origins as one of the first 10.3metre vehicles supplied to London Country in 1973. It is now numbered 3345. *Mike Harris*

Above: Kentish Bus have remained consistently supportive of the Optare MetroRider. No.448 (1448) dates from 1994, having spent a spell with Londonlinks, and was photographed at Bexleyheath in July 1997. *Laurie Rufus*

Left: Kentish Bus operate Croydon area mobility bus routes from their Northfleet base. No.492 (3492) is a Leyland National of 1977 which started life with Southdown, reaching London via Hastings & District in 1991. *Stephen Madden*

LEASIDE

Leaside Bus Co Ltd, 16 Watsons Road, London, N22 4TZ

Leaside was purchased by the Cowie group on 29th September 1994, taking 523 vehicles.

    Following livery experiments in the summer of 1995, traditional London red has been augmented by yellow relief in the form of a flying sash towards the rear of vehicles and across the roof. Some interchange of vehicles has taken place with Cowie South London, and with County Bus. In January 1998 Leaside is due to absorb the London-based operations of Kentish Bus at Cambridge Heath.

    The fleet operates from garages at Clapton, Enfield, Palmers Green, Tottenham and Wood Green.

Just before the Cowie group changed its marketing identity to Arriva in October 1997, Leaside vehicles started to appear with a new style of fleetname. Metrobus M747 demonstrates that fleetname style together with the subsequently added Arriva logo. *Colin Lloyd*

Facing page: Leaside's renewed contract for route 38 imposes an increased vehicle requirement which has been met in part by standard Routemasters transferred from South London. RM1725, at Victoria in August 1997, shows the route branding which has been introduced. *Laurie Rufus*

The autumn of 1995 saw the arrival of 13 DAF DB250 double-deckers bodied by Northern Counties with Leaside. They entered service on route 263, on which DBS2 was found at North Finchley. *Russell Upcraft*

A substantial order for 40 Leyland Olympians with Alexander bodywork was fulfilled for Leaside in 1992. They are used on high-intensity route 253, and include L317, which was observed leaving Aldgate. *Russell Upcraft*

Leaside took the first fourteen low-floor Scania vehicles with Wright Pathfinder bodywork delivered to London Buses in 1994 shortly before the fragmentation of the fleet. SLW2 poses at Silver Street in April 1997. *Colin Brown*

The 307 route, formed from the eastern end of the 107, now sees operation by Plaxton-bodied 9.8metre Dennis Darts, classified as the LDR class in London. LDR5 carries the Cowie group insignia which has quickly become a thing of the past. *Capital Transport*

A cascading of vehicles between Cowie group subsidiaries in London during 1996 sent seven Carlyle-bodied Dennis Darts to Enfield where they replaced Optare StarRiders on route 192. DT62 demonstrates the new order of the day on this route. *Capital Transport*

The standard MCW Metrorider has become a fairly rare sight in London. Leaside's MR105 is one of three which have been retained to operate the DHSS shuttle service from Clapton garage, as seen in Waterloo Road in October 1996. *Mike Harris*

Several Routemasters in various fleets have received Super-Rear advertising in connection with the use of sulphur-free fuel. Leaside's RML2492 at Green Park shows this display, which includes contravision treatment on the windows. *Capital Transport*

RV1 is one of thirty AEC Regent Vs with Park Royal bodywork which entered service with East Kent in 1966. Transferred from Leaside to County in October 1997, it is used solely for private hire and special events. *Capital Transport*

A number of Leaside vehicles forming a private hire fleet have received maroon and off-white livery coupled with Leaside Travel fleetnames. M625, new in 1981, was registered at a time when advance registrations were only being issued in small batches. Here it is seen at St Ignatius College on route 617, a schoolday variant of the 217 (which is otherwise worked by MTL London). It has since passed to County ownership. *Mike Harris*

LIMEBOURNE

Q Drive Coaches Ltd, Silverthorne Road, Battersea, London, SW8 3HE

Although both London Buslines and Berks Bucks Bus Company were sold to CentreWest on 20th March 1996, the London coach business operated by Q Drive was retained. At the same time, it was announced that route C10 had been won and it was decided that a bus operation would be set up to operate the route from the Battersea base. The route was taken over in May 1996 using six new Optare MetroRiders in a livery of red with beige skirt and green trim. The livery was the first by a contract operator to utilise an 80% red livery as laid down by LT for buses operating contracts within central London. The company has since been successful in winning tendered routes 42 and 156, both operated by low-floor Dennis Darts. Route C3 was additionally taken up in October 1997. The operation remains under the control of Q Drive Coaches Ltd of Wokingham in Surrey.

Limebourne took over route C10 in May 1996 using new Optare MetroRiders. N203MWW crosses Lambeth Bridge in August 1997. The 42 was gained from Kentish Bus in April 1997, and resulted in the purchase of eight new low-floor Dennis Darts with Plaxton bodywork. P308HDP is seen in Mansell Street in the following month. *Geoff Rixon/Mike Harris*

LONDON BUSLINES

Berks Bus Co Ltd, Middlesex Business Centre, Bridge Road, Southall, Middlesex, UB2 4AB

In the first round of LT tendering, Len Wright gained LT route 81 (Hounslow and Slough) from July 1985. Nine former London Fleetlines were acquired and repainted into a yellow and brown livery with London Buslines logos. With the acquisition of more tendered routes, the fleet was expanded with additional Fleetlines from London and Manchester as well as new Leyland Lynxes and Mercedes-Benz minibuses. New Dennis Darts were purchased during 1996, improving the age profile of the fleet. On 20th March 1996 Q Drive, which included Berks Bucks and London Buslines, was purchased by CentreWest, though remaining as a separate company operationally. During the summer of 1997 some rationalisation of operations has taken place with CentreWest.

LT routes operated are 105, 203, 258, 285, 490, 980–92. Other routes operated are Surrey County Council Sunday services 441, 446, 456, 461 and K3. The fleet bears a livery of yellow and brown with light brown and orange relief; Mobility buses are yellow and red. Route 285 dedicated vehicles (611–25) are yellow with red and maroon relief. The depot is at Southall (Bridge Road).

On 23rd August 1997 the eastern arm of route 90 was taken over by London Buslines and assigned new number 490. Nine low-floor 10metre Dennis Darts with Marshall Capital bodywork were purchased for the purpose, of which DML639 was located in Twickenham during September 1997. *Geoff Rixon*

London Buslines hold the present contract for route 285, using Plaxton-bodied Dennis Darts such as 613, which was passing the Fighting Cocks pub in Kingston in July 1997. *Stephen Madden*

The operation of route 105 having been taken over by CentreWest from London & Country in November 1995, three further low-floor Dennis Darts with Plaxton body-work were introduced in the spring of 1997, also in L&C livery. On 13th September 1997 operation of the route passed to London Buslines, on which date L239 was found at Greenford Broadway. *Colin Brown*

LONDON CENTRAL

London Central Bus Co Ltd, One Warner Road, London, SE5 9LU

London Central was purchased by the Go Ahead Group on 18th October 1994, taking 498 vehicles. These included the largest contingent of Routemasters to be taken by any of the subsidiaries.

Routemasters used on routes 12 and 36 have received branded liveries for these routes. Livery has otherwise remained traditional London red with white relief, accompanied by a stylised fleet logo based on a Thames clipper.

To date, few vehicles have left the fleet; rather, success in tendering has led to an increase in the overall fleet size. The purchase by the Go Ahead group of London General has resulted in many central administrative functions moving to the Mitcham base of London General during 1997, though some offices remain based at Camberwell.

The fleet operates from garages at Bexleyheath, Camberwell, New Cross and Peckham.

London Central are building up a substantial fleet of Volvo Olympians with Northern Counties Palatine I bodywork. NV62, from the 1997 delivery, demonstrates that the livery style of London General, with yellow coachline on the skirt, is now appearing on London Central vehicles now that both operators are under common ownership. It is seen in Dulwich
Capital Transport

Facing page: The AV class of nine Volvo Olympians with Alexander single-door bodywork delivered in 1995 has so far remained unique in the London Central fleet. AV3 passes through Bermondsey in this view.
Malc McDonald

The 24 single-door Optare Spectras of 1992/3 are chiefly intended for use on route 3, though in July 1997 SP3 was found working on the 40. No further examples have appeared in London, and Stagecoach East London sold their dual-door example in the spring of 1997.
Stephen Madden

London Central remains a major user of the Leyland Titan, and has a high proportion of the later examples, such as T1070. Now that the Stagecoach companies are increasingly cascading their examples to provincial fleets, it seems probable that London Central will emerge as the last stronghold of the type in London.
Mike Harris

London Central's Routemasters now carry route branding for the 12 and 36. RML2400, a mere 31-year-old, shows the former style in Walworth Road.
Malc McDonald

L261, one of the 1986/7 batch of Leyland Olympians with Eastern Coach Works bodywork, is fitted with high-backed seating. It ran with its original registration for less than three months before receiving a mark originally on a Routemaster.
Richard Godfrey

All of London Central's 28 Optare
MetroRiders are concentrated at
Bexleyheath garage. MRL136, the oldest
of them, was tracked down at Ferrier
Estate, Kidbrooke in July 1996.
Mike Harris

During the past year a number of the MA
class of Mercedes-Benz 811Ds with
Alexander bodywork have been transferred from London General to London
Central. MA131 was one of the first
examples to change hands in 1996.
Stephen Madden

LONDON COACHES

London Coaches (Kent) Ltd, Lower Road, Northfleet, Kent, DA11 9SN

London Coaches was set up in 1986 and privatised to a management-led team on 29th May 1992. In February 1992, LT contract route 726 had been gained, part of which was worked from Lower Road, Northfleet, where an increasing London commuter network had been developed.

During 1995 and 1996 the balance of work on 726 and all the coaching operations were moved to Northfleet, where an associated company, London Coaches (Kent) was set up, trading as North Kent Express. When this had been completed in September 1996, the London operation consisted only of sight-seeing work. In March 1997 the sightseeing work of Blue Triangle was purchased and in December the London operation was purchased by Arriva. Vehicles carry a livery of red and cream.

London Coaches (Kent) now operate the orbital 726 route entirely from their Northfleet base with twelve DAF SB220 vehicles bodied by Ikarus, such as DK9. The 726 was proposed for withdrawal by London Transport in the autumn of 1997, not for the first time, but appears to have had a stay of execution.
Stephen Madden

Routemasters are less common in the London Coaches fleet now, but the ten which were rebuilt with an extra bay in 1990 all survive. ERM242, with driver's windscreen open, approaches the southern end of Park Lane on a fine day in August 1997. *Stephen Madden*

Below left: The more recent recruits to the sightseeing fleet comprise Metrobuses, mostly from other London fleets. All of them have received a new covering at the front of the upper-deck, which does not seem to sit as happily on the design as it might. MB245 also shows that it has retained its dual-door configuration. *Stephen Madden*

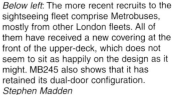

Right: In 1994, London Coaches bought seven MCW Metroliners, converting them to open-top with maximised upper-deck capacity for use on sightseeing work. ML6 had gained allover advertising for Madame Tussauds, including contravision lower-deck window displays, when met in July 1997. The sticker in the front windscreen confirms that it is, appropriately, working on a Baker Street diagram. *Stephen Madden*

LONDON & COUNTRY

London & Country Ltd, Lesbourne Road, Reigate, Surrey, RH2 7LE

Following the sale of London Country South West to the Drawlane Group in February 1988, a new fleetname, London & Country, was adopted from April 1989. Already heavily involved in LT tendered work, the Company acquired a mixed fleet of second-hand vehicles from Manchester, Nothern General, Southdown & Strathclyde. The West Surrey operations of Alder Valley were bought in December 1990 and a considerable exchange of vehicles occured within the newly renamed British Bus plc. In recent years, investment in new buses has been very noticeable. On 18th June 1996, British Bus was purchased by the Cowie Group plc, now Arriva Passenger Services.

LT routes operated are 85, 465, 627, H27, H28, H29, K5, K6, R61, R62. Other routes are County Council services in Surrey and commercial services.

From 30th August 1997 London & Country also oversees the residual Londonlinks operation, although this retains separate status at present.

The fleet is painted in two-tone green with red relief. Because vehicles used on LT work represent only a small part of the company's operations, this listing only covers those buses employed on LT contract routes from the depots at Hounslow and Leatherhead. The full fleet is covered in the London Country Bus Handbook.

No.402 is a Mercedes-Benz 709D of 1992 with Dormobile bodywork, one of the last built before that firm ceased production. A tail-lift is fitted as part of the requirement for route R61, on which it was loading in Richmond Station in September 1997.
Geoff Rixon

Facing page:
Amongst the earlier Volvo Citybuses with East Lancs bodywork purchased by London & Country was 611, found on route 85 in July 1997. Many later examples of the type have since passed to associated operators.
Stephen Madden

LONDON GENERAL

London General Transport Services Ltd, 25 Raleigh Gardens, Mitcham, Surrey, CR4 3NS

London General was purchased by a management-led team on 2nd November 1994, taking 636 vehicles, and thus becoming the largest of the privatised London companies. In May 1996 the company was in turn purchased by the Go-Ahead Group, and some rationalisation with London Central has since taken place at the organisational level.

Traditional London livery of red with white relief has been retained, accompanied by a fleetname logo incorporating a vertical orange stripe. Major orders are now being delivered, chiefly in association with the retention of LT contracts in the Sutton area.

The fleet operates from garages at Battersea Bridge, Merton, Putney, Stockwell, Sutton and Waterloo. Major maintenance of Battersea Bridge and Waterloo vehicles is undertaken at Stockwell.

At the end of 1996 London General purchased 44 low-floor Dennis Darts with Plaxton Pointer bodywork in association with retained LT routes in the Sutton and Merton areas. LDP3 is one of the first batch of 9.2metre vehicles with 32-seat bodywork. *Gerald Mead*

A substantial order is also being delivered for Volvo Olympians with Northern Counties Palatine bodywork. So far, 42 vehicles have arrived, of which NV130 is one of the newest. In this July 1997 view it is still in its first few weeks of service. *Stephen Madden*

London General have started to dispose of a few Metrobuses, though M812, new in 1983, should be safe for a little while yet. Those sold have found their way both to northern members of the Go-Ahead group and, somewhat aptly, to Metrobus of Orpington for their South Coast fleet. *Stephen Madden*

Right: The 39 Volvo Citybuses which were purchased by London General from 1989 to 1991 all carry Northern Counties bodywork, and a high proportion have received Routemaster registrations. VC34 however still carries its original identity. *Stephen Madden*

RMLs used on route 11 from Waterloo carry route branding, as shown here by RML2648 turning into Victoria Bus Station from Buckingham Palace Road.
Russell Upcraft

Two Metrobuses have been converted to open-top. M241 (locally identified as OM241), carrying General fleetnames, was converted for a tourist service in the Medway Towns worked by London General during the summer of 1996. Just before going to Kent it was photographed in Pall Mall. *Stephen Madden*

The Red Arrow fleet of Leyland Nationals was rebuilt to Greenway specification by East Lancs between 1992 and 1994. GLS479 has more recently received a revised fleetname style. *Stephen Madden*

Right: Dennis Dart DW46, with Wright bodywork, shows the appearance created by painting the destination surround area in red rather than retaining the original, and still more usual, matt black as it comes along London Road, Mitcham in May 1997. *Mike Harris*

With silhouette figures on its side to promote its accessibility, VWL1 is rarely seen on ordinary service owing to problems with its ramp. It is seen in October 1997 outside the Epsom branch of Sainsbury's on a special service to the rival Tesco store at New Malden. *Gerald Mead*

LONDONLINKS

Londonlinks Ltd, Invicta House, Armstrong Road, Maidstone, Kent, ME15 6TY

Londonlinks was established by the British Bus Group in January 1995 to take over most of the London-based operations of Kentish Bus and London & Country. In April 1996, the former Kentish Bus contracts, based at Dunton Green, passed back to that company. Administration, which from the start was under the wing of Kentish Bus at Northfleet, moved to Maidstone in October 1995 when that aspect was merged with Maidstone & District. In June 1996 control of British Bus interests passed to the Cowie Group (now Arriva). During the second half of 1997, there has been some rationalisation of work between Londonlinks and adjacent Cowie group companies; by January 1998, control of Londonlinks will have been assumed by London & Country again.

Vehicles operate in a livery of light green with dark green and red relief, and are based at Beddington Farm Road, Croydon.

Londonlinks have introduced route branding for their operations on the 127. Volvo B6 No.205, with Northern Counties Paladin body, was found at Whytecliffe Road, Purley in July 1997. *Mike Harris*

From a series of Volvo Citybuses bodied by Northern Counties for London & Country, eight remain in the Londonlinks fleet. No.625 takes the sun in Tooting during September 1997. *Gerald Mead*

Facing page: Four Dennis Dart 9metre vehicles with Plaxton Pointer bodywork delivered in 1995 bore Kent registrations, reflecting the fact that control of Londonlinks moved to Maidstone in that autumn. No.162 was in Station Road, West Croydon in May 1997. *Mike Harris*

Left: The only Leyland National to have survived with Londonlinks in substantially unrebuilt condition is No.331, which started life in 1977 with London Country Bus Services at Crawley. In August 1997 it was about to depart from West Croydon Bus Station. *Stephen Madden*

Five MCW Metroriders remain with Londonlinks, of which two have passed from Kentish Bus in the past year. No.865 was new in 1988. *Stephen Madden*

LONDON PRIDE

Ensign Bus Services Ltd, Unit 3, Allbright Industrial Estate, Ferry Lane, Rainham, Essex, RM13 9BU

Ensign Bus Services operate a substantial network of sightseeing tours and private hire work under the London Pride fleetname, the ordinary bus operation having been sold (as Frontrunner South East) in December 1990 to become what is now Capital Citybus. The fleet once contained a large number of ex-London Buses Fleetlines, but MCW Metrobuses and Metroliners are now in favour, supported by a number of Dennis Dominators and Leyland Titans.

Most vehicles carry a livery of red with silver relief, but those on former Cityrama tours have a deep cream relief.

Several Dennis Dominators have found their way into London Pride's fleet, and most have been converted to part-open-top layout. Alexander-bodied No.231 was acquired from Kelvin Central. Note the colour-coded destination blinds which are now used for the company's various tourist routes.
Stephen Madden

MCW Metrobus No.371, converted to open-top after arrival from Grey-Green in 1996, also has an offside door, in common with several other vehicles in the fleet. It was caught passing through Trafalgar Square in May 1997.
Stephen Madden

A small proportion of the fleet comprises covered-top vehicles, such as No.107, a Dennis Dominator with Northern Counties bodywork acquired from Thamesdown in 1995. The slipboard in the windscreen indicates that local fares are available.
Stephen Madden

LONDON UNITED AND WESTLINK

London United Busways Ltd, Wellington Road, Fulwell, Middlesex, TW2 5NX
Stanwell Bus Co Ltd, 6 Pulborough Way, Hounslow, Middlesex, TW4 6DE

London United was purchased by a management-led team on 5th November 1994, taking 464 vehicles. These included 194 Dennis Darts, by far the largest gathering of the type in the former LBL fleet.

Following trials, traditional London livery of red with white relief has been developed. Routemasters have grey relief and deep yellow transfers; Darts used for bus work have white roofs; some other vehicles have silver grey roof, grey upper-deck window-surrounds, and a thin white band below the upper-deck windows and above the grey skirt. Airbus vehicles are all-red with deep yellow lettering.

In addition to the usual ebb and flow of LT contracts, the Airbus operation has been revised and updated with 19 new Volvo Olympians carrying Alexander Royale bodywork. A new Airbus Direct service, furnished by specially-converted Dennis Darts, provides a more personalised link between the terminals of Heathrow Airport and hotels in Central London.

In September 1995 the holding company of London United purchased Stanwell Bus. This company had been bought by a management-led team on 20th January 1994, taking 119 vehicles. Ownership of the fleet passed to the West Midlands Travel group on 24th March 1994; they, in turn, were purchased by the National Express group early in April 1995. In the summer of 1997, Transdev, a French-based holding company, purchased the London United group.

Increasing rationalisation now occurs between the fleets. Many LSs surplus to Westlink requirements have been rebuilt to Urban Bus specification and transferred to London United. The Westlink livery of red with white and turquoise relief is now being amended to come more into line with London United styles.

The London United fleet operates from garages at Fulwell, Hounslow and Shepherds Bush. Airbus vehicles are based at West Ramp, Heathrow and maintained at Stamford Brook. The Westlink fleet operates from garages at Kingston and Hounslow Heath, although all major maintenance is undertaken at the latter.

Thirteen Westlink Leyland Nationals have been rebuilt as urban buses for the main London United fleet. LS268, one of six which spent a period with West Midlands during their time of owning Westlink, accepts custom at Richmond Station shortly after its conversion. *Geoff Rixon*

Facing Page: The 23 all-Leyland Olympians of 1989 have moved to Hounslow garage and most now carry branding for route 140. L296 works its way south from Harrow Weald in September 1997. *Capital Transport*

Two batches of Alexander-bodied Volvo Olympians have been received during the past year. The more recent batch, bodied in Belfast, is being placed on route 57, as shown by VA24 at Kingston in December 1997. *Geoff Rixon*

Two batches of Volvo Olympians were bodied by Alexander to Royale design to modernise the Airbus fleet in 1995/6. A124 was the first of the second batch. This view at Heathrow Central shows the sponsorship of Airbus routes by Toshiba. *Tony Wilson*

Amongst the standard Metrobuses with London United, M1251 has been fitted with high-backed seating. In July 1997 it was found on temporary loan to Westlink following their assumption of the contract for route 57. *Stephen Madden*

Two of the reserve fleet of RMs were retrieved by London United at the start of 1997 to meet increased requirements, and underwent partial refurbishment before entering service. RM2033 shows its pristine state at Marble Arch in August 1997. *Stephen Madden*

The Leyland Lynx is very much a minority vehicle in London. LX4, unusually working the 237 at Hounslow in April 1997, is one of six with London United, who have the largest such holding of the red fleets. *Colin Brown*

Eight low-floor Dennis Darts received Wright Crusader bodies in 1996 for use at Hounslow. As has become fashionable, they were registered in Northern Ireland. CD7 carries logos which indicate its accessibility to the disabled. *Stephen Madden*

London United took a substantial proportion of the first Dennis Darts to arrive in London at the start of the decade. Duple provided bodies on the first 28 (including an ex-demonstrator), and Carlyle the remaining 140. DT162, at Surbiton in July 1997, shows the recent upgrading of the K1 route from Metroriders. *Geoff Rixon*

Many of the DT class have been upgraded with dual-purpose seating, air-conditioning and large luggage racks for the Airbus Direct service, as shown by Duple-bodied DT21. Some have subsequently reverted to normal bus use, albeit retaining the new seating. *Stephen Madden*

Right: The application of new livery to LS7 belies its status as the oldest Leyland National in London. New high-back seats were fitted in 1996 when it was returned to service after four years in store. *Stephen Madden*

Six Optare Excels have been added to the Westlink fleet to augment route 371, and carry dedicated route identification, with different messages on each vehicle. XL1 pauses at Ham in July 1997. *Geoff Rixon*

In similar fashion, the eight Optare-bodied MAN vehicles which now form the MV class (having originally been classified as VA) have received individual route branding. MV4 was found working north to Kingston at Ham in July 1997. *Geoff Rixon*

London United continued their love affair with the Dennis Dart by taking a good number of the Plaxton-bodied series. DR65 carries Heathrow Connection logos, though working on local route H32 in this June 1997 shot at Southall. *Colin Brown*

Westlink Optare Delta DA3 is seen in April 1997 at Slough High Street, near the westernmost extremes of coverage by the former LBL subsidiaries.
Colin Brown

Facing page: All over advertisements are not permitted within the central LT area, but Westlink's Leyland National LS112 works far enough out to avoid this restriction and is seen advertising the Epsom firm of John Ashley.
Stephen Madden

Left: The first examples of the DR class were bodied by Reeve Burgess before production was moved to the main Plaxton site at Scarborough. DR14, one of several moved across from London United in 1996, shows the new Westlink fleetname applied to old-style livery in this view at Hounslow West Station.
Colin Brown

Westlink have converted three of their MCW Metroriders for wheelchair access by installing a tail lift. At the same time, the vehicles have been reclassified from MRL to MRW. One of these, MRW4 (ex-MRL80) is seen at Twickenham on their regular route, partly funded by the London Borough of Richmond. The re-registration with LBR letters reflects this. *Geoff Rixon*

MAIDSTONE & DISTRICT

The Maidstone & District Motor Services Ltd, Invicta House, Armstrong Road, Maidstone, Kent, ME15 6TY

Maidstone & District, now a member of the Arriva group, gained their first LT contract in June 1997 as a result of a rationalisation of operations in West Kent by the then Cowie Group plc. Most weekday journeys on route 402 between Bromley North and Tunbridge Wells were transferred from Kentish Bus, together with associated workings on schoolday routes 408 and 420. Kentish Bus continue to work on some trips on 402, including the weekday evening and Sunday service.

Maidstone & District also operate Green Line services from the Maidstone area into Victoria.

The 402 group is worked from M&D's Tunbridge Wells garage with five Leyland Olympians in dark green and Regency cream livery, coupled with special route-branding. When occasion requires, other vehicles from the M&D fleet are substituted.

Maidstone & District's assumption of most journeys on the 402 from June 1997 partially created a historical throwback to some workings of the 1930s. Leyland Olympian 5903 with Northern Counties bodywork is one of five vehicles in dedicated livery for the service, and was seen at Bromley South in September. For a few weeks before M&D took over these workings, the vehicles had been on loan to Kentish Bus at Dunton Green. *Colin Brown*

102

METROBUS

Metrobus Ltd, Oak Farm, Farnborough Hill, Orpington, Kent, BR6 6DA

Following the collapse of the Orpington & District Bus Company in February 1981, operations were taken over by the Cranleigh-based Tillingbourne Bus Company from 2nd March 1981. A new company was formed, that of Tillingbourne (Metropolitan) Ltd, to provide peak-hour services between Forestdale and Croydon. Forestdale, a large housing estate five miles from the nearest railway station, had never been served by London Transport services. The new Company worked hard to restore public confidence and by the end of 1981 operated three successful routes: the 353 from Croydon to Orpington, the 355 linking Croydon to Forestdale and the 357 Croydon via Forestdale to Orpington. All three became part of the LT network in 1985.

Following a management-led buy out on 24th September 1983, Metrobus Ltd was born and has since gone from strength to strength. Having successfully gained routes 61 and 361 from August 1986, thirteen former London Fleetlines were acquired and subsequent gains saw the introduction of Leyland Lynxes and Olympians, Optare MetroRiders and Excels, Dennis Darts and, most recently, new Volvo Olympians.

LT routes operated are 64, 138, 146, 161, 181, 261, 284, 630, 693, with 233 to follow in 1998. Routes 351, 352, 353, 354, 356, 358, 361, 654 are also operated with LT agreement. The fleet is in blue and yellow livery, and is kept at Oak Farm, Green Street Green.

During 1997 the operations of East Surrey, South Godstone were acquired. These are being kept separate as Metrobus East Surrey. Metrobus have also taken over much of the work of Leisurelink, Newhaven, and have established a further subsidiary of Metrobus South Coast with a depot at Lewes, from which recently-gained East Sussex County Council work is also operated. These two fleets are not covered in this book.

Metrobus purchased ten Optare Excels in 1996, of which P507OUG is seen at Kentish Way, Bromley in September 1997. Note the light blue sash amidships which draws attention to the low-floor capability of the vehicle.
Mike Harris

Facing page: The latest new arrivals in the Metrobus fleet are Volvo Olympians with East Lancs Pyoneer bodywork for use on newly gained route 64. R837MFR represents the type at Addington Village. *Gerald Mead*

Left: In 1991, Metrobus acquired two Leyland Lynxes from Miller, Foxton, to add to their four existing examples. F166SMT heads south at Bromley South Station in July 1997. *Mike Harris*

Below: The 146 was one of the first routes to be tendered, and was worked by Crystals for many years. More recently it has passed to Metrobus, who use Reeve Burgess-bodied Dennis Darts such as J701EMX seen by Kennedy's at Bromley, which remains a rare unspoilt example of a traditional town centre butcher's shop. *Gerald Mead*

METROLINE

Metroline Travel Ltd, 118–122 College Road, Harrow, Middlesex, HA1 1DB

Metroline was purchased by a management-led team on 7th October 1994, taking 386 vehicles. On 28th November 1994, Atlas Bus was purchased from the Pullmans Group, together with 26 Leyland Titans.

After a period of experiments, red livery with white relief has been augmented by a dark blue skirt. The separate Atlas Bus operation was wound up in August 1996, its Harlesden base having already been vacated in January 1996.

The holding company of Metroline Holdings plc has also purchased the coach fleet of Brent's of Watford. In June 1997, Metroline Holdings plc was floated on the Stock Exchange.

The fleet operates from garages at Cricklewood, Edgware, Harrow Weald, North Wembley and Willesden. Major maintenance of vehicles based at North Wembley and of single-deckers from Edgware is undertaken at Harrow Weald; double-deckers from Edgware are maintained at Cricklewood. Vehicles are also allocated to the Contract Services (formerly Commercial Services) fleet, now based at Cricklewood.

Route gains in the summer of 1997 led to a substantial influx of new low-floor Dennis Darts with Metroline. DL18, at Kingshill Avenue, Yeading in September 1997, is one of twenty-one 10metre vehicles with Plaxton bodywork; note how the fleetname has been adapted to publicise the type of vehicle. *Colin Brown*

Metroline have fourteen of the low-floor Dennis Lances bodied by Wright for London Buses in 1993/4. LLW30, showing the use of its exit ramp, has a non-matching registration because the appropriate number was not available from the DVLC. *Capital Transport*

Facing page: Twenty-two Volvo Olympians with Alexander bodywork were purchased in the autumn of 1996 to replace Leyland Titans on route 52. AV21, at Kensal Rise in March 1997, was used as a pilot vehicle for route branding which has since been applied to all of the batch. Note the misspelling of Kensington on this one. The registrations of this batch appeared in an unusual order in an attempt to secure some degree of matching, as a result of which this penultimate vehicle in the order carried the first registration.
Colin Brown

Left: As they receive new livery, Metroline's RMLs are acquiring fleetnames which promote the feature of "serving the West End", as well as route descriptions common to both their normal routes, the 6 and 98. RML2695 with deficient fleet number heads along Oxford Street in August 1997. *Laurie Rufus*

Route 302 took over the northern functions of the 52 when it was created in 1993, and for a while was worked by Dennis Lances before standard Metrobuses took over in February 1995. M87 pulls up at Deansbrook Road in May 1997. *Colin Brown*

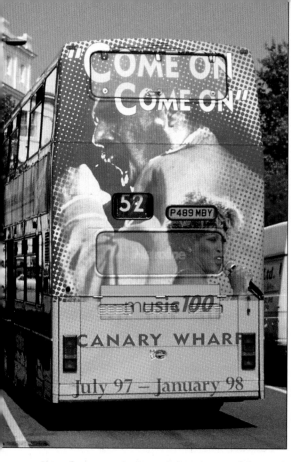

Above: Super-rear advertisements have become all the rage lately, falling as they do within the livery regulations imposed by LT. Most include contravision treatment of the windows. AV9, at Hyde Park Corner in August 1997, encourages the public to visit the Music 100 event at Canary Wharf. *Laurie Rufus*

Right: Vehicles dedicated to driver-training work are still permitted to carry all-over advertising. M409 publicises the AA/Vodaphone travel news service on local radio. *Stephen Madden*

Facing page: Metroline operate a number of courtesy services for superstores in their area. In September 1997 DT103 leaves Brent Cross, whence a network of routes is provided for the Tesco store. Note how the route display is used to reflect the identity of the service.
Colin Brown

Left: Metroline have started to dispose of their once-substantial fleet of Carlyle-bodied Dennis Darts. DT157, the last of the batch to join the fleet, passes through the forecourt of Edgware Station.
Tony Wilson

Below: October 1997 saw the introduction of new routes 189 and 316. Dual-door low-floor Dennis Darts with Plaxton bodies are used. DLD24 is seen at Brent Cross.
Colin Brown

Left: The Leyland Titans which Metroline acquired from Atlas Bus with route 52 in 1996 are rapidly disappearing from the fleet, and those that remain are now in the Contract Services section, as evidenced by their fleetname. T302, in Kensington Church Street on 20th July 1997, was performing special short workings on London United route 27 whilst the Underground was disrupted for the weekend. *Mike Harris*

Above: M1429 has received high-back seating and seat belts and is assigned to the Contract Services fleet with a modified livery for private hire and school contract work. It was caught at Trafalgar Square in September 1997. *Stephen Madden*

MTL LONDON

MTL London Northern Ltd, 17-19 Highgate Hill, London N19 5NA

London Northern was purchased by MTL Trust Holdings on 26th October 1994, taking 341 vehicles. The operations of London Suburban Bus, already owned by MTL, were absorbed on a staged basis up to June 1996. R&I Tours were taken over in October 1995, and absorbed into the MTL London fleet in June 1996. In August 1997 coaching operations in London were discontinued.

    The fleet operates from garages at Holloway, North Acton and Potters Bar. Traffic area boundaries mean that vehicles based at Potters Bar are licensed in the Eastern traffic area. Holloway garage has the largest daily vehicle turn-out of any London garage.

The newest of 24 Marshall-bodied MAN vehicles in the MTL London fleet, of which fifteen were absorbed from R&I Tours in 1996, MM278 was caught on the outskirts of Kingsbury in May 1997. MTL London have opted for unrelieved red livery for the majority of their fleet. *Colin Brown*

Of the former London Suburban fleet, sixteen Volvo Olympians with Northern Counties Palatine 2 bodywork have survived following takeover by MTL London. V216 was an unusual visitor to the C2 route in August 1997; normally this route is the province of the DNL class. *Stephen Madden*

Facing page: Earlier repaints carried MTL London Northern fleetnames; the shorter version was adopted during 1995. When new, M1083 was the last of a series of standard vehicles before a batch of 22 with Cummins engines was delivered to what has now become the South London fleet. *Stephen Madden*

Left: Ten of the 1991 batch of Scania N113s with Alexander bodywork form the allocation for peak-hours route X43, which was introduced to capitalise on the red route traffic management scheme. Based at Potters Bar, all but one carry this dedicated livery; S11 is seen at Islington. *Gerald Mead*

RML2295, with the earlier version of the fleetname, represents operation on what will be MTL London's sole surviving two-man route after the 139 receives single-deckers. The bus is seen at Marble Arch in August 1997. *Stephen Madden*

Two of the three DAF SB220 vehicles which joined the fleet in 1996 carry Optare Delta bodywork. Formal fleet numbers were allocated only after some time in stock. DAF 849 is seen at Waltham Cross. *Russell Upcraft*

Facing Page: The third DAF SB220 has Ikarus bodywork, and came from R&I Tours in 1996. DAF539 encounters a damp day at Hertford Bus Station. Note how the route suffix is shown as part of the destination display. *Russell Upcraft*

Left: Amongst the Dennis Darts acquired from R&I Tours were six with Duple bodywork completed by Carlyle in 1990. DC216 was found at Kensal Rise in March 1997.
Colin Brown

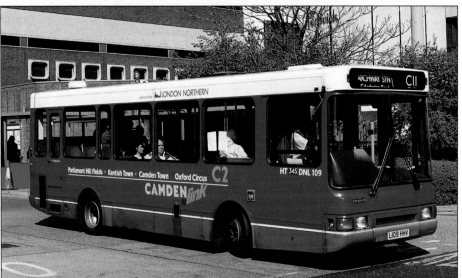

Nineteen Dennis Darts with Northern Counties Paladin bodies were amongst the last delivered to London Buses before the main fleets were privatised; all came to what was then London Northern. DNL109 carries dedicated livery for the C2 route, but was found working on the C11 at Brent Cross in April 1997.
Colin Brown

Above: Five MAN single-deckers with Optare bodywork purchased in 1995 by R&I Tours passed to MTL London when the fleet was taken over. The first of these, MV249, enters the bus lane at Ealing Common in September 1997 on its way to Brent Cross along the busy North Circular Road. *Geoff Rixon*

Left: A sole Marshall Minibus was delivered to MTL London in 1996 for use on local route PB1 at Potters Bar. A somewhat dusty MC1 carries appropriate route branding towards the rear of each side. *Richard Godfrey*

Something of a surprise when delivered in 1993 were twenty Wright-bodied Mercedes-Benz 811D vehicles. MW18, the first of the batch, stands in Waltham Cross Bus Station in September 1997, and is particularly remarkable for still carrying the London Northern insignia on its windscreen. *Russell Upcraft*

Standard Plaxton-bodied Dennis Darts from the R&I fleet formed the DP class when they passed to MTL London, and more have since been purchased. DP241 decants its load at Kings Cross Station. *Mike Harris*

Above: Representing the Marshall-bodied MAN single-deckers acquired from R&I Tours in 1996, MM260 is at Shepherds Bush Green on the 95, for which R&I had gained the contract. *Malc McDonald*

MRL223 seen at Wood Green is one of two Optare MetroRiders bought by MTL in 1997 to meet an increased requirement at Potters Bar for route W4. They joined 13 similar vehicles, with minor bodywork differences at Potters Bar and Holloway. MTL has another three Optare MetroRiders at the former R&I depot at North Acton, these being classified OM. *Malc McDonald*

NETWORK WATFORD

LDT Ltd, Castle Street, Luton, LU1 3AJ

LDT Ltd, known as 'The Shires', was formed from the former London Country North West and Luton & District fleets, and adopted its present trading name of 'The Shires' in April 1995, together with local marketing identities. Compared with the size of the company, the LT element of its operations is small. The Company is owned by Arriva, the new trading name for the former Cowie Group plc.

London Country North West gained an involvement in LT minibus work in 1986, though this ceased in 1988. Subsequently, routes 142 and 340 were gained and allocated to Watford garage. The green and grey privatisation livery was changed to blue and yellow with grey skirt when operations were relaunched in April 1995. Watford operations, previously known as Watfordwide and from 1993 Watford Bus, were marketed as `Network Watford' from this date. The contract for route 142 has recently been renewed.

In addition, Network Watford work route 350 with LT agreement, and other local services in and around Watford, both commercial and on behalf of Hertfordshire County Council. The depot is at St Albans Road, Garston.

Network Watford, the local marketing identity of The Shires, provide various Leyland Olympians for their two LT routes. Leyland-bodied 5121 carries the new livery introduced in 1995, though this is likely to be replaced by Arriva colours in the coming months. *Capital Transport*

Facing Page: When there is a shortage of the official allocation of Olympians, rare appearances are made by other double-deck types based at Watford garage. ECW bodied VR 5016 is seen on one such rare working in October 1997. *Colin Brown*

NOSTALGIABUS

Nostalgiabus Ltd, Unit 2, Abbey Industrial Estate, 24 Willow Lane, Mitcham

Nostalgiabus has during the past year gained LT contracts for school journeys on routes 127, 156 and 613, alongside other work for Surrey County Council, private hire operations and summer Sunday work on 70D and 710. The fleet is, as the name implies, centred on vintage vehicles, though some more modern machines have been acquired for the latest route gains.

Various liveries are carried, generally reflecting the previous or original ownership of vehicles, though the vehicles which are generally used on LT work are in red with cream and/or gold relief.

In December 1997, Nostalgiabus introduced commercial service 306 covering part of London & Country route 406. Partly worked by one-man vehicles and partly by Routemasters, RMC1462 is seen on it at Surbiton. *Geoff Rixon*

Two Olympians with Alexander bodies were purchased by Nostalgiabus in 1997 from MTL Liverpool following the winning of LT contracts for school journeys. *David Stewart*

Nostalgiabus acquired B102SED, a Leyland Olympian with East Lancs bodywork, from Warrington in 1996 for rail replacement and private hire work. More recently it has also appeared on LT school route 613. *Richard Godfrey*

SOUTH LONDON

South London Transport Ltd, Brighton Road, South Croydon, Surrey, CR2 6EL

South London was purchased by the Cowie group on 10th January 1995, taking 447 vehicles. These included the largest contingent of Olympians (161) to be taken by any of the subsidiaries. Some interchange of vehicles has since taken place with Leaside, and during the summer of 1997 some of the workings of Londonlinks were absorbed, followed by Kentish Bus route 19 in October 1997. In November 1997 a change of group identity to Arriva was approved by shareholders, and a new fleetname style is now being introduced.

From the autumn of 1995, traditional red livery with white relief has been augmented by a yellow flying sash towards the rear of the vehicle, carried over the roof. The fleet operates from garages at Battersea, Brixton, Croydon, Norwood and Thornton Heath.

Several of South London's ECW-bodied Leyland Olympians have received registrations from Routemasters. The mark now on L219 came from an RMC, and effectively disguises the fact that this vehicle is now into middle age.
Stephen Madden

Facing page: With the dissolution of much of the Londonlinks operation during the summer of 1997, 36 Volvo Citybuses with East Lancs bodywork passed to South London, and have now started to receive that operator's livery. VE682 loads at Waterloo Station in September 1997.
Mike Harris

South London's Metrobus M399, at Morden Station in May 1997, displays the final form of London-based livery within the Cowie group. The Cowie element of the fleetname is now disappearing quickly, to be superseded by Arriva logos. *Mike Harris*

Only two of the three Metrobuses ordered for evaluation of future vehicle types in 1984 were ever built. M1441, with Gardner 6LXB engine and Voith D851 gearbox, heads south for Old Coulsdon, still carrying the pre-privatisation fleet logo. *John Miller*

Right: Routemasters used on the 159 have gained standard livery during the past year, replacing the special scheme which had been used for that route since the contract started in 1994. RM275 is still essentially in original condition after 37 years and one of only a handful remaining with plain front windows. *Stephen Madden*

During 1996 seven of the DRL class were moved from Leaside to South London to increase capacity on the 412 route. An anonymous-looking DRL42 touts for custom at Fairfield Halls, Croydon in July 1997. *Mike Harris*

Seven DAF/Ikarus vehicles (of which two have subsequently left) were brought to South London to replace trains between West Croydon and Wimbledon during the construction of Tramlink. DIB4, at West Croydon Bus Station in September 1997, came from Birmingham Omnibus. *Mike Harris*

SOVEREIGN

London Sovereign Ltd, Station Road, Borehamwood, Herts, WD6 1HB
Sovereign Buses (Harrow) Ltd, Babbage Road, Stevenage, Herts, SG1 2EQ

Sovereign Bus & Coach was established in January 1989 as the western part of the former London Country North East. Now forming part of the Blazefield Group, the Company has two separate divisions employed on LT work: Sovereign Harrow and London Sovereign, the latter being the former fleet of BTS, Borehamwood.

The Harrow operation was set up in December 1990 for locally-based LT contracts gained at that time. Borehamwood Travel Services was formed with twenty vehicles from the fleet of C J Franklin of Borehamwood in August 1984. BTS ran an emergency service on route 292 during the London Country North East strike of January 1988 and took over the route formally from February 1988 until it was lost on tender from November 1993. Before losing this route, the Company gained the contract to operate crew route 13 (Golders Green to Aldwych) using RMLs leased from London Buses. Blazefield Holdings, the owners of Sovereign, acquired BTS in August 1994 and the trading name was changed from BTS to London Sovereign in September 1996.

LT routes operated are 13, 114, 606 (London Sovereign), 398, H10, H11, H13, H17 (Sovereign Harrow). London Sovereign also operate Hertfordshire County Council route 861.

The London Sovereign fleet is in poppy red livery with yellow relief and housed at Station Road, Borehamwood. The Harrow fleet is in blue and cream and housed at Pinner Road, Harrow.

Fourteen Leyland Olympians with Northern Counties bodywork provide London Sovereign's allocation on route 114. The first of the batch, L139 pauses at Porlock Avenue, Harrow in April 1997. *Colin Brown*

Facing page: Three Leyland Titans are to be found with London Sovereign, of which T57 is the sole instance of Park Royal bodywork. All three buses have been converted to single-entrance. *Capital Transport*

RML2598 represents the nineteen RMLs with London Sovereign; three others were declared surplus to requirements and returned to LTB in mid-1997. All carry branding for their work on the 13, on which weekday evening and Sunday work is now in the hands of one-man vehicles from MTL London. It is seen in Baker Street. *Capital Transport*

Sovereign (Harrow) was set up in December 1990 for local routes gained at that time. This is a Mercedes-Benz 709D with Reeve Burgess bodywork, drawn from a larger batch of such vehicles in the main Sovereign fleet. It is seen at Ruislip Lido. *Capital Transport*

STAGECOACH EAST LONDON AND SELKENT

East London Bus & Coach Co Ltd, 2-4 Clements Road, Ilford, Essex, IG1 1BA
South East London & Kent Bus Co Ltd, 180 Bromley Road, London, SE26 2XA

East London was purchased by the Stagecoach Group on 6th September 1994, taking 595 vehicles, and Selkent on the same date, with 414 vehicles. Major fleet updating is now in hand; all but one of East London's Metroriders have gone, and significant inroads to the fleet of Leyland Titans are under way, many of them being cascaded to other Stagecoach companies.

Vehicles lost their white relief stripes and grey skirts very quickly, both through full and partial repaints, and gained Stagecoach logos. From the end of 1994 East London Routemasters appeared with cream relief bands instead of white, and gold logos.

A handful of East London vehicles, both owned and loaned, have carried corporate Stagecoach livery and have been so used outside the inner London area. Selkent trainers also carry corporate livery.

In July 1997 East London took over control of Docklands Transit following its purchase by Stagecoach Holdings. Full integration took place in October 1997.

The East London fleet operates from garages at Barking, Bow, Leyton, Romford, Stratford and Upton Park. Stratford vehicles are maintained at Bow. The Selkent fleet operates from garages at Bromley, Catford and Plumstead.

The Stagecoach group has a general preference for Alexander bodywork. SLD3 was one of the first examples of the new ALX200 design on a low-floor Dennis Dart SLF chassis. This view at Walthamstow in May 1997 clearly shows the route insignia used on the 230. *Colin Brown*

All but one of the low-floor Scanias with Wright bodywork in the Stagecoach East London fleet were delivered after privatisation in 1994. SLW22 was found at East Ham on their normal haunt of route 101. *Capital Transport*

At short notice, Stagecoach East London took over the London City Airport courtesy service in the spring of 1997. Seven dual-door low-floor Dennis Darts with Alexander ALX200 bodywork were promptly drafted in, painted in a special livery for the service; two more have followed since. *Mike Harris*

Facing page: Recent orders for Volvo Olympians have specified bodywork by both Alexander and Northern Counties. VA63, seen at the foot of Ludgate Hill, is one of the latest batch of 38 bodied by Alexander to dual-door specification.
Stephen Madden

Left: Newer Leyland Titans from Stagecoach East London are gradually being cascaded to provincial operators within the group. T819 may well find itself moving in the coming months. Its registration is from a short series which were obtained in 1983 when it proved necessary to advance the licensing of seven vehicles before the change of year-indicator.
Stephen Madden

Facing page: East London took the majority of the Scanias which joined London fleets earlier in the decade. S27 came from a batch of twenty with Alexander bodies, of which ten others are now with MTL London. *John Miller*

Above: Three Routemaster coaches provide back-up for the busy 15 route. RMC1456 is kept in lovingly fine condition, even if purists may object to its carrying red livery and an alien registration. One of the three now carries Green Line livery again. *Stephen Madden*

Facing page: New contracts in the Barking area in 1993 led to the arrival of large quantities of Dennis Darts. DRL136 is a 9metre example with Plaxton Pointer bodywork seen at Upton Park. Such local marketing names as East London Hoppa are now falling out of use.
Capital Transport

Some of the Dennis Darts for the Barking scheme were bodied by Wright. As is usual, they were registered in Northern Ireland. DWL25 represents the body-builder's work on 9metre chassis, only found in two of the former LBL fleets.
Capital Transport

The largest fleet of Optare Deltas in London resides with Stagecoach East London. DA23, new in 1992, was one of twenty allocated to Seven Kings garage until its closure in 1993, when the batch moved to Barking. *Tony Wilson*

The loss of several contracts coupled with the usual needs of fleet updating have had the effect of giving Stagecoach Selkent the youngest age profile of the major fleets. Dennis Dart No.615, with Alexander Dash bodywork, has arrived at Eltham High Street during its first few weeks in service. *Mike Harris*

DT33 is one of the survivors of a class which was once rather more numerous in south east London. An appearance on route 54 is a rare event, this route normally being worked by Olympians. *Mike Harris*

Facing page: The twelve Dennis Lances with Plaxton Verde bodywork which form the LV class were until recently earmarked for transfer elsewhere, never having been accepted fully on the 208. They have now found a new home on the 227, which was transferred from Kentish Bus in November 1997. *Mike Harris*

Facing page: After a period during which all their Park Royal-bodied Titans had been disposed of, Selkent have regained several of the type from East London to meet revised requirements. T214 came south of the river in the closing weeks of 1996. *Colin Brown*

Left: Selkent received new Volvo Olympians with Northern Counties bodywork during the autumn of 1997. An early arrival was VN85, terminating at Shoreditch in September 1997. These vehicles have reverted to the tradition of class prefixes, Selkent having for a while moved to a system based simply on fleet numbers. *Malc McDonald*

TELLINGS-GOLDEN MILLER

Tellings-Golden Miller Ltd, 20A Wintersells Road, Byfleet, Surrey, KT14 7LF

In June 1985, Tellings Coaches of Byfleet took control of the stage carriage operations of Golden Miller of Feltham. Five Bristol RE buses were purchased to operate the four routes, but these were soon sold. Two of the routes were transferred in October 1987 to Fountain Coaches, which operated from the former Golden Miller premises. The remaining two routes, the 602 (Feltham to Shepperton) and the 606 (Staines to Stanwell Moor) were retained, and the businesses of Tellings Coaches and Golden Miller were merged. The new Company gained the contracts to run LT routes 116 and 117 from Brentford to Staines, but these were taken over by London & Country from 23rd February 1992.

The Company gained their latest LT tendered route with the acquisition of new route S3 between Belmont and Worcester Park from April 1995. Three new Plaxton Beaver-bodied Mercedes-Benz 811Ds were purchased for this contract. LT route 235 has been awarded from January 1998. Surrey County Council routes 501, 511, 513, 521, 551, 564, 691 and 740 are also operated. Fleet livery is blue and white with yellow relief, and vehicles are garaged at Wintersells Road, Byfleet.

Facing page: Deliveries to Tellings-Golden Miller have included the first examples of Plaxton Beaver 2 bodywork on LT routes. P704LCF is a 31-seater built on the Mercedes-Benz Vario chassis, and was caught in Portsmouth Road, Kingston in August 1997. *Geoff Rixon*

Left: Other vehicles used on LT work are older MCW Metroriders, such as E808UDT, which was acquired from Cardiff Bluebird in 1994. Here it is seen at Carshalton Beeches in October 1997. *Richard Godfrey*

THAMESWAY

Essex Buses Ltd, Stapleford Close, New Writtle Street, Chelmsford, Essex, CM2 0SD

In July 1990 the LT routes and other western operations of Eastern National passed to the new Thamesway company, since when the LT operations have expanded. This has resulted in the arrival of many new Mercedes-Benz minibuses, together with a substantial intake of Dennis Darts. From 1st December 1995 the Company was re-united with Eastern National to become Essex Buses Ltd, but both retain their individual names.
  LT routes operated are 191, 193, 214, 362, 379, 389, 399, 462, D8, W9, W11, W12, W13, 951-959, 961.

In 1996 Thamesway refreshed their LT fleet with fifteen Dennis Darts on which Plaxton Pointer bodywork was mounted. No.980 rounds the bend in Church Street, Enfield in June 1997. *Russell Upcraft*

Thamesway's purple and yellow livery has now been applied to most of the fleet. In this shot at Walthamstow in April 1997, Mercedes-Benz 709D No. 306, with Reeve Burgess Beaver bodywork, also shows the FirstBus logo which forms an integral part of the new fleetname. *Colin Brown*

Now a rare example of Robin Hood body-work in the major London fleets, Mercedes-Benz 609D No. 261 was new in 1987, and reached Thamesway from South Wales Transport in 1994. It was caught in Clements Road, Ilford in July 1997.
Mike Harris

One of nine Marshall-bodied Mercedes-Benz Varios delivered to Thamesway in the late summer of 1997, No.413 was displayed at the Bus & Coach Show at Birmingham in October 1997.
Marshall Specialist Vehicles

THORPE'S

F E Thorpe & Sons Ltd, 272 Latimer Road, North Kensington, London, W10 6QY

Frank E Thorpe & Sons Ltd started as a small private coach company back in 1968. As well as private hire work, the mixed fleet of coaches and minibuses was also used for school and local authority contracts. The company moved into LT work in October 1992 with the winning of the tender to operate the inter-station mobility route, marketed as Stationlink. The route was originally run with three former LBL Optare City Pacer mobility buses. Following this successful venture into bus work, LT route C4 (Putney Pier to Hurlingham) was gained from April 1995. The Stationlink circular route was retained upon re-tender and was subsequently revamped to run both clockwise and anti-clockwise. The route was also numbered, becoming the SL1 and SL2. New low floor wheelchair-accessible vehicles were specified and new Optare Excels were bought, the first of the type to appear on the streets of London.

In August 1997 Thorpe took over the LT contracts of Javelin Coaches, Wandsworth. LT routes operated are now 871-886, 904, 905, 926, 928, 938-946, 963-965, 967-969, 974-979, C4, SL1, SL2. Other local authority contracts are also operated. Vehicles carry red and white or red and yellow livery, and are garaged at Latimer Road, North Kensington.

When the contract for Stationlink services was renewed with Thorpe's in 1996, four Optare Excels were purchased. The first of these, N100FET makes its way through Lambeth in July 1996. *Malc McDonald*

FLEET LISTS

Standard body codes are used in the following fleet lists, showing the body type, seating capacity and entrance position in that order.

Body Type

Single-deck bus	B
Single-deck coach	C
Convertible open-top double-deck bus	CO
Dual-purpose vehicle	DP
Dual-purpose double-deck vehicle	DPH
Highbridge double-deck bus	H
Open-top double-deck bus	O
Partial open-top double-deck bus	PO

The further prefix 'F' is used for full-fronted vehicles where this is not normal for the type

Seating capacity

For double-deckers the upper-deck capacity is shown first, followed by that for the lower deck. Standee capacities have not been shown as there are sometimes local variations between the licensed capacity of a vehicle and the operational capacity agreed with road staff.

Entrance position

Separate entrance and exit (front and centre) with doors	D
Front entrance with platform doors	F
Rear entrance without doors	R
Rear entrance with platform doors	RD

The further suffix 'L' indicates a vehicle fitted with a wheelchair tail-lift. 'T' indicates a vehicle which contains a toilet compartment. '+' indicates a vehicle fitted with an offside door.

Fleet number suffixes

Vehicle restricted to staff bus duties	s
Vehicle restricted to training work	t
Vehicle unlicensed long-term	u
Vehicle withdrawn for disposal	w

ARMCHAIR (Buses)

Reg	Type	Body	Seating	Year	Notes
RIB8739	Leyland Atlantean AN68A/1R	Eastern Coach Works	H43/31F	1976	Ex Ribble, 1992
GIL8496	Leyland Atlantean AN68A/1R	East Lancashire	H45/29D	1978	Ex South Yorkshire, 1991
GIL2603	Leyland Atlantean AN68A/1R	Roe	H45/31F	1979	Ex South Yorkshire, 1990
GIL2604	Leyland Atlantean AN68A/1R	Roe	H45/31F	1979	Ex South Yorkshire, 1990
GIL2605	Leyland Atlantean AN68A/1R	Roe	H45/31F	1979	Ex South Yorkshire, 1990
C449SJU	Ford Transit 190D	Robin Hood	B16F	1985	Ex Easton, Ramsgate, 1996
C322RPE	Ford Transit 190D	Carlyle	B16F	1986	Ex London Buslines, 1995
D829UTF	Ford Transit 190D	Carlyle	B16F	1986	Ex London Buslines, 1995
E991NMK	Leyland Swift LBM6T/2RA	Wadham Stringer Vanguard II	B37F	1988	
G94VMM	Mercedes-Benz 709D	Reeve Burgess Beaver	B25F	1989	

Leyland Olympian ONCL10/1RZ — Alexander RL — H47/30F — 1990

G361YUR	G363YUR	G365YUR	G367YUR	G369YUR	G371YUR
G362YUR	G364YUR	G366YUR	G368YUR	G370YUR	G372YUR

H755DTM — Mercedes-Benz 811D — Reeve Burgess Beaver — B33F — 1990

Leyland Olympian ON2R50C13Z4 — Leyland — H47/31F — 1991

H546GKX	H549GKX	H552GKX	H556GKX	H559GKX	H563GKX
H547GKX	H550GKX	H553GKX	H557GKX	H561GKX	H564GKX
H548GKX	H551GKX	H554GKX	H558GKX	H562GKX	

Dennis Dart SFD412BR5 — Plaxton Pointer — B37F* — 1996 — * P154-60MLE are B39F

P27MLE	P29MLE	P32MLE	P35MLE	P156MLE	P158MLE	P160MLE
P28MLE	P31MLE	P34MLE	P154MLE	P157MLE	P159MLE	

Dennis Dart SFD212BR1 — Plaxton Pointer — B35F — 1997

P675RWU	P679RWU	P683RWU	P687RWU	P691RWU	P695RWU	P699RWU
P676RWU	P680RWU	P684RWU	P688RWU	P692RWU	P696RWU	
P677RWU	P681RWU	P685RWU	P689RWU	P693RWU	P697RWU	
P678RWU	P682RWU	P686RWU	P690RWU	P694RWU	P698RWU	

Volvo Olympian — Northern Counties Palatine 2 — H47/29F — 1997

R417SOY	R418SOY	R419SOY	R420SOY

Previous Registrations

GIL2603	YKY669T	GIL2605	YKY671T	RIB8739	SFV435P	
GIL2604	YKY670T	GIL8496	UDT185S			

The coach fleet is listed in the London Coach Handbook.

15	JJG15P	Leyland Atlantean AN68/1R	Eastern Coach Works	O43/31F	1976	Ex East Kent, 1992
47	XMD47A	Leyland Titan PD2/12	Metro-Cammell	O32/26RD	1956	Ex preservation, 1991
78	GHV78N	Daimler Fleetline CRL6	Park Royal	O44/27D	1975	Ex London Buslines, 1991
109	KJD109P	Leyland Fleetline FE30ALR	Park Royal	O45/25D	1976	Ex Fire Research Establishment, Borehamwood (npsv), 1990
133	OUC33R	Leyland Fleetline FE30ALR	MCW	O44/35F	1976	Ex Filer, Ilfracombe, 1994; Gardner engine
206	MPJ206L	Leyland Atlantean AN68A/1RSp	MCW	O43/29D	1972	Ex London Country North West, 1991
247	OJD247R	Leyland Fleetline FE30ALR	MCW	O44/24D	1977	Ex Mott, Stoke Mandeville, 1994
321	THX321S	Leyland Fleetline FE30ALR	MCW	O44/24D	1977	Ex Universitybus, Hatfield, 1995
361	OJD361R	Leyland Fleetline FE30ALR	Park Royal	PO44/27D	1977	Ex London Buses, 1991; Gardner engine
441	MLH441L	Daimler Fleetline CRG6LXB	MCW	PO44/24D	1973	Ex Morgan, Staplehurst, 1994; Gardner engine
488	MLH488L	Daimler Fleetline CRL6	MCW	H44/24D	1973	Ex London United, 1993
498	THX498S	Leyland Fleetline FE30ALR	Park Royal	O44/27D	1977	Ex Filer, Ilfracombe, 1994
526	THM526M	Daimler Fleetline CRL6	MCW	O44/29F	1973	Ex Kime, Folkingham, 1994
545	THX545S	Leyland Fleetline FE30ALR	Park Royal	PO44/24D	1977	Ex Mott, Stoke Mandeville, 1994
548	THM548M	Daimler Fleetline CRL6	MCW	O44/32F	1973	Ex Filer, Ilfracombe, 1994
853	PFN853	AEC Regent V 2LD3RA	Park Royal	FO40/32F	1959	Ex preservation, 1991
958	KUC958P	Daimler Fleetline CRL6	MCW	O44/24D	1975	Ex Maidstone & District, 1994
DM934	SMU934N	Daimler Fleetline CRL6	Park Royal	PO44/27D	1974	Ex Woolley, Llanedwen, 1994
DM1033	GHV33N	Daimler Fleetline CRL6	Park Royal	O44/27D	1975	Ex London Buslines, 1991
DM1147	KUC147P	Daimler Fleetline CRL6	Park Royal	O45/32F	1975	Ex London Pride, Rainham, 1997
DM1155	KUC155P	Daimler Fleetline CRL6	Park Royal	O44/27D	1975	Ex Home James, Totton, 1995
DM1787	GHM787N	Daimler Fleetline CRL6	MCW	O44/27D	1974	Ex London Buses, 1993
DM2556	THX556S	Leyland Fleetline FE30ALR	Park Royal	O44/27D	1978	Ex MTL London, 1995
DM2600	THX600S	Leyland Fleetline FE30ALR	Park Royal	H44/27D	1978	Ex John Penrose School, Harefield (npsv), 1995
DM3898	KLL898N	Daimler Fleetline CRL6	Park Royal	O44/27D	1974	Ex London Buslines, 1996
DMS1020	GHV20N	Daimler Fleetline CRL6	Park Royal	O45/28D	1974	Ex Gilmurray, Sturry, 1995
DMS1530	THM530M	Daimler Fleetline CRL6	MCW	O44/29F	1973	Ex Kime, Folkingham, 1994
DMS1854	GHM854N	Daimler Fleetline CRL6	MCW	O44/24D	1975	Ex Buckland & Hetherington, West Wittering, 1995
DMS1979	KUC979P	Leyland Fleetline FE30ALR	MCW	PO44/24D	1976	Ex London Buses, 1991
DMS2002	KJD2P	Leyland Fleetline FE30ALR	MCW	O44/29F	1976	Ex Scutt, Owston Ferry, 1995
DMS2012	KJD12P	Leyland Fleetline FE30ALR	MCW	O44/29F	1976	Ex Cook, Biggleswade, 1995
DMS2058	KJD58P	Leyland Fleetline FE30ALR	Park Royal	O44/24D	1976	Ex Manning, Challow, 1996
DMS2168	OJD168R	Leyland Fleetline FE30AGR	MCW	O44/24D	1976	Ex MTL London, 1995
DMS2205	OJD205R	Leyland Fleetline FE30AGR	MCW	O44/24D	1977	Ex London Buses, 1992
DMS2235	OJD235R	Leyland Fleetline FE30AGR	MCW	O44/28D	1977	Ex Easton, Ramsgate, 1997
DMS2253	OJD253R	Leyland Fleetline FE30ALR	MCW	O44/24D	1977	Ex Adams, Handley, 1996
DMS2326	THX326S	Leyland Fleetline FE30ALR	MCW	O44/24D	1978	Ex London Buses, 1992
DMS2365	OJD365R	Leyland Fleetline FE30ALR	Park Royal	O44/24D	1977	Ex Thomas, West Ewell, 1994
DMS2376	OJD376R	Leyland Fleetline FE30ALR	Park Royal	O44/24D	1977	Ex Garratt, Leicester, 1996
DMS2390	OJD390R	Leyland Fleetline FE30ALR	Park Royal	O45/29F	1977	Ex Wealden PSV, Five Oak Green, 1995

DMS2396	OJD396R	Leyland Fleetline FE30ALR	Park Royal	O44/27D	1977	Ex Easton, Ramsgate, 1997
DMS2412	OJD412R	Leyland Fleetline FE30ALR	Park Royal	O44/24D	1977	Ex London Buses, 1992
DMS2447	OJD447R	Leyland Fleetline FE30ALR	Park Royal	O44/24D	1977	Ex London Buses, 1992
DMS2484	THX484S	Leyland Fleetline FE30ALR	Park Royal	O44/24D	1977	Ex Garratt, Leicester, 1996
DMS2534	THX534S	Leyland Fleetline FE30ALR	Park Royal	H44/27D	1978	Ex preservation, 1996
DMS2595	THX595S	Leyland Fleetline FE30ALR	Park Royal	O44/27D	1978	Ex London Buses, 1993
RM236	LDS236A	AEC Routemaster 5RM	Park Royal	H36/28R	1960	Ex Cadbury, Bournville (npsv), 1995
RMF588	FPT588C	AEC Routemaster	Park Royal	O41/31F	1965	Ex Wright, Rainham, 1992
RMF592	FPT592C	AEC Routemaster	Park Royal	H41/31F	1965	Ex preservation, 1995
	KLL902N	Daimler Fleetline CRL6	Park Royal	H44/27D	1975	Ex London Buslines, 1996
	KJD80P	Leyland Fleetline FE30ALR	Park Royal	H44/24D	1976	Ex Hunter, Garston, 1997
	THX478S	Leyland Fleetline FE30ALR	Park Royal	H44/24D	1977	Ex preservation, 1996
	THX531S	Leyland Fleetline FE30ALR	Park Royal	H44/27D	1977	Ex Eastern Counties, 1996
	THX566S	Leyland Fleetline FE30ALR	Park Royal	O44/27D	1978	Ex Mather, Poulton, 1996
	THX576S	Leyland Fleetline FE30ALR	Park Royal	H44/27D	1978	Ex Lambert, Harlow, 1996

Previous registrations

KLL898N	GHV7N
KLL902N	GHV41N
LDS236A	VLT272
XMD47A	KCH106

CAPITAL CITYBUS

100	JHE144W	MCW Metrobus DR104/6	MCW	H46/31F	1981	Ex MTL, Liverpool, 1996
101	JHE171W	MCW Metrobus DR104/6	MCW	H46/31F	1981	Ex South Yorkshire, 1991
102	JHE172W	MCW Metrobus DR104/6	MCW	H46/31F	1981	Ex South Yorkshire, 1991
104	JHE194W	MCW Metrobus DR104/6	MCW	H46/31F	1981	Ex Mainline, Sheffield, 1994
105	JHE138W	MCW Metrobus DR104/6	MCW	H46/31F	1981	Ex Stevensons, Uttoxeter, 1995
106	JHE157W	MCW Metrobus DR104/6	MCW	H46/31F	1981	Ex South Yorkshire, 1991
107	G107FJW	MCW Metrobus DR102/70	MCW	H43/30F	1989	Ex Optare, Leeds, 1992
109	JHE152W	MCW Metrobus DR104/6	MCW	H46/31F	1981	Ex MTL, Liverpool, 1996
110	JHE170W	MCW Metrobus DR104/6	MCW	H46/31F	1981	Ex South Yorkshire, 1991
111	JHE156W	MCW Metrobus DR104/6	MCW	H46/31F	1981	Ex MTL, Liverpool, 1996
112	GRA102V	MCW Metrobus DR102/4	MCW	H43/30F	1980	Ex Derby, 1990

113-120		MCW Metrobus DR104/6	MCW	H46/31F	1981	Ex South Yorkshire, 1991

113	JHE169W	115	JHE182W	117	JHE147W	119	JHE149W
114	JHE162W	116	JHE146W	118	JHE148W	120	JHE150W

121	G121YEV	Leyland Olympian ONCL10/1RZ	Alexander RL	H47/30F	1990
122	G122YEV	Leyland Olympian ONCL10/1RZ	Alexander RL	H47/30F	1990
123	G123YEV	Leyland Olympian ONCL10/1RZ	Alexander RL	H47/30F	1990
125	G125YEV	Leyland Olympian ONCL10/1RZ	Alexander RL	H47/30F	1990
126	G126YEV	Leyland Olympian ONCL10/1RZ	Alexander RL	H47/30F	1990
128	G128YEV	Leyland Olympian ONCL10/1RZ	Alexander RL	H47/30F	1990
129	J129YRM	Leyland Olympian ON2R50C13Z4	Northern Counties Palatine	H47/30F	1991
130	J130YRM	Leyland Olympian ON2R50C13Z4	Northern Counties Palatine	H47/30F	1991
131	J131YRM	Leyland Olympian ON2R50C13Z4	Northern Counties Palatine	H47/30F	1991
132	J132YRM	Leyland Olympian ON2R50C13Z4	Northern Counties Palatine	H47/30F	1991
133	G133ATW	Leyland Olympian ONCL10/1RZ	Northern Counties Palatine	H45/30F	1989
134	J134YRM	Leyland Olympian ON2R50C13Z4	Northern Counties Palatine	H47/30F	1991
135	J135YRM	Leyland Olympian ON2R50C13Z4	Northern Counties Palatine	H47/30F	1991

136-158 Leyland Olympian ON2R50C13Z4 Leyland H47/29F 1991

136	J136YRM	140	J140YRM	144	J144YRM	148	J148YRM	152	J152YRM	156	J156YRM
137	J137YRM	141	J141YRM	145	J145YRM	149	J149YRM	153	J153YRM	157	J157YRM
138	J138YRM	142	J142YRM	146	J146YRM	150	J150YRM	154	J154YRM	158	J158YRM
139	J139YRM	143	J143YRM	147	J247YRM	151	J151YRM	155	J155YRM		

159-165 Leyland Olympian ON2R50C13Z4 Northern Counties Palatine 1 H47/30F 1992

159	K888TTT	160	K888ELR	161	K888TWY	162	K888LAD	163	K888PFD	164	K888BFG	165	K888BWU

166	K888TKS	Leyland Olympian ON2R50C13Z4	Northern Counties Palatine 2	H46/29F	1993	
167	L888YTT	Volvo Olympian YN2RV18Z4	Northern Counties Palatine 2	H47/29F	1993	
168	L888TTT	Volvo Olympian YN2RV18Z4	Northern Counties Palatine 2	H47/29F	1993	
169	E964PME	Leyland Olympian ONLXB/1RH	Optare	H47/29F	1988	Ex Ensign, Rainham, 1994
170	E470SON	MCW Metrobus DR102/63	MCW	H45/30F	1988	Ex London Buses, 1992
171	E461SON	MCW Metrobus DR102/63	MCW	H45/30F	1988	Ex London Buses, 1992
172	C372CAS	Leyland Olympian ONLXB/1RH	Alexander RL	H47/25F	1986	Ex Highland Scottish, 1992
173	C373CAS	Leyland Olympian ONLXB/1RH	Alexander RL	H47/25F	1986	Ex Highland Scottish, 1992
174	C374CAS	Leyland Olympian ONLXB/1RH	Alexander RL	DPH47/25F	1986	Ex Highland Scottish, 1992
175	DAE510W	MCW Metrobus DR103/4	MCW	DPH43/29F	1980	Ex MTL, Liverpool, 1996
176	DAE512W	MCW Metrobus DR103/4	MCW	DPH43/30F	1980	Ex MTL, Liverpool, 1996
177	DAE513W	MCW Metrobus DR103/4	MCW	DPH43/30F	1980	Ex MTL, Liverpool, 1996
178	E478SON	MCW Metrobus DR102/63	MCW	H45/30F	1988	Ex London Buses, 1992
179	E472SON	MCW Metrobus DR102/63	MCW	H45/30F	1988	Ex London Buses, 1992
180	A183WEV	Leyland Olympian ONLXB/1R	Alexander RL	H45/34F	1984	Ex Highland Scottish, 1992
181	J181HME	Dennis Dominator DDA2004	Northern Counties Palatine 1	H45/29F	1991	
182	J182HME	Dennis Dominator DDA2004	Northern Counties Palatine 1	H45/29F	1991	
183	B443CKW	Dennis Dominator DDA901	Alexander RH	H46/32F	1984	Ex Mainline, Sheffield, 1994
184	B444CKW	Dennis Dominator DDA901	Alexander RH	H46/32F	1984	Ex Mainline, Sheffield, 1994
185	DEM83X	Dennis Dominator DDA145	Alexander RH	H45/33F	1982	Ex Kelvin Central Buses, 1995
187	CHF347X	Dennis Dominator DDA157	Alexander RH	H45/33F	1982	Ex Kelvin Central Buses, 1995

188	CHF348X	Dennis Dominator DDA157	Alexander RH	H45/33F	1982	Ex Kelvin Central Buses, 1995
189	CHF349X	Dennis Dominator DDA157	Alexander RH	H45/33F	1982	Ex Kelvin Central Buses, 1995
190	B440CKW	Dennis Dominator DDA901	Alexander RH	H46/32F	1984	Ex Mainline, Sheffield, 1994

191-198		Dennis Dominator DDA1023	East Lancs	H45/31F	1988	Ex Southampton Citybus, 1992

191	F291PTP	193	F293PTP	195	F295PTP	197u	F297PTP
192	F292PTP	194	F294PTP	196	F296PTP	198	F298PTP

199	CHF353X	Dennis Dominator DDA157	Alexander RH	H45/33F	1982	Ex Kelvin Central Buses, 1995
200	CHF350X	Dennis Dominator DDA157	Alexander RH	H45/33F	1982	Ex Kelvin Central Buses, 1995
201	CHF351X	Dennis Dominator DDA157	Alexander RH	H45/33F	1982	Ex Kelvin Central Buses, 1995
202	B102WUW	Dennis Dominator DDA1001	Northern Counties	H43/31F	1984	Ex London Coaches, 1993
203	B103WUW	Dennis Dominator DDA1001	Northern Counties	H43/31F	1984	Ex London Coaches, 1993

223-238		Volvo Olympian	Alexander (Belfast)	H47/25D	1997	Red livery

223	P223MPU	226	P226MPU	229	P229MPU	232	P232MPU	235	P235MPU	238	P238MPU
224	P224MPU	227	P227MPU	230	P230MPU	233	P233MPU	236	P236MPU		
225	P225MPU	228	P228MPU	231	P231MPU	234	P234MPU	237	P237MPU		

239-249		Volvo Olympian YN2RV18Z4	Northern Counties Palatine 1	H47/27D	1996	

239	P239HMD	241	N241CMP	243	P243HMD	245	P245HMD	247	N247CMP	249	P249HMD
240	P240HMD	242	P242HMD	244	N244CMP	246	P246HMD	248	P248HMD		

250	J135PVC	Leyland Olympian ON2R50C13Z4	Leyland	H47/25D	1991	Ex Volvo, Warwick, 1991; red livery

251-274		Dennis Dominator DDA2001	Northern Counties Palatine	H47/29D	1990/1	* Red livery

251	H251KVX	255	H255KVX	259	H259KVX	263	H263KVX	267	H267KVX	271	H271KVX
252	H252KVX	256	H256KVX	260	H460JVX	264	H264KVX	268*	H268KVX	272	H272KVX
253	H253KVX	257	H257KVX	261	H261KVX	265	H265KVX	269	H269KVX	273	H273KVX
254	H254KVX	258	H258KVX	262	H262KVX	266	H266KVX	270	H270KVX	274*	H274KVX

276	FUT36V	MCW Metrobus DR102/14	MCW	H45/27D	1980	Ex Leicester, 1990
277	FUT37V	MCW Metrobus DR102/14	MCW	H45/27D	1980	Ex Leicester, 1990

279-294		MCW Metrobus DR102/71	MCW	H46/31F	1988	

279	F279NHJ	282	F282NHJ	284	F284NHJ	286	F286NHJ	288	F288NHJ	290	F290NHJ	293	F293NHJ
280	F280NHJ	283	F283NHJ	285	F285NHJ	287	F287NHJ	289	F289NHJ	291	F291NHJ	294	F294NHJ
281	F281NHJ												

295-299		MCW Metrobus DR104/3	MCW	H46/30F	1980	Ex South Yorkshire, 1988

295	JWF495W	296	JWF496W	297	JWF497W	298	JWF498W	299	JWF499W

340-348			Dennis Dominator DDA1024		East Lancs				H46/33F	1989	Ex Leicester Citybus, 1996	
340	F140MBC	342	F142MBC	345	F145MBC	347	F147MBC	348	F148MBC			
341	F141MBC	344	F144MBC									

401-416			Dennis Arrow SFD121BR2		Northern Counties Palatine 2				H47/35F*	1996	* 413-6 are H47/33F	
401	P401PLE	404	P404PLE	407	P407PLE	409	P409PLE	411	P411PLE	413	P413MTW	415	P415MTW
402	P402PLE	405	P405PLE	408	P408PLE	410	P410PLE	412	P412PLE	414	P414MTW	416	P416MTW
403	P403PLE	406	P406PLE									

417-426			Dennis Arrow SFD121BR3		East Lancs Pyoneer				H49/28D*	1997	* 426 is H52/25D	
417	P417PVW	419	P419PVW	421	P421PVW	423	P423PVW	425	P425PVW			
418	P418PVW	420	P420PVW	422	P422PVW	424	P424PVW	426	R426SOY			

601-620			Mercedes-Benz 811D		Plaxton Beaver				B28F	1992	610 is in red livery	
601	J601HMF	605	J605HMF	611	J611HMF	613	J613HMF	616	J616HMF	618	J618HMF	
602	J602HMF	610	J610HMF	612	J612HMF	615	J615HMF	617	J617HMF	620	J620HMF	

621-630			Optare MetroRider		Optare				B28F	1992		
621	J621HMH	623	J623HMH	625	J625HMH	627	J627HMH	629	J629HMH			
622	J622HMH	624	J624HMH	626	J626HMH	628	J628HMH	630	J630HMH			

631	J631HMH	Mercedes-Benz 811D		Alexander AM		B28F	1992	
632	J632HMH	Mercedes-Benz 811D		Alexander AM		B28F	1992	
633	J633HMH	Mercedes-Benz 811D		Alexander AM		B28F	1992	
669	J459JOW	Dennis Dart 9SDL3011		Wadham Stringer Portsdown		B37F	1991	Ex Wealden PSV, Five Oak Green, 1995
670	L670SMC	Dennis Dart 9SDL3034		Northern Counties Paladin		B31F	1994	

671-680			Volvo B6-41		Alexander Dash				B31F	1994		
671	L671RMD	673	L673RMD	675	L675RMD	677	L677RMD	679	L679RMD			
672	L672RMD	674	L674RMD	676	L676RMD	678	L678RMD	680	L680RMD			

681	L281RML	Volvo B6-50		Northern Counties Paladin		B39F	1994	
682	L888JTC	Volvo B6-50		Northern Counties Paladin		B39F	1994	
683	L888AMY	Volvo B6-50		Northern Counties Paladin		B39F	1994	
684	L4GML	Volvo B6-50		Northern Counties Paladin		B31F	1994	Ex Flightparks, Horley, 1996
685	L5GML	Volvo B6-50		Northern Counties Paladin		B31F	1994	Ex Flightparks, Horley, 1996
686	L6GML	Volvo B6-50		Northern Counties Paladin		B31F	1994	Ex Flightparks, Horley, 1996
701	P701HMT	Optare L1070		Optare Excel		B33F	1996	
702	P702HMT	Optare L1070		Optare Excel		B33F	1996	
703	P703HMT	Optare L1070		Optare Excel		B33F	1996	
704	P704HMT	Optare L1070		Optare Excel		B33F	1996	

705-717		Dennis Dart SLF		East Lancs Spryte		B37-	1998	On Order	
705		707	709		711	713		715	717
706		708	710		712	714		716	

738	KRS538V	Leyland National 2 NL106L11/1R		B44F	1980	Ex Bluebird Northern, 1993
739	KRS539V	Leyland National 2 NL106L11/1R		B44F	1980	Ex Bluebird Northern, 1993
740	KRS534V	Leyland National 2 NL106L11/1R		B44F	1980	Ex Bluebird Northern, 1993
741	KRS541V	Leyland National 2 NL106L11/1R		B44F	1980	Ex Bluebird Northern, 1993
742	MSO11W	Leyland National 2 NL106L11/1R		B44F	1980	Ex Bluebird Northern, 1993
744	GUW454W	Leyland National 2 NL106AL11/2R		B41F	1981	Ex London Buses, 1994
748	B358LOY	Leyland National 2 NL116TL11/3R		B48F	1984	Ex British Airways, 1993
749	B359LOY	Leyland National 2 NL116TL11/3R		B48F	1984	Ex British Airways, 1993
750	NLP389V	Leyland National 2 NL116L11/3R		B49F	1980	Ex British Airways, 1993
751	NLP391V	Leyland National 2 NL116L11/3R		B49F	1980	Ex British Airways, 1993
797	D497MYS	Volvo B10M-61	Duple Dominant	B55F	1986	Ex Eastbourne, 1996
799	D499MYS	Volvo B10M-61	Duple Dominant	B55F	1986	Ex Eastbourne, 1996
913	ALD913B	AEC Routemaster 5RM	Park Royal	H36/28R	1964	Ex preservation, 1996
920	VLT120	AEC Routemaster 5RM	Park Royal	H36/28R	1959	Ex preservation, 1996

Previous Registrations

A183WEV	A980OST	KRS541V	GSO7V	P405PLE	P905HMH	P410PLE	P910HMH
DEM83X	ACM768X	P401PLE	P901HMH	P406PLE	P906HMH	P411PLE	P911HMH
KRS534V	GSO1V	P402PLE	P902HMH	P407PLE	P907HMH	P412PLE	P912HMH
KRS538V	GSO4V	P403PLE	P903HMH	P408PLE	P908HMH		
KRS539V	GSO5V	P404PLE	P904HMH	P409PLE	P909HMH		

Special liveries

East London livery: 172/5/7/80/5/8/9/99, 201, 402-6.

On order

27 Dennis Arrow - East Lancs Pyoneer

CAPITAL LOGISTICS (LT Bus Fleet)

CS1	L204ULX	Mercedes-Benz 709D	Plaxton Beaver	B18FL	1993	
CS2	L205ULX	Mercedes-Benz 709D	Plaxton Beaver	B18FL	1993	
CS3	L206ULX	Mercedes-Benz 709D	Plaxton Beaver	B18FL	1993	
CS4	P255MLE	Mercedes-Benz 711D	Plaxton Beaver	B20FL	1997	
CS5	P456MLE	Mercedes-Benz 711D	Plaxton Beaver	B20FL	1997	
CS6	H837GLD	Mercedes-Benz 609D	North Western Coach Sales	C13F	1991	Ex Marton, West Drayton, 1992

CENTREWEST

BL2-91 — Bristol LH6L — Eastern Coach Works — B39F* — 1976-77 — * BL36 and 81 are DP40F Ex London Buses, 1994

2t	KJD402P	28t	KJD428P	35t	KJD435P	65t	OJD65R	85t	OJD85R
4t	KJD404P	34t	KJD434P	36t	KJD436P	81t	OJD81R	91t	OJD91R

D33-41 — Dennis Dart SFD412BR5 — Plaxton Pointer — B37F — 1996

33	133CLT	35	N635ACF	37	N637ACF	39	P409MLA	41	P411MLA
34	N634ACF	36	N636ACF	38	P408MLA	40	P410MLA		

DLP1 — P41MLE — Dennis Dart SFD112BR1 — Plaxton Pointer — B27D — 1996 — On extended loan from London Transport

DM117-157 — Dennis Dart SFD112 — Marshall Capital — B31F — 1997

117	P117NLW	123	P123NLW	129	P129NLW	135	P135NLW	141	P141NLW	147	P247OEW	153	P153NLW
118	P118NLW	124	P124NLW	130	P130NLW	136	P136NLW	142	P142NLW	148	P148NLW	154	P154NLW
119	P119NLW	125	P125NLW	131	P131NLW	137	P137NLW	143	P143NLW	149	P149NLW	155	P255RFL
120	P120NLW	126	P126NLW	132	P132NLW	138	P138NLW	144	P144NLW	150	P150NLW	156	P156NLW
121	P121NLW	127	P127NLW	133	P133NLW	139	P139NLW	145	P145NLW	151	P151NLW	157	P157NLW
122	P122NLW	128	P128NLW	134	P134NLW	140	P140NLW	146	P146NLW	152	P152NLW		

DML165-190 — Dennis Dart SLF — Marshall Capital — B37F — 1998 — On Order

165	R165TLM	169	R169TLM	173	R173TLM	177	R177TLM	181	R181TLM	185	R185TLM	189	R189TLM
166	R166TLM	170	R170TLM	174	R174TLM	178	R178TLM	182	R182TLM	186	R186TLM	190	R190TLM
167	R167TLM	171	R171TLM	175	R175TLM	179	R179TLM	183	R183TLM	187	R187TLM		
168	R168TLM	172	R172TLM	176	R176TLM	180	R180TLM	184	R184TLM	188	R188TLM		

DP1-32 — Dennis Dart 9SDL3053 — Plaxton Pointer — B32F — 1995

1	N801FLW	6	N806FLW	11	N811FLW	16	N816FLW	21	N821FLW	26	N826FLW	31	N831FLW
2	N802FLW	7	N807FLW	12	N812FLW	17	N817FLW	22	N822FLW	27	N827FLW	32	N832FLW
3	N803FLW	8	N808FLW	13	N813FLW	18	N818FLW	23	N823FLW	28	N828FLW		
4	N804FLW	9	N809FLW	14	N814FLW	19	N819FLW	24	N824FLW	29	N829FLW		
5	N805FLW	10	N810FLW	15	N815FLW	20	N820FLW	25	N825FLW	30	N830FLW		

DW1-14 — Dennis Dart 8.5SDL3003 — Wright Handybus — B30F — 1990 — Ex London Buses, 1994

1	JDZ2301	3	JDZ2303	5	JDZ2305	7	JDZ2307	9	JDZ2309	11	JDZ2311	13	JDZ2313
2	JDZ2302	4	JDZ2304	6	JDZ2306	8	JDZ2308	10	JDZ2310	12	JDZ2312	14	JDZ2314

DW15-126   Dennis Dart 8.5SDL3003*   Wright Handybus   B26F   1990-92   Ex London Buses, 1994 * DW92-9/101-14 are 8.5SDL3010, DW115-25 are 8.5SDL3015, DW126 is 8.5SDL3018

15	JDZ2315	27	JDZ2327	39	JDZ2339	79	JDZ2379	91	JDZ2391	103	KDZ5103	115	LDZ9115
16	JDZ2316	28	JDZ2328	40	JDZ2340	80	JDZ2380	92	JDZ2392	104	KDZ5104	116	LDZ9116
17	JDZ2317	29	JDZ2329	41	JDZ2341	81	JDZ2381	93	JDZ2393	105	KDZ5105	117	LDZ9117
18	JDZ2318	30	JDZ2330	42	JDZ2342	82	JDZ2382	94	JDZ2394	106	KDZ5106	118	LDZ9118
19	JDZ2319	31	JDZ2331	43	JDZ2343	83	JDZ2383	95	JDZ2395	107	KDZ5107	119	LDZ9119
20	JDZ2320	32	JDZ2332	72	JDZ2372	84	JDZ2384	96	JDZ2396	108	KDZ5108	120	LDZ9120
21	JDZ2321	33	JDZ2333	73	JDZ2373	85	JDZ2385	97	JDZ2397	109	KDZ5109	121	LDZ9121
22	JDZ2322	34	JDZ2334	74	JDZ2374	86	JDZ2386	98	JDZ2398	110	KDZ5110	122	LDZ9122
23	JDZ2323	35	JDZ2335	75	JDZ2375	87	JDZ2387	99	JDZ2399	111	KDZ5111	123	LDZ9123
24	JDZ2324	36	JDZ2336	76	JDZ2376	88	JDZ2388	100	JDZ2300	112	KDZ5112	124	LDZ9124
25	JDZ2325	37	JDZ2337	77	JDZ2377	89	JDZ2389	101	KDZ5101	113	LDZ9113	125	LDZ9125
26	JDZ2326	38	JDZ2338	78	JDZ2378	90	JDZ2390	102	KDZ5102	114	LDZ9114	126	LDZ9126

DW162-170   Dennis Dart 8.5SDL3015   Wright Handybus   B29F*   1993   * DW169/70 are B26F Ex London Buses, 1994

162	NDZ3162	164	NDZ3164	166	NDZ3166	168	NDZ3168	170	NDZ3170
163	NDZ3163	165	NDZ3165	167	NDZ3167	169	NDZ3169		

L1	P401MLA	Dennis Dart SFD212BR1	Plaxton Pointer	B34F	1996	
L2	P402MLA	Dennis Dart SFD212BR1	Plaxton Pointer	B34F	1996	
L3	P403MLA	Dennis Dart SFD212BR1	Plaxton Pointer	B34F	1996	
L4	P404MLA	Dennis Dart SFD212BR1	Plaxton Pointer	B34F	1996	
L5	P405MLA	Dennis Dart SFD212BR1	Plaxton Pointer	B34F	1996	
L6	P406MLA	Dennis Dart SFD212BR1	Plaxton Pointer	B34F	1996	
LA24	L24GAN	Leyland Olympian ON2R50C13Z4	Alexander RH	H45/29F	1993	Ex London Buslines, 1997
LA25	L25GAN	Leyland Olympian ON2R50C13Z4	Alexander RH	H45/29F	1993	Ex London Buslines, 1997
LA26	L26GAN	Leyland Olympian ON2R50C13Z4	Alexander RH	H45/29F	1993	Ex London Buslines, 1997
LA27	L27GAN	Leyland Olympian ON2R50C13Z4	Alexander RH	H45/29F	1993	Ex London Buslines, 1997
LA28	L28GAN	Leyland Olympian ON2R50C13Z4	Alexander RH	H45/29F	1993	Ex London Buslines, 1997

LA46-54   Leyland Olympian ONCL10/1RZ   Alexander RL   H47/28F   1989   Ex London Buslines, 1997

46	G46XLO	48	G48XLO	50	G50XLO	52	G52XLO	54	G54XLO
47	G47XLO	49	G49XLO	51	G51XLO	53	G53XLO		

LC1	N921LUF	LDV 400	Crystals	DP10FL	1995
LC2	N922LUF	LDV 400	Crystals	DP10FL	1995
LC3	N923LUF	LDV 400	Crystals	DP10FL	1995

LLW11-24 Dennis Lance SLF 11SDA3202 Wright Pathfinder 320 B34D* 1993-94 Ex London Buses, 1994 *LLW13 is B31D

11	ODZ8911	13	ODZ8913	15	ODZ8915	17	ODZ8917	19	ODZ8919	21	ODZ8921	23	ODZ8923
12	ODZ8912	14	ODZ8914	16	ODZ8916	18	ODZ8918	20	ODZ8920	22	ODZ8922	24	ODZ8924

LN29-45 Leyland Olympian ON2R50C13Z4 Northern Counties H47/30F 1990 Ex London Buslines, 1996/7

29	H129FLX	32	H132FLX	35	H135FLX	38	H138FLX	41	H141FLX	44	H144FLX
30	H130FLX	33	H133FLX	36	H136FLX	39	H139FLX	42	H142FLX	45	H145FLX
31	H131FLX	34	H134FLX	37	H137FLX	40	H140FLX	43	H143FLX		

LS444t	GUW444W	Leyland National 2 NL106AL11/2R (Volvo)	DP43F	1981	Ex London Buses, 1994
LS470t	GUW470W	Leyland National 2 NL106AL11/2R (Volvo)	DP43F	1981	Ex London Buses, 1994
LS472t	GUW472W	Leyland National 2 NL106AL11/2R (Volvo)	DP43F	1981	Ex London Buses, 1994
LS497t	GUW497W	Leyland National 2 NL106AL11/2R (Volvo)	DP43F	1981	Ex London Buses, 1994
LS503t	503CLT	Leyland National 2 NL106AL11/2R (Volvo)	DP43F	1981	Ex London Buses, 1994
LS504t	GUW504W	Leyland National 2 NL106AL11/2R (Volvo)	DP43F	1981	Ex London Buses, 1994
LX10	810DYE	Leyland Lynx LX112TL11ZR1R Leyland	DP48F	1987	Ex London Buses, 1994
LX11	811DYE	Leyland Lynx LX112TL11ZR1R Leyland	DP48F	1987	Ex London Buses, 1994

M285-583 MCW Metrobus DR101/12* MCW H43/28D 1980 Ex London Buses, 1994
(M385 ex London General, 1996)
*M523/83 are DR101/14

285	BYX285V	330	EYE330V	349	GYE349W	371	GYE371W	413	GYE413W	451	GYE451W	497	GYE497W
291	BYX291V	337	EYE337V	358	GYE358W	374	GYE374W	414	GYE414W	452	GYE452W	498	GYE498W
305	BYX305V	338	EYE338V	360	GYE360W	383	GYE383W	418	GYE418W	465	GYE465W	499	GYE499W
308	BYX308V	339	EYE339V	362	GYE362W	385	GYE385W	421	GYE421W	470	GYE470W	504	GYE504W
311	BYX311V	340	EYE340V	364	GYE364W	390	GYE390W	425	GYE425W	486	GYE486W	505	GYE505W
316	EYE316V	343	EYE343V	368	GYE368W	393	GYE393W	427	GYE427W	487	GYE487W	523	GYE523W
319	EYE319V	345	EYE345V	369	GYE369W	397	GYE397W	434	GYE434W	489	GYE489W	583	GYE583W
329	EYE329V	347	GYE347W	370	GYE370W	406	GYE406W	442	GYE442W	494	GYE494W		

M843-952 MCW Metrobus DR101/16 MCW H43/28D 1983 Ex London Buses, 1994

843	OJD843Y	860	OJD860Y	874	OJD874Y	884	OJD884Y	892	A892SUL	938	A938SUL
851	OJD851Y	861	OJD861Y	875	OJD875Y	885	OJD885Y	893	A893SUL	941	A941SUL
857	OJD857Y	866	OJD866Y	882	OJD882Y	886	OJD886Y	898	A898SUL	943	A943SUL
859	OJD859Y	872	OJD872Y	883	OJD883Y	887	OJD887Y	901	A901SUL	952	A952SUL

M979-1438 MCW Metrobus DR101/17* MCW H43/28D 1984-86 Ex London Buses, 1994
*M1049/51/4 are DR101/19

979	A979SYF	1201	B201WUL	1258	B258WUL	1338u	C338BUV	1380	C380BUV	1418u	C418BUV
1049	A749THV	1244	B244WUL	1259	B259WUL	1340u	C340BUV	1382	C382BUV	1419t	C419BUV
1051	A751THV	1245	B245WUL	1260t	B260WUL	1375	C375BUV	1384u	C384BUV	1420	C420BUV
1054	A754THV	1246	B246WUL	1267	B267WUL	1376	C376BUV	1400	C400BUV	1421	C421BUV
1144	B144WUL	1247	B247WUL	1328u	C328BUV	1377	C377BUV	1412u	C412BUV	1422u	C422BUV
1199	B199WUL	1256	B256WUL	1335u	C335BUV	1378	C378BUV	1415	C415BUV	1438	C438BUV

MA1-107 Mercedes-Benz 811D Alexander AM B28F* 1988-89 Ex London Buses, 1994 * MA1/2/10/2/51/5 are B26F, MA3-7 are B26FL, MA101 is DP28F

1	F601XMS	26	F626XMS	45	F645XMS	56	F656XMS	69	F669XMS	80	F680XMS	92	F692XMS
2	F602XMS	33	F633XMS	46	F946BMS	57	F657XMS	70	F670XMS	81	F681XMS	101	VLT31
3	F603XMS	35	F635XMS	48	F948BMS	58	F658XMS	71	F671XMS	82	F682XMS	106	F706XMS
4	F604XMS	36	F636XMS	49	F949BMS	59	F659XMS	72	F672XMS	83	F683XMS	107	F707XMS
5	F605XMS	37	F637XMS	50	F950BMS	62	F662XMS	73	F673XMS	84	F684XMS		
6	F606XMS	38	F638XMS	51	F951BMS	64	F664XMS	74	F674XMS	85	F685XMS		
7	F607XMS	40	F640XMS	52	F952BMS	65	F665XMS	75	F675XMS	86	F686XMS		
10	F610XMS	42	F642XMS	53	F953BMS	66	F666XMS	77	F677XMS	88	F688XMS		
12	F612XMS	43	F643XMS	54	F954BMS	67	F667XMS	78	F678XMS	89	F689XMS		
23	F623XMS	44	F644XMS	55	F955BMS	68	F668XMS	79	F679XMS	91	F691XMS		

ML101-116 Marshall Minibus Marshall B26F 1997 On order

101	R101VLX	104	R104VLX	107	R107VLX	110	R110VLX	113	R113VLX	116	R116VLX
102	R102VLX	105	R105VLX	108	R108VLX	111	R211VLX	114	R114VLX		
103	R103VLX	106	R706VLX	109	R109VLX	112	R112VLX	115	R115VLX		

MM1-10 Mercedes-Benz 811D Marshall C16 B28F 1995/96

1	N521REW	3	N523REW	5	N525REW	7	N527REW	9	P489CEG
2	N522REW	4	N524REW	6	N526REW	8	P488CEG	10	P490CEG

MM25	P825NAV	Mercedes-Benz 0814	Marshall	B28F	1997	
MM26	P826NAV	Mercedes-Benz 0814	Marshall	B28F	1997	
MT8	G538GBD	Mercedes-Benz 709D	Reeve Burgess Beaver	B18FL	1989	Ex London Buses, 1994
MW17	LDZ9017	Mercedes-Benz 811D	Wright	B26F	1992	Ex London Buses, 1994
RF326u	MLL963	AEC Regal IV 9821LT	Metro-Cammell	B39F	1952	Ex preservation, 1996
RH1	C501DYM	Iveco Daily 49.10	Robin Hood City Nippy	DP21F	1986	On extended loan from preservation, 1996
RM1292u	NVS485	AEC Routemaster 5RM	Park Royal	H36/28R	1962	Ex London Transport Buses, 1997
RM1676u	676DYE	AEC Routemaster 5RM	Park Royal	H36/28R	1963	Ex London Transport Buses, 1997
RMC1492u	492CLT	AEC Routemaster 6RM	Park Royal	H32/25RD	1962	Ex London Buses, 1994
RMC1510	510CLT	AEC Routemaster 6RM	Park Royal	O32/25RD	1962	Ex London Buses, 1994; Cummins engine

RML885-2740 AEC Routemaster 7RM (Cummins) Park Royal H40/32R 1961-67 Ex London Buses, 1994

885	WLT885	2352	CUV352C	2388	JJD388D	2476	JJD476D	2522	JJD522D	2609	NML609E	2677	SMK677F
2268	CUV268C	2357	CUV357C	2390	JJD390D	2480	JJD480D	2530	JJD530D	2623	NML623E	2687	SMK687F
2278	CUV278C	2365	JJD365D	2405	JJD405D	2486	JJD486D	2542	JJD542D	2647	NML647E	2717	SMK717F
2281	CUV281C	2369	JJD369D	2428	JJD428D	2490	JJD490D	2553	JJD553D	2656	NML656E	2724	SMK724F
2291	CUV291C	2374	JJD374D	2442	JJD442D	2498	JJD498D	2555	JJD555D	2664	SMK664F	2735	SMK735F
2309	CUV309C	2378	JJD378D	2467	JJD467D	2501	JJD501D	2559	JJD559D	2667	SMK667F	2740	SMK740F
2313	CUV313C	2379	JJD379D	2473	JJD473D	2506	JJD506D	2602	NML602E	2672	SMK672F		

RW54-88 Renault-Dodge S75 Wright B28F* 1990 Ex London Buses, 1994 * RW86/8 are DP28F

54	HDZ5454	59	HDZ5459	66	HDZ5466	72	HDZ5472	76	HDZ5476	80	HDZ5480
55	HDZ5455	60	HDZ5460	68	HDZ5468	73	HDZ5473	77	HDZ5477	83	HDZ5483
56	HDZ5456	61	HDZ5461	70	HDZ5470	74	HDZ5474	78	HDZ5478	86	HDZ5486
58	HDZ5458	62	HDZ5462	71	HDZ5471	75	HDZ5475	79	HDZ5479	88	HDZ5488

V1-12 Volvo Olympian YN2RV18Z4 Northern Counties Palatine 2 H43/29F 1995

1	N301JBV	3	N303JBV	5	N305JBV	7	N307JBV	9	N309JBV	11	N311JBV
2	N302JBV	4	N304JBV	6	N306JBV	8	N308JBV	10	N310JBV	12	N312JBV

V41-55 Volvo Olympian Northern Counties Palatine 2 DPH43/29F 1996

41	P241UCW	44	P244UCW	47	P247UCW	50	P250UCW	53	P253UCW
42	P242UCW	45	P245UCW	48	P248UCW	51	P251UCW	54	P254UCW
43	P243UCW	46	P246UCW	49	P249UCW	52	P252UCW	55	P255UCW

Previous registrations

NVS485	292CLT	**133CLT**	N633ACF	**810DYE**	D106NDW
VLT31	F701XMS, F903CMS	**503CLT**	GUW503W	**811DYE**	D111NDW

Special liveries

Cream: BL85.
Route 607 livery: V41-55.
Blue with route A10 branding: L1-6.

On order

34 Dennis Dart SLF

COUNTY BUS (LT and Leaside Travel vehicles)

DI4	P754RWU	DAF DE33WSSB3000	Ikarus 350	C53F	1997	Ex Leaside, 1997
DIB56	J56GCX	DAF SB220LC550	Ikarus Citibus	B48F	1992	Ex South London, 1997
DIB124	K124TCP	DAF SB220LC550	Ikarus Citibus	B48F	1992	Ex South London, 1997
DIB926	J926CYL	DAF SB220LC550	Ikarus Citibus	B48F	1992	Ex Grey-Green, 1997
DIB927	J927CYL	DAF SB220LC550	Ikarus Citibus	B48F	1992	Ex Grey-Green, 1997
DIB928	J928CYL	DAF SB220LC550	Ikarus Citibus	B48F	1992	Ex Grey-Green, 1997
DP1	N551LUA	DAF DE33WSSB3000	Plaxton Première 350	C49F	1996	Ex Leaside, 1997
DP2	N552LUA	DAF DE33WSSB3000	Plaxton Première 350	C49F	1996	Ex Leaside, 1997
DP3	P753RWU	DAF DE33WSSB3000	Plaxton Première 350	C53F	1997	Ex Leaside, 1997

DP301-313		Dennis Dart 9SDL3002*	Plaxton Pointer	B35F	1991	* 302-7/13 are 9SDL3011; 309 rebodied 1992

DP301 J301WHJ	DP303 J303WHJ	DP305 J305WHJ	DP307 J307WHJ	DP309 J309WHJ	DP311 J311WHJ	DP313 J313WHJ
DP302 J302WHJ	DP304 J304WHJ	DP306 J306WHJ	DP308 J308WHJ	DP310 J310WHJ	DP312 J312WHJ	

DP323	K323CVX	Dennis Dart 9SDL3011	Plaxton Pointer	B35F	1992

DP324-334		Dennis Dart SFD212	Plaxton Pointer	B34F	1996

DP324 P324HVX	DP326 P326HVX	DP328 P328HVX	DP330 P330HVX	DP332 P332HVX	DP334 P334HVX
DP325 P325HVX	DP327 P327HVX	DP329 P329HVX	DP331 P331HVX	DP333 P833HVX	

DPL406-414		Dennis Dart 9.8SDL3018	Plaxton Pointer	B40F	1993

DPL406 K406FHJ	DPL408 K408FHJ	DPL410 K410FHJ	DPL412 K412FHJ	DPL414 K414FHJ
DPL407 K407FHJ	DPL409 K409FHJ	DPL411 K411FHJ	DPL413 K413FHJ	

DW314	J314XVX	Dennis Dart 9SDL3011	Wright Handybus	B35F	1992	
DW315	J315XVX	Dennis Dart 9SDL3011	Wright Handybus	B35F	1992	
DW316	J316XVX	Dennis Dart 9SDL3011	Wright Handybus	B35F	1992	
DW317	J317XVX	Dennis Dart 9SDL3011	Wright Handybus	B35F	1992	
ELW266	M266VPU	Dennis Lance 11SDA3201	Wright Pathfinder 320	B40F	1994	
ELW267	M267VPU	Dennis Lance 11SDA3201	Wright Pathfinder 320	B40F	1994	
ELW268	M268VPU	Dennis Lance 11SDA3201	Wright Pathfinder 320	B40F	1994	
ELW269	M269VPU	Dennis Lance 11SDA3201	Wright Pathfinder 320	B40F	1994	
LR4	TPD104X	Leyland Olympian ONTL11/1R	Roe	H43/29F	1982	Ex London Country North East, 1989
LR5	TPD105X	Leyland Olympian ONTL11/1R	Roe	H43/29F	1982	Ex London Country North East, 1989
LR15	TPD115X	Leyland Olympian ONTL11/1R	Roe	H43/29F	1982	Ex London Country North East, 1989
LR23	TPD123X	Leyland Olympian ONTL11/1R	Roe	H43/29F	1982	Ex London Country North East, 1989
M1	GBU1V	MCW Metrobus DR101/6	MCW	H43/30F	1979	Ex Leaside, 1997
M4	GBU4V	MCW Metrobus DR101/6	MCW	H43/30F	1979	Ex Leaside, 1997

M5	GBU5V	MCW Metrobus DR101/6	MCW	H43/30F	1979	Ex Leaside, 1997
M8	GBU8V	MCW Metrobus DR101/6	MCW	H43/30F	1979	Ex Leaside, 1997
M9	GBU9V	MCW Metrobus DR101/6	MCW	H43/30F	1979	Ex Leaside, 1997
M170	BYX170V	MCW Metrobus DR101/9	MCW	H43/28D	1979	Ex Leaside, 1997
M175	BYX175V	MCW Metrobus DR101/9	MCW	H43/28D	1979	Ex Leaside, 1997
M537	GYE537W	MCW Metrobus DR101/14	MCW	H43/28D	1981	Ex Leaside, 1997
M573	GYE573W	MCW Metrobus DR101/14	MCW	H43/28D	1981	Ex Leaside, 1997
M625	KYO625X	MCW Metrobus DR101/14	MCW	H43/28D	1981	Ex Leaside, 1997
M649	KYV649X	MCW Metrobus DR101/14	MCW	H43/28D	1981	Ex Leaside, 1997
M1248	B248WUL	MCW Metrobus DR101/17	MCW	H43/28D	1985	Ex Leaside, 1997
M1367	C367BUV	MCW Metrobus DR101/17	MCW	DPH43/28D	1985	Ex Leaside, 1997
M1379	VLT88	MCW Metrobus DR101/17	MCW	DPH43/28F	1985	Ex Leaside, 1997
M1398	C398BUV	MCW Metrobus DR101/17	MCW	H43/28D	1985	Ex Leaside, 1997
M1437	VLT12	MCW Metrobus DR101/17	MCW	DPH43/24F	1986	Ex Leaside, 1997
MB722	L722OVX	Iveco Turbo Daily 59.12	Marshall C31	B25F	1994	
MB723	L722PHK	Iveco Turbo Daily 59.12	Marshall C31	B25F	1994	

MB918-938		Mercedes-Benz 709D	Reeve Burgess Beaver*	B23F	1989-92	* MB933-8 are Plaxton Beaver

MB918 G918UPP	MB925 G925WGS	MB928 G928WGS	MB931 G931WGS	MB934 J934WHJ	MB937 J937WHJ
MB919 G919UPP	MB926 G926WGS	MB929 G929WGS	MB932 G932WGS	MB935 J935WHJ	MB938 J938WHJ
MB924 G924WGS	MB927 G927WGS	MB930 G930WGS	MB933 J933WHJ	MB936 J936WHJ	

MBT713	L713OVX	Iveco Turbo Daily 59.12	Marshall C31C	B18FL	1994
MBT714	L714OVX	Iveco Turbo Daily 59.12	Marshall C31C	B18FL	1994
MBT715	L715OVX	Iveco Turbo Daily 59.12	Marshall C31C	B18FL	1994
MBT716	L716OVX	Iveco Turbo Daily 59.12	Marshall C31C	B18FL	1994

MD601-612		Mercedes-Benz 811D	Reeve Burgess Beaver	B28F	1991

MD601 J601WHJ	MD603 J603WHJ	MD605 J605WHJ	MD607 J607WHJ	MD609 J609WHJ	MD611 J611WHJ
MD602 J602WHJ	MD604 J604WHJ	MD606 J606WHJ	MD608 J608WHJ	MD610 J610WHJ	MD612 J612WHJ

RMC1453	453CLT	AEC Routemaster 6RM	Park Royal	H32/25RD	1962	Ex Leaside, 1997
RMC1464	464CLT	AEC Routemaster 6RM (Iveco)	Park Royal	O36/25RD	1962	Ex Leaside, 1997
RV1	GJG750D	AEC Regent V 2D3RA	Park Royal	H40/32F	1966	Ex Leaside, 1997

SLF419-431		Dennis Dart SFD322 BR1	Plaxton Pointer	B43F	1996

SLF419 P419HVX	SLF421 P421HVX	SLF423 P423HVX	SLF425 P425HVX	SLF427 P427HVX	SLF429 P429HVX	SLF431 P431HVX
SLF420 P420HVX	SLF422 P422HVX	SLF424 P424HVX	SLF426 P426HVX	SLF428 P428HVX	SLF430 P430HVX	

T69	70CLT	Leyland Titan TNLXB2RRSp	Park Royal	O44/26D	1979	Ex Leaside, 1997	
T83	CUL83V	Leyland Titan TNLXB2RRSp	Park Royal	O44/26D	1979	Ex Leaside, 1997	
T100	CUL100V	Leyland Titan TNLXB2RRSp	Park Royal	O44/26D	1979	Ex Leaside, 1997	
TPL1	124CLT	Leyland Tiger TRCTL11/3ARZM	Plaxton Paramount 3200 3	C53F	1989	Ex Leaside, 1997	
TPL2	361CLT	Leyland Tiger TRCTL11/3ARZM	Plaxton Paramount 3200 3	C53F	1989	Ex Leaside, 1997	
TPL8	VLT18	Leyland Tiger TRCL10/3ARZA	Plaxton Paramount 3200 3	C53F	1991	Ex Leaside, 1997	
VPL1	C874CYX	Volvo B10M-61	Plaxton Paramount 3200 2	C53F	1986	Ex Leaside, 1997	
VPL2	C876CYX	Volvo B10M-61	Plaxton Paramount 3200 2	C53F	1986	Ex Leaside, 1997	

		Dennis Dart SLF		Plaxton Pointer		B35F	1997
	R416COO	R419COO	R422COO	R424COO	R426COO	R428COO	R430COO
	R417COO	R420COO	R423COO	R425COO	R427COO	R429COO	R431COO
	R418COO	R421COO					

Previous registrations

VLT12	C437BUV	**VLT88**	C379BUV	**124CLT**	G661WMD
VLT18	H643GRO	**70CLT**	CUL69V	**361CLT**	G662WMD

Special liveries

Allover advertisement: LR4/5/15, MB918/32.
LT Mobility Bus: MBT713-6.
Leaside Travel : DI4, DP1-3, M170/5/537/73/625/49/1248/367/79/98/437, T69/83/100, TPL1/2/8, VPL1/2.

The full fleet is listed in the London Country Bus Handbook

CRYSTALS (LT contract fleet)

	L68DPE	Mercedes-Benz 709D	Crystals	DP18FL	1994	
	L76DPE	Mercedes-Benz 709D	Crystals	DP18FL	1994	
	L168EKR	Mercedes-Benz 711D	Crystals	B18FL	1994	Ex Crystals, Doncaster (demonstrator), 1994
	M569TJL	Mercedes-Benz 709D	Crystals	B19FL	1995	
	N601JGP	Mercedes-Benz 709D	Crystals	B25F	1995	
	N602JGP	Mercedes-Benz 709D	Crystals	B25F	1995	
	N603JGP	Mercedes-Benz 709D	Crystals	B25F	1995	
	N604JGP	Mercedes-Benz 811D	Crystals	B29F	1995	
	N605JGP	Mercedes-Benz 811D	Crystals	B29F	1995	
	N606JGP	Mercedes-Benz 811D	Crystals	B29F	1995	
	P347HKU	Mercedes-Benz 711D	Crystals	B—F	1997	
	P348HKU	Mercedes-Benz 711D	Crystals	B—F	1997	

EPSOM BUSES (Bus fleet)

D600RGJ	Bedford YMT	Plaxton Derwent II		B60F	1987
E204YGC	Mercedes-Benz 709D	Reeve Burgess Beaver		DP25F	1988
E205YGC	Mercedes-Benz 709D	Reeve Burgess Beaver		DP25F	1988
E206BGN	Mercedes-Benz 709D	Reeve Burgess Beaver		DP25F	1988
F207DGT	Mercedes-Benz 709D	Reeve Burgess Beaver		DP25F	1988
F208GGH	Mercedes-Benz 709D	Robin Hood		B26F	1988
F209GGH	Mercedes-Benz 709D	Robin Hood		B26F	1988
H210UGO	Mercedes-Benz 709D	Phoenix		B26F	1988

	Optare MetroRider MR03	Optare		B26F	1991	Ex London General, 1997
H679YGO	H681YGO	H683YGO	H685YGO	H687YGO		H689YGO
H680YGO	H682YGO	H684YGO	H686YGO	H688YGO		

H947JPA	Mercedes-Benz 709D	Reeve Burgess		B25F	1990	Ex O'Reilly & King, Little Bookham, 1997
K593BEG	Mercedes-Benz 709D	Marshall C19		B27F	1992
K892CSX	Dennis Dart 9.8SDL3017	Alexander Dash		B40F	1992
K112NGK	Dennis Dart 9.8SDL3012	Plaxton Pointer		B40F	1993
K113NGK	Dennis Dart 9.8SDL3012	Plaxton Pointer		B40F	1993
K321GEW	Dennis Dart 9.8SDL3017	Marshall C27		B40F	1993
L894NAV	Mercedes-Benz 709D	Marshall C19		B27F	1993
M960CGF	Dennis Dart 9.8SDL3040	Plaxton Pointer		B40F	1994
N401SPA	Dennis Dart 9.8SDL3054	Plaxton Pointer		B40F	1995
N402SPA	Dennis Dart 9.8SDL3054	Plaxton Pointer		B40F	1995
P570APJ	Mercedes-Benz 709D	Plaxton Beaver		B23F	1997
R211MGT	Mercedes-Benz 0814D	UVG Citi-Star		B29F	1997
R212MGT	Mercedes-Benz 0814D	UVG Citi-Star		B29F	1997
R213MGT	Mercedes-Benz 0814D	UVG Citi-Star		B29F	1997

The coach fleet is listed in the London Coach Handbook.

GREY-GREEN

104	E104JYV			Volvo B10M-50				Alexander RV			H43/35F	1987
105	E105JYV			Volvo B10M-50				Alexander RV			H43/35F	1987
107	E107JYV			Scania K92CRB				East Lancs			H45/31F	1988
109	E109JYV			Scania N112DRB				East Lancs			H46/29F	1988
110	E110JYV			Scania N112DRB				East Lancs			H46/29F	1988
111	E111KYN			Scania N112DRB				East Lancs			H46/29F	1988
112	E112KYN			Scania N112DRB				East Lancs			H46/29F	1988
113	E113KYN			Scania N112DRB				East Lancs			H46/29F	1988
114	E114KYN			Scania N112DRB				East Lancs			H46/29F	1988

115-144		Volvo B10M-50		Alexander RV			H46/29D	1988	* Red livery (136 is fitted with an East Lancs top deck following accident damage)

115*	F115PHM	120	F120PHM	125*	F125PHM	130	F130PHM	135	F135PHM	140	F140PHM
116*	F116PHM	121	F121PHM	126	F126PHM	131	F131PHM	136	F136PHM	141	F141PHM
117*	F117PHM	122	F122PHM	127	F127PHM	132	F132PHM	137	F137PHM	142	F142PHM
118*	F118PHM	123*	F123PHM	128	F128PHM	133	F133PHM	138	F138PHM	143	F143PHM
119*	F119PHM	124	F124PHM	129	F129PHM	134	F134PHM	139	F139PHM	144	F144PHM

145	G145TYT	Volvo B10M-50	Alexander RV		H46/29D	1990
146	G146TYT	Volvo B10M-50	Alexander RV		H46/29D	1990
147	G147TYT	Volvo B10M-50	Alexander RV		H46/29D	1990
148	G148TYT	Volvo B10M-50	Alexander RV		H46/29D	1990

149-158		Volvo B10M-50		Alexander RV		H46/33F	1990

149	G149TYT	151	G151TYT	153	G153TYT	155	H155XYU	157	H157XYU
150	G150TYT	152	G152TYT	154	G154TYT	156	H156XYU	158	H158XYU

159	L159GYL	Scania N113DRB	Northern Counties Palatine 1	H42/25D	1994
160	L160GYL	Scania N113DRB	Northern Counties Palatine 1	H42/25D	1994
161	L161GYL	Scania N113DRB	Northern Counties Palatine 1	H42/25D	1994

163-172		Volvo B10M-61		East Lancs EL2000 (1992)		H44/30D	1985

163	B863XYR	165	B865XYR	167	B867XYR	170	B870XYR	172	B872XYR
164	B864XYR	166	B866XYR	168	B868XYR	171	B871XYR		

178	M178LYP	Scania N113DRB				Northern Counties Palatine 1			H42/25D	1995			
179	M179LYP	Scania N113DRB				Northern Counties Palatine 1			H42/25D	1995			
180	M180LYP	Scania N113DRB				Northern Counties Palatine 1			H42/25D	1995			
181	N181OYH	Scania N113DRB				Northern Counties Palatine 1			H42/25D	1996			
182	N182OYH	Scania N113DRB				Northern Counties Palatine 1			H42/25D	1996			
183	N183OYH	Scania N113DRB				Northern Counties Palatine 1			H42/25D	1996			

401-415 — Leyland Olympian ON2R50C13Z4 — Northern Counties — H47/30F — 1990 — Ex County, 1991

401	H101GEV	403	H103GEV	405	H105GEV	407	H107GEV	409	H109GEV	412	H112GEV	414	H114GEV
402	H102GEV	404	H104GEV	406	H106GEV	408	H108GEV	410	H110GEV	413	H113GEV	415	H115GEV

912-925 — Volvo B10M-55 — East Lancs EL2000 — B41F — 1990

912	H912XYT	914	H914XYT	916	H916XYT	918	H918XYT	920	H920XYT	922	H922XYT	925	H925XYT
913	H913XYT	915	H915XYT	917	H917XYT	919	H919XYT	921	H921XYT	923	H923XYT		

934-941 — Dennis Dart 9SDL3024 — Plaxton Pointer — B31F — 1993

934	L934GYL	936	L936GYL	938	L938GYL	940	L940GYL	
935	L935GYL	937	L937GYL	939	L939GYL	941	L941GYL	

950	M950LYR	Dennis Dart 9.8SDL3040	Plaxton Pointer	B40F	1995

952-968 — Dennis Dart SFD212BR1 — Alexander ALX200 — B36F — 1997

952	P952RUL	955	P955RUL	958	P958RUL	961	P961RUL	964	P964RUL	967	P967RUL
953	P953RUL	956	P956RUL	959	P959RUL	962	P962RUL	965	P965RUL	968	P968RUL
954	P954RUL	957	P957RUL	960	P960RUL	963	P963RUL	966	P966RUL		

The coach fleet is listed in the London Coach Handbook.

Reg	Chassis	Body	Seating	Year	Notes
F924ABV	Talbot-Pullman Freeway	TBP	DP19F	1989	Ex Walker, Stanford-le-Hope, 1996
F310OVW	MCW Metrorider MF150/112	MCW	B24F	1988	
F312PEV	Scania N113DRB	Alexander RH	H47/33F	1989	
F314RHK	Scania N113DRB	Alexander RH	H47/33F	1989	
J51GCX	DAF SB220LC550	Ikarus Citibus	B48F	1992	Ex Strathclyde, 1994
J52GCX	DAF SB220LC550	Ikarus Citibus	B48F	1992	Ex Strathclyde, 1994
J582WVX	Mercedes-Benz 709D	Alexander AM	B25F	1991	
J583WVX	Mercedes-Benz 709D	Alexander AM	B25F	1991	
L475GOV	Talbot-Pullman Freeway	TBP	B18FL	1994	
L476GOV	Talbot-Pullman Freeway	TBP	B18FL	1994	
M52WEV	LDV 400	LDV	16	1995	Ex Harris Coaches, West Thurrock, 1995
M649RCP	DAF DB250RS505	Northern Counties Palatine 2	H47/30F	1995	Ex Bee-Line, 1996
N25COO	LDV 400	LDV	16	1995	Ex Harris Coaches, West Thurrock, 1996
P317KTW	DAF DE02RSDB250	Northern Counties Palatine 2	H47/30F	1996	
P318KTW	DAF DE02RSDB250	Northern Counties Palatine 2	H47/30F	1996	
P320KAR	Optare L1070	Optare Excel	B35F	1996	
P321KAR	Optare L1070	Optare Excel	B35F	1996	
P322KAR	Optare L1070	Optare Excel	B35F	1996	
P323KAR	Optare L1070	Optare Excel	B35F	1996	

	Optare L1070	Optare Excel	B33F	1997	
P324NHJ	P326NHJ	P328NHJ	P330NHJ	P332NHJ	P334NHJ
P325NHJ	P327NHJ	P329NHJ	P331NHJ	P333HBC	

	DAF DE02RSDB250	Northern Counties Palatine 2	H43/25D	1997
P335ROO				
P336ROO				
P337ROO				

	Volvo Olympian	East Lancs Pyoneer	H51/28D	1997		
P338ROO	P340ROO	P342ROO	P344ROO	P346ROO	P348ROO	P350ROO
P339ROO	P341ROO	P343ROO	P345ROO	P347ROO	P349ROO	

	Volvo Olympian	East Lancs Pyoneer	H51/35F	1997
P351ROO	P353ROO	R355XVX	R357XVX	R359XVX
P352ROO	R354XVX	R356XVX	R358XVX	

Special liveries

LTS rail : J582WVX.
ASDA Gala Bingo Club : J583WVX.
White: M52WEV, N25COO.

KENTISH BUS

AN210w	EPH210V	Leyland Atlantean AN68A/1R	Roe	H43/30F	1979	Ex London Country, 1986
AN221w	EPH221V	Leyland Atlantean AN68A/1R	Roe	H43/30F	1980	Ex London Country, 1986
AN276w	KPJ276W	Leyland Atlantean AN68A/1R	Roe	H43/30F	1981	Ex London Country, 1986

115	L115YVK	Dennis Dart 9SDL3034	Northern Counties Paladin	B35F	1994	
116	L116YVK	Dennis Dart 9SDL3034	Northern Counties Paladin	B35F	1994	
117	L117YVK	Dennis Dart 9SDL3034	Northern Counties Paladin	B35F	1994	
118	L118YVK	Dennis Dart 9SDL3034	Northern Counties Paladin	B35F	1994	
119	L119YVK	Dennis Dart 9SDL3034	Northern Counties Paladin	B35F	1994	

514-556 Leyland Olympian ON2R50C13Z4 * Northern Counties Palatine 1 H47/27D 1990 * 514/41/3/4/6-54/6 are ONCL10/1RZ

514	G514VBB	**521**	G521VBB	**528**	G528VBB	**535**	G535VBB	**542**	G542VBB	**549**	G549VBB	**556**	G556VBB
515	G515VBB	**522**	G522VBB	**529**	G529VBB	**536**	G536VBB	**543**	G543VBB	**550**	G550VBB		
516	G516VBB	**523**	G523VBB	**530**	G530VBB	**537**	G537VBB	**544**	G544VBB	**551**	G551VBB		
517	G517VBB	**524**	G524VBB	**531**	G531VBB	**538**	G538VBB	**545**	G545VBB	**552**	G552VBB		
518	G518VBB	**525**	G525VBB	**532**	G532VBB	**539**	G539VBB	**546**	G546VBB	**553**	G553VBB		
519	G519VBB	**526**	G526VBB	**533**	G533VBB	**540**	G540VBB	**547**	G547VBB	**554**	G554VBB		
520	G520VBB	**527**	G527VBB	**534**	G534VBB	**541**	G541VBB	**548**	G548VBB	**555**	G555VBB		

610-618 Leyland Olympian ONLXB/1R Eastern Coach Works H45/32F 1984/85 Ex Northumbria, 1990/91

610w	A240GHN	**612w**	A242GHN	**614w**	A244GHN	**617w**	B247NVN			
611w	A241GHN	**613w**	A243GHN	**615w**	B245NVN	**618w**	B248NVN			

721-734 Volvo Citybus B10M-50 Alexander RV H47/29D 1989 Ex Londonlinks, 1997

721	F101TML	**724**	F104TML	**726**	F106TML	**728**	F108TML	**730**	F110TML	**733**	F113TML
723	F103TML	**725**	F105TML	**727**	F107TML	**729**	F109TML	**732**	F112TML		

869w	F932LKE	MCW Metrorider MF154/13	MCW	B33F	1988	Ex Boro'line Maidstone, 1992
1154	J154NKN	Mercedes-Benz 814D	Dormobile Routemaker	B33F	1992	Ex Crossways, Swanley, 1996

1444-1453 Optare MetroRider MR17 Optare B29F 1994 Ex Londonlinks, 1996/7

1444	M444HPF	**1446**	M446HPF	**1448**	M448HPF	**1450**	M450HPF	**1452**	M452HPG
1445	M445HPF	**1447**	M447HPF	**1449**	M449HPF	**1451**	M451HPF	**1453**	M453HPG

1801-1808 Optare MetroRider MR15 Optare B29F 1996

1801	N801BKN	**1803**	N803BKN	**1805**	N805BKN	**1807**	N807BKN
1802	N802BKN	**1804**	N804BKN	**1806**	N806BKN	**1808**	N808BKN

1844	E34NEF	MCW Metrorider MF154/9		MCW				DP31F	1988	Ex Londonlinks, 1995		
1852	N852YKE	Optare MetroRider MR13		Optare				B25F	1995	Ex Londonlinks, 1996		
1862	F862LCU	MCW Metrorider MF158/15		MCW				B31F	1988	Ex Maidstone & District, 1997		
1863	F863LCU	MCW Metrorider MF158/15		MCW				B31F	1988	Ex Maidstone & District, 1997		
1864	F864LCU	MCW Metrorider MF158/15		MCW				B31F	1988	Ex Londonlinks, 1995		
1866	G866TCU	Optare MetroRider MR01		Optare				B31F	1989	Ex Londonlinks, 1995		
1886	H886CCU	Optare MetroRider		Optare				B25F	1991			
1887	H887CCU	Optare MetroRider		Optare				B25F	1991			
1889	H889CCU	Optare MetroRider		Optare				B25F	1991			
1890	H890CCU	Optare MetroRider		Optare				B25F	1991			
1961	J961JNL	Optare MetroRider		Optare				B25F	1991			
1962	J962JNL	Optare MetroRider		Optare				B25F	1991			
1970	J970JNL	Optare MetroRider		Optare				B25F	1991			
1973	J973JNL	Optare MetroRider		Optare				B25F	1991			
1974	J974JNL	Optare MetroRider		Optare				B25F	1991			
1975	J975JNL	Optare MetroRider		Optare				B25F	1991			
1977	L837MWT	Optare MetroRider MR01		Optare				B31F	1993	Ex Darlington, 1995		
1978	L838MWT	Optare MetroRider MR01		Optare				B31F	1993	Ex Londonlinks, 1995		
2209	TIB5905	Leyland Tiger TRCTL11/3RH		Duple 320				C53F	1986	Ex London Country, 1986		
2830	TIB5903	Volvo B10M-61		Van Hool Alizée				C53F	1988	Ex Jason, St Mary Cray, 1993		
2831	TIB5904	Volvo B10M-61		Van Hool Alizée				C53F	1988	Ex Jason, St Mary Cray, 1993		
3053	H813EKJ	Leyland Lynx LX2R11G15Z4S		Leyland				B49F	1991	Ex Boro'line Maidstone, 1992		
3054	H815EKJ	Leyland Lynx LX2R11G15Z4S		Leyland				B49F	1991	Ex Boro'line Maidstone, 1992		

3056-3065		Leyland Lynx LX2R11C15Z4S		Leyland				B49F	1989	Ex Boro'line Maidstone, 1992 (3065 ex Maidstone & District, 1997)		
3056	G36VME	3058	G38VME	3060	G40VME	3062	G42VME	3064	G44VME			
3057	G37VME	3059	G39VME	3061	G41VME	3063	G43VME	3065	G45VME			

3087	G217LGK	Dennis Dart 9SDL3002		Duple/Carlyle Dartline				B36F	1990	Ex R&I Tours, London NW10, 1995		
3093	G123RGT	Dennis Dart 9SDL3002		Duple/Carlyle Dartline				B36F	1990	Ex R&I Tours, London NW10, 1995		
3095	G125RGT	Dennis Dart 9SDL3002		Duple/Carlyle Dartline				B36F	1990	Ex R&I Tours, London NW10, 1995		
3096	G126RGT	Dennis Dart 9SDL3002		Duple/Carlyle Dartline				B36F	1990	Ex R&I Tours, London NW10, 1995		
3097	G127RGT	Dennis Dart 9SDL3002		Duple/Carlyle Dartline				B36F	1990	Ex R&I Tours, London NW10, 1995		
3098	G128RGT	Dennis Dart 9SDL3002		Duple/Carlyle Dartline				B36F	1990	Ex R&I Tours, London NW10, 1995		

3112-3159		Dennis Dart 9SDL3034		Northern Counties Paladin				B35F	1994			
3112	L112YVK	3129	L129YVK	3134	L134YVK	3139	L139YVK	3144	L144YVK	3150	L150YVK	3157	L157YVK
3113	L113YVK	3130	L130YVK	3135	L135YVK	3140	L140YVK	3145	L145YVK	3152	L152YVK	3158	L158BFT
3114	L114YVK	3131	L131YVK	3136	L136YVK	3141	L141YVK	3146	L146YVK	3153	L153YVK	3159	L159BFT
3127	L127YVK	3132	L132YVK	3137	L137YVK	3142	L142YVK	3148	L148YVK	3154	L154YVK		
3128	L128YVK	3133	L133YVK	3138	L138YVK	3143	L143YVK	3149	L149YVK	3155	L155YVK		

3137/8 are on loan to Maidstone & District

3184	P184LKL	Dennis Dart SFD212BR1	Plaxton Pointer	B37F	1996	
3185	P185LKL	Dennis Dart SFD212BR1	Plaxton Pointer	B37F	1996	
3186	P186LKJ	Dennis Dart SFD322BR1	Plaxton Pointer	B40F	1997	
3187	P187LKJ	Dennis Dart SFD322BR1	Plaxton Pointer	B40F	1997	
3188	P188LKJ	Dennis Dart SFD322BR1	Plaxton Pointer	B40F	1997	
3189	P189LKJ	Dennis Dart SFD322BR1	Plaxton Pointer	B40F	1997	
3190	P190LKJ	Dennis Dart SFD322BR1	Plaxton Pointer	B40F	1997	
3191	P191LKJ	Dennis Dart SFD322BR1	Plaxton Pointer	B40F	1997	

| 3250-3259 | | Scania L113CRL | Wright Access Ultralow | B43F | 1995 | |

| 3250 | N250BKK | 3252 | N252BKK | 3254 | N254BKK | 3256 | N256BKK | 3258 | N258BKK |
| 3251 | N251BKK | 3253 | N253BKK | 3255 | N255BKK | 3257 | N257BKK | 3259 | N259BKK |

3335	SIB6705	Leyland National 10351A/1R	East Lancs (1992)	B41F	1978	Ex Londonlinks, 1996
3336	SIB6706	Leyland National 2 NL106AL11/1R	East Lancs (1992)	B41F	1981	Ex Londonlinks, 1996
3337	SIB6707	Leyland National 2 NL106AL11/1R	East Lancs (1992)	B41F	1981	Ex Londonlinks, 1996
3338	SIB6708	Leyland National 2 NL106AL11/1R	East Lancs (1992)	B41F	1982	Ex Londonlinks, 1996
3345	SIB6715	Leyland National 1051/1R/0402	East Lancs (1993)	B41F	1973	Ex Londonlinks, 1996
3346	SIB6716	Leyland National 1051/1R/0402	East Lancs (1993)	B41F	1974	Ex Londonlinks, 1996
3361	PDZ6261	Leyland National 10351/1R	East Lancs (1994)	B41F	1977	Ex Londonlinks, 1996
3362	PDZ6262	Leyland National 10351/1R	East Lancs (1994)	B41F	1977	Ex Londonlinks, 1996
3492	RUF42R	Leyland National 11351/2R		B25DL	1977	Ex London Buses, 1993
3493	THX202S	Leyland National 10351A/2R		B21DL	1978	Ex London Buses, 1993
3494	YYE290T	Leyland National 10351A/2R		B21DL	1979	Ex London Buses, 1993

| 5557-5565 | | Volvo Olympian YN2RC16Z4 | Northern Counties Palatine 2 | H47/30F | 1994 | |

| 5557 | L557YCU | 5559 | L559YCU | 5562 | L562YCU | 5564 | L564YCU |
| 5558 | L558YCU | 5561 | L561YCU | 5563 | L563YCU | 5565 | L565YCU |

5601	WDC219Y	Leyland Olympian ONLXB/1R	Eastern Coach Works	H44/32F	1983	Ex Northumbria, 1991
5608	CEF231Y	Leyland Olympian ONLXB/1R	Eastern Coach Works	H45/32F	1983	Ex Northumbria, 1991
5616	B246NVN	Leyland Olympian ONLXB/1R	Eastern Coach Works	H45/32F	1985	Ex Northumbria, 1991
5619	B256RAJ	Leyland Olympian ONLXB/1R	Eastern Coach Works	H45/32F	1985	Ex Northumbria, 1990
5620	C257UAJ	Leyland Olympian ONLXB/1R	Eastern Coach Works	H45/32F	1985	Ex Northumbria, 1991

| 5751-5762 | | Leyland Olympian ONLXB/1RH | Optare | H47/29F | 1988/89 | Ex Boro'line Maidstone, 1992 |

| 5751 | E151OMD | 5753 | E153OMD | 5755 | E155OMD | 5757 | E157OMD | 5759 | E159OMD | 5761 | E161OMD |
| 5752 | E152OMD | 5754 | E154OMD | 5756 | E156OMD | 5758 | E158OMD | 5760 | E160OMD | 5762 | F991UME |

5765	H765EKJ	Leyland Olympian ON2R50C13Z4		Northern Counties				H47/30F	1991	Ex Boro'line Maidstone, 1992			
5766	H766EKJ	Leyland Olympian ON2R50C13Z4		Northern Counties				H47/30F	1991	Ex Boro'line Maidstone, 1992			
5767	H767EKJ	Leyland Olympian ON2R50C13Z4		Northern Counties				H47/30F	1991	Ex Boro'line Maidstone, 1992			
5768	H768EKJ	Leyland Olympian ON2R50C13Z4		Northern Counties				H47/30F	1991	Ex Boro'line Maidstone, 1992			
5769	H769EKJ	Leyland Olympian ON2R50C13Z4		Northern Counties				H47/30F	1991	Ex Boro'line Maidstone, 1992			
5770	H770EKJ	Leyland Olympian ON2R50C13Z4		Northern Counties				H47/30F	1991	Ex Boro'line Maidstone, 1992			
6172	XPG172T	Leyland Atlantean AN68A/1R		Park Royal				H43/30F	1979	Ex Londonlinks, 1997			
6186	XPG186T	Leyland Atlantean AN68A/1R		Roe				H43/30F	1979	Ex Londonlinks, 1996			

6220-6282		Leyland Atlantean AN68A/1R		Roe				H43/30F	1979/81	Ex London Country, 1986			
6220	EPH220V	6232	EPH232V	6270	KPJ270W	6271	KPJ271W	6274	KPJ274W	6277	KPJ277W	6282	KPJ282W

7631-7643		Volvo Citybus B10M-50		Northern Counties				H45/31F	1989	Ex Londonlinks, 1996/7			
7631	G631BPH	7633	G633BPH	7635	G635BPH	7637	G637BPH	7639	G639BPH	7641	G641BPH	7643	G643BPH
7632	G632BPH	7634	G634BPH	7636	G636BPH	7638	G638BPH	7640	G640BPH	7642	G642BPH		

7702	G641CHF	Volvo Citybus B10M-50	East Lancs	H49/39F	1989	Ex North Western, 1996
7703	G642CHF	Volvo Citybus B10M-50	East Lancs	H49/39F	1989	Ex North Western, 1996
7706	G648EKA	Volvo Citybus B10M-50	East Lancs	H49/39F	1990	Ex North Western, 1996
7707	G649EKA	Volvo Citybus B10M-50	East Lancs	H49/39F	1990	Ex North Western, 1996
7708	G659DTJ	Volvo Citybus B10M-50	East Lancs	H49/39F	1990	Ex North Western, 1996
7709	G660DTJ	Volvo Citybus B10M-50	East Lancs	H49/39F	1990	Ex North Western, 1996
7722	F102TML	Volvo Citybus B10M-50	Alexander RV	H47/29D	1989	Ex Londonlinks, 1997
7731	F111TML	Volvo Citybus B10M-50	Alexander RV	H47/29D	1989	Ex Londonlinks, 1997
7734	F114TML	Volvo Citybus B10M-50	Alexander RV	H47/29D	1989	Ex Boro'line Maidstone, 1992
7764	E164OMD	Volvo Citybus B10M-61	Alexander RV	H47/37F	1988	Ex Boro'line Maidstone, 1992

Previous registrations

F932LKE	F241JWV, 217UKL	SIB6705	YPF762T	SIB6708	LFR874X	TIB5903	E316OPR
PDZ6261	UPB310S	SIB6706	LFR855X	SIB6715	TPD176M	TIB5904	E319OPR
PDZ6262	UPB313S	SIB6707	JCK850W	SIB6716	UPE196M	TIB5905	C261SPC

Special liveries

Overall advertisement: 6274.
Green Line: 2209, 2830/1.
LT Mobility Bus: 3492-4.
Crossways Business Park: 1154.
Green Traveller: 1978.

LEASIDE

DBS1-13 — DAF DB250RS505* — Northern Counties Palatine 2 — H47/30F — 1995 — * DBS11-13 are DE02RSDB250

1	N601DWY	3	N603DWY	5	N605DWY	7	N607DWY	9	N609DWY	11	N611DWY	13	N613DWY
2	N602DWY	4	N604DWY	6	N606DWY	8	N608DWY	10	N610DWY	12	N612DWY		

DRL49	K549ORH	Dennis Dart 9SDL3016	Plaxton Pointer	B34F	1992	Ex London Buses, 1994
DRL50	K550ORH	Dennis Dart 9SDL3016	Plaxton Pointer	B34F	1992	Ex London Buses, 1994
DRL51	K551ORH	Dennis Dart 9SDL3016	Plaxton Pointer	B34F	1992	Ex London Buses, 1994
DRL52	K552ORH	Dennis Dart 9SDL3016	Plaxton Pointer	B34F	1992	Ex London Buses, 1994

DT58-64 — Dennis Dart 8.5SDL3003 — Carlyle Dartline — B28F — 1990 — Ex South London, 1996

58	H458UGO	59	H459UGO	60	H460UGO	61	H461UGO	62	H462UGO	63	H463UGO	64	H464UGO

L315-354 — Leyland Olympian ON2R50C13Z4 — Alexander RH — H43/25D — 1992 — Ex London Buses, 1994

315	J315BSH	321	J321BSH	327	J327BSH	333	J433BSH	339	J339BSH	345	J345BSH	351	J351BSH
316	J316BSH	322	J322BSH	328	J328BSH	334	J334BSH	340	J340BSH	346	J346BSH	352	J352BSH
317	J317BSH	323	J323BSH	329	J329BSH	335	J335BSH	341	J341BSH	347	J347BSH	353	J353BSH
318	J318BSH	324	J324BSH	330	J330BSH	336	J336BSH	342	J342BSH	348	J348BSH	354	VLT32
319	J319BSH	325	J325BSH	331	J331BSH	337	J337BSH	343	J343BSH	349	J349BSH		
320	J320BSH	326	J326BSH	332	J332BSH	338	J338BSH	344	J344BSH	350	J350BSH		

LDR1-55 — Dennis Dart 9.8SDL3054* — Plaxton Pointer — B40F — 1995/96 — * LDR40-55 are SFD412

1	N671GUM	7	N677GUM	13	N683GUM	19	N689GUM	43	P843PWW	49	P849PWW	55	P855PWW
2	N672GUM	8	N678GUM	14	N684GUM	20	N690GUM	44	P844PWW	50	P850PWW		
3	N673GUM	9	N679GUM	15	N685GUM	21	N691GUM	45	P845PWW	51	P851PWW		
4	N674GUM	10	N680GUM	16	N686GUM	40	P840PWW	46	P846PWW	52	P852PWW		
5	N675GUM	11	N681GUM	17	N687GUM	41	P841PWW	47	P847PWW	53	P853PWW		
6	N676GUM	12	N682GUM	18	N688GUM	42	P842PWW	48	P848PWW	54	P854PWW		

M6t	WYW6T	MCW Metrobus DR101/8	MCW	H43/28D	1978	Ex South London, 1996
M14t	WYW14T	MCW Metrobus DR101/8	MCW	H43/28D	1978	Ex South London, 1995
M51	WYW51T	MCW Metrobus DR101/8	MCW	H43/28D	1979	Ex South London, 1996
M205t	BYX205V	MCW Metrobus DR101/9	MCW	H43/28D	1979	Ex South London, 1997

M220-493 — MCW Metrobus DR101/12 — MCW — H43/28D — 1980 — Ex London Buses, 1994 (M282 ex South London, 1996; M310/89/441/69/91 ex South London, 1995; M220 ex South London, 1997)

220tu	BYX220V	310	BYX310V	382t	GYE382W	422t	GYE422W	445t	GYE445W	478t	GYE478W	493	GYE493W
266	BYX266V	317	EYE317V	389	GYE389W	426t	GYE426W	450t	GYE450W	485t	GYE485W		
282t	BYX282V	353	GYE353W	419	GYE419W	441	GYE441W	469t	GYE469W	491	GYE491W		

M509-798 MCW Metrobus DR101/14 MCW H43/28D 1981-82 Ex London Buses, 1994

No.	Reg	No.	Reg	No.	Reg	No.	Reg	No.	Reg	No.	Reg	No.	Reg
509	GYE509W	587	GYE587W	632	KYV632X	669	KYV669X	712	KYV712X	744	KYV744X	776	KYV776X
510	GYE510W	590	GYE590W	635	KYV635X	672	KYV672X	713	KYV713X	745	KYV745X	777	KYV777X
529	GYE529W	591	GYE591W	636	KYV636X	673	KYV673X	714	KYV714X	746	KYV746X	778	KYV778X
530	GYE530W	593	GYE593W	637	KYV637X	675	KYV675X	715	KYV715X	747	KYV747X	780	KYV780X
531	GYE531W	596	GYE596W	638	KYV638X	676	KYV676X	716	KYV716X	748	KYV748X	781	KYV781X
533	GYE533W	600	GYE600W	641	KYV641X	679	KYV679X	717	KYV717X	749	KYV749X	782	KYV782X
535	GYE535W	602	GYE602W	642	KYV642X	681	KYV681X	718	KYV718X	750	KYV750X	783	KYV783X
536	GYE536W	603	GYE603W	643	KYV643X	684	KYV684X	719	KYV719X	751	KYV751X	784	KYV784X
538	GYE538W	604	GYE604W	644	KYV644X	686	KYV686X	720	KYV720X	752	KYV752X	785	KYV785X
540	GYE540W	605	GYE605W	645	KYV645X	688	KYV688X	721	KYV721X	753	KYV753X	786	KYV786X
543	GYE543W	609	KYO609X	646	KYV646X	689	KYV689X	723	KYV723X	754	KYV754X	787	KYV787X
544	GYE544W	610	KYO610X	647	KYV647X	692	KYV692X	726	KYV726X	756	KYV756X	788	KYV788X
547	GYE547W	611	KYO611X	648	KYV648X	694	KYV694X	727	KYV727X	757	KYV757X	789	KYV789X
548	GYE548W	612	KYO612X	650	KYV650X	698	KYV698X	728	KYV728X	758t	KYV758X	790	KYV790X
549	GYE549W	613	KYO613X	651	KYV651X	699	KYV699X	729	KYV729X	761	KYV761X	791	KYV791X
551	GYE551W	614	KYO614X	652	KYV652X	700	KYV700X	730	KYV730X	762	KYV762X	792	KYV792X
557	GYE557W	615	KYO615X	653	KYV653X	701	KYV701X	731	KYV731X	765	KYV765X	793	KYV793X
559	GYE559W	617	KYO617X	657	KYV657X	702	KYV702X	732	KYV732X	766	KYV766X	795	KYV795X
562	GYE562W	619	KYO619X	658	KYV658X	703	KYV703X	733	KYV733X	767	KYV767X	796	KYV796X
567	GYE567W	622	KYO622X	659	KYV659X	704	KYV704X	734	KYV734X	768	KYV768X	798	KYV798X
569	GYE569W	624	KYO624X	660	KYV660X	705	KYV705X	736	KYV736X	770	KYV770X		
575	GYE575W	626	KYO626X	661	KYV661X	707	KYV707X	737	KYV737X	771	KYV771X		
581	GYE581W	627	KYO627X	663	KYV663X	708	KYV708X	738	KYV738X	772	KYV772X		
582	GYE582W	628	KYO628X	664	KYV664X	709	KYV709X	740	KYV740X	773	KYV773X		
585	GYE585W	630	KYO630X	665	KYV665X	710	KYV710X	742	KYV742X	774	KYV774X		
586	GYE586W	631	KYO631X	666	KYV666X	711	KYV711X	743	KYV743X	775	KYV775X		

No.	Reg	Type	Body	Layout	Year	History
M891	OJD891Y	MCW Metrobus DR101/16	MCW	H43/28D	1983	Ex London Buses, 1994
M903	A903SUL	MCW Metrobus DR101/16	MCW	H43/28D	1983	Ex London Buses, 1994
M919	A919SUL	MCW Metrobus DR101/16	MCW	H43/28D	1983	Ex London Buses, 1994
M929	A929SUL	MCW Metrobus DR101/16	MCW	H43/28D	1983	Ex London Buses, 1994
M936	A936SUL	MCW Metrobus DR101/16	MCW	H43/28D	1983	Ex South London, 1996
M939	A939SUL	MCW Metrobus DR101/16	MCW	H43/28D	1983	Ex London Buses, 1994

M988-1424 MCW Metrobus DR101/17* MCW H43/28D 1984-86 Ex London Buses, 1994 * M1044 is DR101/19

988	A988SYF	1130	B130WUL	1169	B169WUL	1229	B229WUL	1282	B282WUL	1307	C307BUV	1327	C327BUV
996	A996SYF	1131	B131WUL	1170	B170WUL	1231	B231WUL	1283	B283WUL	1308	C308BUV	1332	C332BUV
1000	A700THV	1132	B132WUL	1173	B173WUL	1233	B233WUL	1285	B285WUL	1309	C309BUV	1362	C362BUV
1044	A744THV	1133	B133WUL	1175	B175WUL	1239	B239WUL	1286	B286WUL	1310	C310BUV	1399	C399BUV
1070	B70WUL	1134	B134WUL	1176	B176WUL	1249	B249WUL	1288	B288WUL	1312	C312BUV	1401	C401BUV
1074	B74WUL	1135	B135WUL	1179	B179WUL	1252	B252WUL	1289	B289WUL	1313	C313BUV	1402	C402BUV
1075	B75WUL	1136	B136WUL	1182	B182WUL	1253	B253WUL	1290	B290WUL	1314	C314BUV	1404	C404BUV
1109	B109WUL	1137	B137WUL	1209	B209WUL	1254	B254WUL	1291	B291WUL	1316	C316BUV	1405	C405BUV
1112	B112WUL	1138	B138WUL	1210	B210WUL	1255	B255WUL	1293	B293WUL	1317	C317BUV	1406	C406BUV
1121	B121WUL	1139	B139WUL	1213	B213WUL	1263	B263WUL	1294	B294WUL	1318	C318BUV	1413	C413BUV
1122	B122WUL	1140	B140WUL	1214	B214WUL	1265	B265WUL	1295	B295WUL	1319	C319BUV	1417	C417BUV
1123	B123WUL	1152	B152WUL	1216	B216WUL	1275	B275WUL	1296	B296WUL	1320	C320BUV	1424	C424BUV
1124	B124WUL	1154	B154WUL	1217	B217WUL	1276	B276WUL	1297	B297WUL	1321	C321BUV		
1126	B126WUL	1155	B155WUL	1219	B219WUL	1278	B278WUL	1298	B298WUL	1322	C322BUV		
1127	B127WUL	1162	B162WUL	1221	B221WUL	1279	B279WUL	1299	B299WUL	1323	C323BUV		
1128	B128WUL	1164	B164WUL	1227	B227WUL	1280	B280WUL	1300	B300WUL	1324	C324BUV		
1129	B129WUL	1165	B165WUL	1228	B228WUL	1281	B281WUL	1303	B303WUL	1326	C326BUV		

MR102	F102YVP	MCW Metrorider MF150/115	MCW	B23F	1988	Ex London Buses, 1994
MR104	F104YVP	MCW Metrorider MF150/116	MCW	DP23F	1988	Ex London Buses, 1994
MR105	F105YVP	MCW Metrorider MF150/116	MCW	DP23F	1988	Ex London Buses, 1994
RM5	VLT5	AEC Routemaster 5RM	Park Royal	H36/28R	1959	Ex London Buses, 1994
RM295u	VLT295	AEC Routemaster 5RM	Park Royal	H36/28R	1960	Ex London Transport Buses, 1997
RM311	KGJ142A	AEC Routemaster 5RM (Iveco)	Park Royal	H36/28R	1960	Ex South London, 1996
RM736†u	XYJ418	AEC Routemaster 5RM	Park Royal	H36/28R	1961	Ex London Transport Buses, 1997
RM1125	KGH858A	AEC Routemaster 5RM (Iveco)	Park Royal	H36/28R	1962	Ex South London, 1996
RM1330u	KGH975A	AEC Routemaster 5RM	Park Royal	H36/28R	1962	Ex London Transport Buses, 1997
RM1725	725DYE	AEC Routemaster 5RM (Iveco)	Park Royal	H36/28R	1963	Ex South London, 1996
RM2185	CUV185C	AEC Routemaster 5RM (Iveco)	Park Royal	H36/28R	1965	Ex South London, 1996

† Fitted with plain upper deck front window

RML882-2758 — AEC Routemaster 7RM (Cummins)   Park Royal   H40/32R   1961-68   Ex London Buses, 1994

882	WLT882	2315	CUV315C	2356	CUV356C	2418	JJD418D	2528	JJD528D	2625	NML625E	2685	SMK685F
884	WLT884	2323	CUV323C	2359	CUV359C	2434	JJD434D	2534	JJD534D	2628	NML628E	2688	SMK688F
888	WLT888	2325	CUV325C	2370	JJD370D	2457	JJD457D	2544	JJD544D	2632	NML632E	2708	SMK708F
896	WLT896	2326	CUV326C	2372	JJD372D	2460	JJD460D	2546	JJD546D	2635	NML635E	2716	SMK716F
897	WLT897	2328	CUV328C	2373	JJD373D	2468	JJD468D	2552	JJD552D	2638	NML638E	2742	SMK742F
901	WLT901	2329	CUV329C	2380	JJD380D	2483	JJD483D	2562	JJD562D	2643	NML643E	2746	SMK746F
2261	CUV261C	2330	CUV330C	2386	JJD386D	2492	JJD492D	2567	JJD567D	2655	NML655E	2747	SMK747F
2267	CUV267C	2334	CUV334C	2391	JJD391D	2494	JJD494D	2571	JJD571D	2658	SMK658F	2750	SMK750F
2277	CUV277C	2340	CUV340C	2394	JJD394D	2503	JJD503D	2588	JJD588D	2660	SMK660F	2754	SMK754F
2280	CUV280C	2344	CUV344C	2401	JJD401D	2504	JJD504D	2589	JJD589D	2666	SMK666F	2758	SMK758F
2287	CUV287C	2346	CUV346C	2406	JJD406D	2510	JJD510D	2595	JJD595D	2675	SMK675F		
2292	CUV292C	2350	CUV350C	2408	JJD408D	2518	JJD518D	2597	JJD597D	2678	SMK678F		
2294	CUV294C	2354	CUV354C	2409	JJD409D	2525	JJD525D	2611	NML611E	2682	SMK682F		
2304	CUV304C	2355	CUV355C	2416	JJD416D	2526	JJD526D	2617	NML617E	2684	SMK684F		

SLW1-14 — Scania N113CRL   Wright Pathfinder 320   B37D   1994   Ex London Buses, 1994

1	RDZ1701	3	RDZ1703	5	RDZ1705	7	RDZ1707	9	RDZ1709	11	RDZ1711	13	RDZ1713
2	RDZ1702	4	RDZ1704	6	RDZ1706	8	RDZ1708	10	RDZ1710	12	RDZ1712	14	RDZ1714

T95w   CUL95V   Leyland Titan TNLXB2RRSp   Park Royal   H44/26D   1979   Ex London Buses, 1994

Previous registrations

KGH858A	125CLT	KGJ975A	330CLT	KGJ142A	WLT311	VLT32	J354BSH
XYJ418	WLT736						

Special liveries

Overall advertisements : M14, M282, M382, M422/45/50.
North London College : M317.
White with Arriva lettering: M6.

On order

3 DAF – Northern Counties B–D

LIMEBOURNE

2201	N201MWW	Optare MetroRider	Optare	B29F	1996
2202	N202MWW	Optare MetroRider	Optare	B29F	1996
2203	N203MWW	Optare MetroRider	Optare	B29F	1996
2204	N204MWW	Optare MetroRider	Optare	B29F	1996
2205	N205MWW	Optare MetroRider	Optare	B29F	1996
2206	N206MWW	Optare MetroRider	Optare	B29F	1996

2301-2319   Dennis Dart SFD212   Plaxton Pointer   B33F   1997

2301	P301HDP	2304	P304HDP	2307	P307HDP	2310	R310NGM	2313	R313NGM	2317	R317NGM
2302	P302HDP	2305	P305HDP	2308	P308HDP	2311	R311NGM	2314	R314NGM	2319	R319NGM
2303	P303HDP	2306	P306HDP	2309	R309NGM	2312	R312NGM	2315	R315NGM		

2501-2506   Marshall Midibus   Marshall   B29F   1996   On loan from London General, 1997

| 2501 | P501HEG | 2502 | P502HEG | 2503 | P503HEG | 2504 | P504HEG | 2505 | P505HEG | 2506 | P506HEG |

LONDON BUSLINES

D601-632   Dennis Dart SFD412*   Plaxton Pointer   B37F   1996   *601-610 are 9.8SDL3054

601	N601XJM	606	N606XJM	611	N611XJM	616	N616XJM	621	N621XJM	626	N626XJM	631	P631CGM
602	N602XJM	607	N607XJM	612	N612XJM	617	N617XJM	622	N622XJM	627	P627CGM	632	P632CGM
603	N603XJM	608	N608XJM	613	N613XJM	618	N618XJM	623	N623XJM	628	P628CGM		
604	N604XJM	609	N609XJM	614	N614XJM	619	N619XJM	624	N624XJM	629	P629CGM		
605	N605XJM	610	N610XJM	615	N615XJM	620	N620XJM	625	N625XJM	630	P630CGM		

DML633-653   Dennis Dart SFD212   Marshall Capital   B37F   1997

633	R633VLX	636	R636VLX	639	R639VLX	642	R642TLM	645	R645TLM	648	R648TLM	651	R651TLM
635	R835VLX	637	R637VLX	640	R640VLX	643	R643TLM	646	R646TLM	649	R649TLM	652	R652TLM
634	R634VLX	638	R638VLX	641	R641VLX	644	R644TLM	647	R647TLM	650	R650TLM	653	R653TLM

L7   P407MLA   Dennis Dart SFD212TGD   Plaxton Pointer   B34F   1996   Ex CentreWest, 1997

L225-236   Dennis Dart SFD212TGD   Plaxton Pointer   B35F   1996/97   Ex CentreWest ,1997

225	N225TPK	228	N228TPK	231	N231TPK	234	N234TPK	237	P237NLW
226	N226TPK	229	N229TPK	232	N232TPK	235	N235TPK	238	P238NLW
227	N227TPK	230	N230TPK	233	N233TPK	236	N236TPK	239	P239NLW

551	K651DBL	Renault-Dodge S75	Plaxton Beaver	B18FL	1992
552	K652DBL	Renault-Dodge S75	Plaxton Beaver	B18FL	1992
553	K653DBL	Renault-Dodge S75	Plaxton Beaver	B18FL	1992

LONDON CENTRAL

AN1	VTP258L		Leyland Atlantean AN68R/1		Alexander AL			H—/—D	1972	Ex London Buses, 1995; mobile canteen/restroom		

AV1-9			Volvo Olympian YN2RC16Z4		Alexander Royale			H45/29F	1995			
1	M81MYM	3	M83MYM	5	M85MYM	7	M87MYM	9	WLT789			
2	M82MYM	4	M84MYM	6	M86MYM	8	M91MYM					

DEL1-11			Dennis Dart 9SDL3034		East Lancs EL2000			B34F	1994	Ex London Buses, 1994		
1	L901JRN	3	L903JRN	5	L905JRN	7	L907JRN	9	L909JRN	11	L911JRN	
2	L902JRN	4	L904JRN	6	L906JRN	8	L908JRN	10	L910JRN			

DRL1-16			Dennis Dart 9SDL3011		Plaxton Pointer			B34F	1991	Ex London Buses, 1994		
1	J601XHL	4	J604XHL	7	J607XHL	10	J610XHL	13	J613XHL	16	J616XHL
2	J602XHL	5	J605XHL	8	J608XHL	11	J611XHL	14	J614XHL		
3	J603XHL	6	J606XHL	9	J609XHL	12	J612XHL	15	J615XHL		

DRL88	K588MGT	Dennis Dart 9SDL3024	Plaxton Pointer	B32F	1993	Ex London General, 1997
DRL92	K592MGT	Dennis Dart 9SDL3024	Plaxton Pointer	B32F	1993	Ex London General, 1997

L34-261			Leyland Olympian ONLXB/1RH		Eastern Coach Works			H42/26D*	1986-87	Ex London Buses, 1994 * L261 is DPH42/26D		
34	C34CHM	84	C84CHM	89	C89CHM	95	VLT29	101	C101CHM			
39	C39CHM	85	C85CHM	90	C90CHM	96	C96CHM	138	WLT838			
40	C40CHM	88	C88CHM	93	C93CHM	100	C100CHM	261	2CLT			

LDP45-89			Dennis Dart SFD212BR1		Plaxton Pointer			B33F	1997			
45	R445LGH	53	R453LGH	60	R460LGH	67	R467LGH	74	R474LGH	82	R482LGH	89 R489LGH
46	R446LGH	54	R454LGH	61	R461LGH	68	R468LGH	75	R475LGH	83	R483LGH	
47	R447LGH	55	R455LGH	62	R462LGH	69	R469LGH	76	R476LGH	84	R484LGH	
48	R448LGH	56	R456LGH	63	R463LGH	70	R470LGH	77	R477LGH	85	R485LGH	
49	R449LGH	57	R457LGH	64	R464LGH	71	R471LGH	78	R478LGH	86	R486LGH	
51	R451LGH	58	R458LGH	65	R465LGH	72	R472LGH	79	R479LGH	87	R487LGH	
52	R452LGH	59	R459LGH	66	R466LGH	73	R473LGH	81	R481LGH	88	R488LGH	

MA121-132			Mercedes-Benz 811D		Alexander AM			B28F	1990/91	Ex London General 1996/7		
121	G121PGT	125	H425XGK	129	H429XGK	131	H431XGK					
122	G122PGT	128	H428XGK	130	H430XGK	132	H432XGK					

MRL136-241 — Optare MetroRider MR03 — Optare — B26F — 1990-93 — Ex London Buses, 1994

136	H136UUA	140	H140UUA	158	H158UUA	226	K426HWY	230	K430HWY	234	K434HWY	238	K438HWY
137	H137UUA	155	H155UUA	159	H159UUA	227	K427HWY	231	K431HWY	235	K435HWY	239	K439HWY
138	H138UUA	156	H156UUA	224	K424HWY	228	K428HWY	232	K432HWY	236	K436HWY	240	K440HWY
139	H139UUA	157	H157UUA	225	K425HWY	229	K429HWY	233	K433HWY	237	K437HWY	241	K441HWY

NV1-27 — Volvo Olympian YN2RV18Z4 — Northern Counties Palatine I — H47/30F — 1995

1	M401RVU	5	M405RVU	9	M409RVU	13	N413JBV	17	N417JBV	21	N421JBV	25	N425JBV
2	M402RVU	6	M406RVU	10	WLT990	14	N414JBV	18	N418JBV	22	N422JBV	26	N426JBV
3	M403RVU	7	M407RVU	11	N411JBV	15	WLT815	19	N419JBV	23	N423JBV	27	N427JBV
4	M404RVU	8	M408RVU	12	N412JBV	16	N416JBV	20	N420JBV	24	N424JBV		

NV28-48 — Volvo Olympian YN2RV18Z4 — Northern Counties Palatine I — H48/27D — 1996

28	N528LHG	31	N531LHG	34	N534LHG	37	N537LHG	40	N540LHG	43	N543LHG	46	N546LHG
29	N529LHG	32	N532LHG	35	N535LHG	38	WLT688	41	N541LHG	44	N544LHG	47	N547LHG
30	N530LHG	33	N533LHG	36	N536LHG	39	N539LHG	42	N542LHG	45	N545LHG	48	N548LHG

NV49-99 — Volvo Olympian — Northern Counties Palatine I — H47/27D — 1997/8

49	P549WGT	57	R257LGH	65	R265LGH	73		81		89		97	
50	P550WGT	58	R258LGH	66	R266LGH	74		82		90		98	
51	R251LGH	59	R259LGH	67	R267LGH	75		83		91		99	
52	R252LGH	60	R241LGH	68	R268LGH	76		84		92			
53	R253LGH	61	R261LGH	69	R269LGH	77		85		93			
54	R254LGH	62	R262LGH	70	R270LGH	78		86		94			
55	R255LGH	63	R263LGH	71	R271LGH	79		87		95			
56	R256LGH	64	R264LGH	72	R272LGH	80		88		96			

RM9-2151 — AEC Routemaster 5RM — Park Royal — H36/28R — 1959-65 — Ex London Buses, 1994 * Scania engine † Fitted with plain upper deck front windows

9	VLT9	687	WLT687	967	WLT967	1104	104CLT	1380	380CLT	1977*	ALD977B	2151	CUV151C
71††t	UFF380	758	WLT758	1002†	OYM368A	1119	119CLT	1400	400CLT	1980	ALD980B		
202	VLT202	782*	WLT782	1033	33CLT	1168*	168CLT	1621	KGJ187A	2022*	ALM22B		
436	WLT436	787	WLT787	1058	58CLT	1174	174CLT	1666	666DYE	2051	ALM51B		
478	WLT478	868	WLT868	1062	62CLT	1176	176CLT	1797*	797DYE	2106*	CUV106C		
527	WLT527	872†	WLT872	1082	82CLT	1260	260CLT	1955	ALD955B	2109	CUV109C		
541	WLT541	928	WLT928	1097	97CLT	1305	305CLT	1962	ALD962B	2128	CUV128C		

RML883-2733 — AEC Routemaster 7RM (Cummins) — Park Royal — H40/32R — 1961-67 — Ex London Buses, 1994
† Fitted with plain upper deck front windows

883	WLT883	2314	CUV314C	2362	CUV362C	2474	JJD474D	2551	JJD551D	2601	NML601E	2711	SMK711F
2270	CUV270C	2318	CUV318C	2381	JJD381D	2482	JJD482D	2554	JJD554D	2604	NML604E	2712	SMK712F
2271	CUV271C	2327	CUV327C	2396	JJD396D	2484	JJD484D	2556	JJD556D	2613	NML613E	2714	SMK714F
2273	CUV273C	2332	CUV332C	2397	JJD397D	2499	JJD499D	2560	JJD560D	2614	NML614E	2733	SMK733F
2275†	CUV275C	2335	CUV335C	2400	JJD400D	2507	JJD507D	2578	JJD578D	2629	NML629E		
2276	CUV276C	2336	CUV336C	2411	JJD411D	2513	JJD513D	2583	JJD583D	2630	NML630E		
2279	CUV279C	2338	CUV338C	2440	JJD440D	2515	JJD515D	2584	JJD584D	2673	SMK673F		
2283	CUV283C	2339	CUV339C	2454	JJD454D	2529	JJD529D	2587	JJD587D	2676	SMK676F		
2302	CUV302C	2345	CUV345C	2469	JJD469D	2539	JJD539D	2596	JJD596D	2683	SMK683F		

SP1-25 — DAF DB250WB505 — Optare Spectra — H44/27F — 1992-93 — Ex London Buses, 1994

1	K301FYG	6	K306FYG	10	K310FYG	14	K314FYG	18	18CLT	22	K322FYG
3	K303FYG	7	K307FYG	11	K311FYG	15	K315FYG	19u	19CLT	23	K323FYG
4	K304FYG	8	K308FYG	12	K312FYG	16	K316FYG	20	20CLT	24	K324FYG
5	K305FYG	9	K309FYG	13	K313FYG	17	170CLT	21	K321FYG	25	WLT825

SR11-123 — Mercedes-Benz 811D — Optare StarRider — B26F — 1988-90 — Ex London Buses, 1994

11	F911YWY	21	F921YWY	25	F925YWY	29	F29CWY	45	F45CWY	52	F52CWY	122	G122SMV
14	F914YWY	22	F922YWY	26	F926YWY	30	F30CWY	47	F47CWY	53	F53CWY	123	G123SMV
16	F916YWY	23	F923YWY	27	F927YWY	42	F42CWY	48	F48CWY	62	F162FWY		
19	F919YWY	24	F924YWY	28	F928YWY	43	F43CWY	51	F51CWY	63	F163FWY		

T75-227 — Leyland Titan TNLXB2RRSp — Park Royal — H44/26D* — 1979-80 — * T227 is H44/24D Ex London Buses, 1994

75tu	CUL75V	164t	CUL164V	173t	CUL173V	186u	CUL186V	227u	EYE227V
76t	CUL76V	172t	CUL172V	185u	CUL185V	191tu	CUL191V		

T274-798 — Leyland Titan TNLXB2RR — Leyland — H44/24D* — 1981-83 — Ex London Buses, 1994 * T275 is H44/26D T329, T766 are on loan to Armchair

274u	GYE274W	352t	KYV352X	683t	OHV683Y	713	OHV713Y	737	OHV737Y	766	OHV766Y	787	OHV787Y
275u	GYE275W	356u	KYV356X	685	OHV685Y	715	OHV715Y	739u	OHV739Y	767	OHV767Y	788u	OHV788Y
292u	KYN292X	362t	KYV362X	687	OHV687Y	716	OHV716Y	742u	OHV742Y	768u	OHV768Y	790	OHV790Y
297	KYN297X	369t	KYV369X	693	OHV693Y	717	OHV717Y	747	OHV747Y	773	OHV773Y	792u	OHV792Y
310u	KYN310X	384	KYV384X	694	OHV694Y	718	OHV718Y	750	OHV750Y	774	OHV774Y	793	OHV793Y
312	KYV312X	396u	KYV396X	696	OHV696Y	720u	OHV720Y	752	OHV752Y	775	OHV775Y	794u	OHV794Y
314t	KYV314X	507u	KYV507X	701	OHV701Y	722u	OHV722Y	755u	OHV755Y	776u	OHV776Y	795	OHV795Y
323u	KYV323X	676u	OHV676Y	704	OHV704Y	723u	OHV723Y	756	OHV756Y	778	OHV778Y	796	OHV796Y
325t	KYV325X	677t	OHV677Y	705u	OHV705Y	725	OHV725Y	757	OHV757Y	779	OHV779Y	798	OHV798Y
327u	KYV327X	678	OHV678Y	707u	OHV707Y	732	OHV732Y	763	OHV763Y	781u	OHV781Y		
329	KYV329X	679	OHV679Y	709	OHV709Y	735	WLT735	764	OHV764Y	782	OHV782Y		
336u	KYV336X	681	OHV681Y	712u	OHV712Y	736	WLT736	765u	OHV765Y	786u	OHV786Y		

| T799-1123 | | | | Leyland Titan TNLXB2RR | | | Leyland | | | H44/26D | 1983-84 | Ex London Buses, 1994 |
| | | | | | | | | | | | | * T803 is O44/26D |

799	OHV799Y	893	A893SYE	932	A932SYE	967	A967SYE	1000	ALM1B	1041	A641THV	1074	A74THX
803	OHV803Y	894	A894SYE	933u	A933SYE	968	A968SYE	1001	A601THV	1042	A642THV	1075	A75THX
806	OHV806Y	895	A895SYE	936	A936SYE	969	A969SYE	1002	A602THV	1043	A643THV	1078	A78THX
808u	OHV808Y	897	A897SYE	937	A937SYE	970	A970SYE	1004	A604THV	1044t	A644THV	1080	B80WUV
811u	OHV811Y	898	A898SYE	938	A938SYE	972	A972SYE	1005	A605THV	1046	A646THV	1082	B82WUV
831	A831SUL	901	A901SYE	939	A939SYE	973	A973SYE	1006	A606THV	1047	A647THV	1085	B85WUV
835	A835SUL	906	A906SYE	940	A940SYE	974	A974SYE	1008	A608THV	1051	A651THV	1086	B86WUV
839	A839SUL	907	A907SYE	941u	A941SYE	977	A977SYE	1009	A609THV	1053	A653THV	1087	B87WUV
844	A844SUL	908	A908SYE	942	A942SYE	979	A979SYE	1010	A610THV	1054	A654THV	1088	B88WUV
851	A851SUL	909	A909SYE	943	A943SYE	980	A980SYE	1011	A611THV	1055	A655THV	1090	B90WUV
852	A852SUL	913	A913SYE	946	A946SYE	981	A981SYE	1012	A612THV	1056	A56THX	1094	B94WUV
853	A853SUL	914	A914SYE	947u	A947SYE	982	A982SYE	1014	A614THV	1057	257CLT	1095	B95WUV
863t	A863SUL	915	A915SYE	948	A948SYE	983	A983SYE	1015	A615THV	1058	A58THX	1098	B98WUV
864	A864SUL	916u	A916SYE	952	A952SYE	984	A984SYE	1016	A616THV	1059	A59THX	1102	B102WUV
870	A870SUL	917	A917SYE	954	A954SYE	985	A985SYE	1017	A617THV	1060	A60THX	1104	B104WUV
871	A871SUL	919t	A919SYE	955	A955SYE	986u	A986SYE	1018	A618THV	1061	A61THX	1105	B105WUV
875u	A875SUL	920u	A920SYE	956	A956SYE	987	A987SYE	1019	A619THV	1062	A62THX	1107	B107WUV
886u	A886SYE	923	A923SYE	957	A957SYE	989	A989SYE	1021	A621THV	1063	A63THX	1109	B109WUV
887	A887SYE	924	A924SYE	958	A958SYE	991	A991SYE	1023	A623THV	1064	A64THX	1111	B111WUV
888	A888SYE	927	A927SYE	959	A959SYE	992	A992SYE	1024	A624THV	1068	A68THX	1120	B120WUV
889	A889SYE	928	A928SYE	962u	A962SYE	993	A993SYE	1033	A633THV	1070	A70THX	1123	B123WUV
890u	A890SYE	929	A929SYE	963u	A963SYE	994	A994SYE	1037	A637THV	1071	A71THX		
891u	A891SYE	930	A930SYE	964u	A964SYE	995	A995SYE	1038	A638THV	1072	A72THX		
892	A892SYE	931	A931SYE	966	A966SYE	997	A997SYE	1040	A640THV	1073	A73THX		

| T1129 | WDA4T | Leyland Titan TNLXB1RF | Park Royal | DPH43/29F | 1979 | Ex London Buses, 1994 |
| VC2 | G102NGN | Volvo CityBus B10M-50 | Northern Counties | DPH45/35D | 1989 | Ex London General, 1997 |

Previous registrations

ALM1B	A600THV	N424JBV	N426JBV	VLT29	C95CHM	WLT838	C138CHM
KGJ187A	621DYE	N425JBV	N427JBV	WLT688	N538LHG	WLT990	M410RVU
N416JBV	N421JBV	N426JBV	N420JBV	WLT735	OHV735Y	2CLT	D261FUL
N420JBV	N422JBV	N427JBV	N423JBV	WLT736	OHV736Y	170CLT	K317FYG
N421JBV	N424JBV	OYM368A	2CLT	WLT789	M89MYM	257CLT	A57THX
N422JBV	N416JBV	UFF380	VLT71	WLT815	N415JBV		
N423JBV	N425JBV	VLT9	VLT9, OYM374A	WLT825	K325FYG		

Special liveries

Overall advertisements: T76, T172.
Docklands Express : NV1-10.

BE112	VDV112S	Bristol VRT/SL3/6LXB	Eastern Coach Works	PO43/31F	1978	Ex Northern, Anston, 1996
BE168	VTV168S	Bristol VRT/SL3/6LXB	Eastern Coach Works	PO43/31F	1978	Ex Northern, Anston, 1996
BE184	AET184T	Bristol VRT/SL3/6LXB	Eastern Coach Works	PO43/31F	1979	Ex Northern, Anston, 1996
BE284	MDM284P	Bristol VRT/SL3/6LXB	Eastern Coach Works	PO43/31F	1975	Ex Northern, Anston, 1996
BW21	PJJ21S	Bristol VRT/SL3/6LXB	Willowbrook	O43/31F	1978	Ex East Kent, 1996
BW75	RVB975S	Bristol VRT/SL3/6LXB	Willowbrook	O43/31F	1978	Ex East Kent, 1994
BW76	RVB976S	Bristol VRT/SL3/6LXB	Willowbrook	O43/31F	1978	Ex East Kent, 1994
BW79	TFN979T	Bristol VRT/SL3/6LXB	Willowbrook	O43/31F	1978	Ex South Coast Buses, 1994
BW82	TFN982T	Bristol VRT/SL3/6LXB	Willowbrook	O43/31F	1978	Ex East Kent, 1996
BW85	TFN985T	Bristol VRT/SL3/6LXB	Willowbrook	H43/31F	1978	Ex South Coast Buses, 1994
BW86	TFN986T	Bristol VRT/SL3/6LXB	Willowbrook	O43/31F	1978	Ex East Kent, 1993
BW87	TFN987T	Bristol VRT/SL3/6LXB	Willowbrook	H43/31F	1978	Ex South Coast Buses, 1994
BW88	TFN988T	Bristol VRT/SL3/6LXB	Willowbrook	O43/31F	1978	Ex East Kent, 1996
BW89	TFN989T	Bristol VRT/SL3/6LXB	Willowbrook	H43/31F	1978	Ex East Kent, 1993
BW91	TFN991T	Bristol VRT/SL3/6LXB	Willowbrook	H43/31F	1978	Ex East Kent, 1993
DM404	JGF404K	Daimler Fleetline CRG6LXB	Park Royal	O44/24D	1972	Ex Wright & Biddell, Rainham, 1997
DM1110	GHV110N	Daimler Fleetline CRL6	Park Royal	O44/27D	1975	Ex Wright & Biddell, Rainham, 1997
DM1111	GHV111N	Daimler Fleetline CRL6	Park Royal	O44/27D	1975	Ex Wright & Biddell, Rainham, 1997
DM1537	THM537M	Daimler Fleetline CRL6	MCW	O44/24D	1974	Ex Wright & Biddell, Rainham, 1997
DS3t	KJF300V	Volvo B58-56	Duple Dominant	C53F	1980	Ex London Buses, 1992
ERM80	VLT80	AEC Routemaster 5RM	Park Royal	O44/32R	1959	Ex London Buses, 1992
ERM84	VLT84	AEC Routemaster 5RM	Park Royal	O44/32R	1959	Ex London Buses, 1992
ERM90	VLT90	AEC Routemaster 5RM	Park Royal	O44/32R	1959	Ex London Buses, 1992
ERM94	VLT94	AEC Routemaster 5RM	Park Royal	O44/32R	1959	Ex London Buses, 1992
ERM143	VLT143	AEC Routemaster 5RM	Park Royal	O44/32R	1959	Ex London Buses, 1992
ERM163	VLT163	AEC Routemaster 5RM	Park Royal	O44/32R	1959	Ex London Buses, 1992
ERM235	VLT235	AEC Routemaster 5RM	Park Royal	O44/32R	1960	Ex London Buses, 1992
ERM237	VLT237	AEC Routemaster 5RM	Park Royal	O44/32R	1960	Ex London Buses, 1992
ERM242	VLT242	AEC Routemaster 5RM	Park Royal	O44/32R	1960	Ex London Buses, 1992
ERM281	VLT281	AEC Routemaster 5RM	Park Royal	O44/32R	1960	Ex London Buses, 1992
MB20u	UKA20V	MCW Metrobus DR101/3	MCW	H43/30F	1980	Ex MTL, Liverpool, 1997
MB21u	UKA21V	MCW Metrobus DR103/2	MCW	H43/30F	1980	Ex MTL, Liverpool, 1997
MB22u	UKA22V	MCW Metrobus DR103/2	MCW	H43/30F	1980	Ex MTL, Liverpool, 1997
MB23	UKA23V	MCW Metrobus DR103/2	MCW	H43/30F	1980	Ex MTL, Liverpool, 1997
MB24	WYW24T	MCW Metrobus DR101/8	MCW	PO43/28D	1979	Ex Leaside, 1995
MB121	BYX121V	MCW Metrobus DR101/9	MCW	PO43/28D	1979	Ex South London, 1996
MB123	BYX123V	MCW Metrobus DR101/9	MCW	PO43/28D	1979	Ex Leaside, 1995
MB143	BYX143V	MCW Metrobus DR101/9	MCW	CPO43/28D	1979	Ex Leaside, 1996
MB185	BYX185V	MCW Metrobus DR101/9	MCW	PO43/28D	1979	Ex South London, 1996
MB245	BYX245V	MCW Metrobus DR101/12	MCW	PO43/28D	1980	Ex Leaside, 1996
MB304	BYX304V	MCW Metrobus DR101/12	MCW	CPO43/28D	1980	Ex South London, 1996

MB495	GYE495W	MCW Metrobus DR101/12	MCW		PO43/28D	1980	Ex South London, 1996
MB539	GYE529W	MCW Metrobus DR101/14	MCW		PO43/28D	1981	Ex South London, 1996
MB553	GYE553W	MCW Metrobus DR101/14	MCW		PO43/28D	1981	Ex South London, 1996
MB558	GYE558W	MCW Metrobus DR101/14	MCW		PO43/28D	1981	Ex South London, 1996
MB840	OJD840Y	MCW Metrobus DR101/16	MCW		PO43/28D	1983	Ex South London, 1996
ML5	C915BPW	MCW Metroliner DR130/6	MCW		O63/16F	1986	Ex Ambassador, Norwich, 1994
ML6	C916BPW	MCW Metroliner DR130/6	MCW		O63/16F	1986	Ex Ambassador, Norwich, 1994
ML7	C917BPW	MCW Metroliner DR130/6	MCW		O63/16F	1986	Ex Ambassador, Norwich, 1994
ML8	C918BPW	MCW Metroliner DR130/6	MCW		O63/16F	1986	Ex Ambassador, Norwich, 1994
ML9	B238LRA	MCW Metroliner DR130/7	MCW		O63/23F	1985	Ex Monetgrange, Nottingham, 1994
ML10	B240LRA	MCW Metroliner DR130/7	MCW		O63/23F	1985	Ex Monetgrange, Nottingham, 1994
ML11	B241LRA	MCW Metroliner DR130/7	MCW		O63/23F	1985	Ex Monetgrange, Nottingham, 1994
RCL2220	CUV220C	AEC Routemaster 8RM	Park Royal		CO40/27RD	1965	Ex London Buses, 1992
RCL2240	CUV240C	AEC Routemaster 8RM	Park Royal		CO36/27RD	1965	Ex London Buses, 1992
RCL2241	CUV241C	AEC Routemaster 8RM	Park Royal		CO36/27RD	1965	Ex London Buses, 1992
RCL2243	CUV243C	AEC Routemaster 8RM	Park Royal		CO36/27RD	1965	Ex London Buses, 1992
RCL2245	CUV245C	AEC Routemaster 8RM	Park Royal		CO40/27RD	1965	Ex London Buses, 1992
RCL2248	CUV248C	AEC Routemaster 8RM	Park Royal		CO36/27RD	1965	Ex London Buses, 1992
RCL2250	CUV250C	AEC Routemaster 8RM	Park Royal		CO36/27RD	1965	Ex London Buses, 1992
RCL2259	CUV259C	AEC Routemaster 8RM	Park Royal		CO36/27RD	1965	Ex London Buses, 1992
RM307	WLT307	AEC Routemaster 5RM	Park Royal		O36/10RL	1960	Ex London Buses, 1992
RM313	WLT313	AEC Routemaster 5RM	Park Royal		CO36/26RD	1960	Ex London Buses, 1992
RM398	WLT398	AEC Routemaster 5RM	Park Royal		CO36/26RD	1960	Ex London Buses, 1992
RM438	WLT438	AEC Routemaster 5RM	Park Royal		CO36/26RD	1960	Ex London Buses, 1992
RM450	WLT450	AEC Routemaster 5RM	Park Royal		O36/10RL	1960	Ex London Buses, 1992
RM479	WLT479	AEC Routemaster 5RM	Park Royal		CO36/26RD	1960	Ex London Buses, 1992
RM545	WLT545	AEC Routemaster 5RM (DAF)	Park Royal		H36/28R	1960	Ex London Buses, 1992
RM710	WLT710	AEC Routemaster 5RM	Park Royal		CO36/26RD	1961	Ex London Buses, 1992
RM752	WLT752	AEC Routemaster 5RM	Park Royal		O36/28R	1961	Ex London Buses, 1992
RM1864	864DYE	AEC Routemaster 5RM	Park Royal		O36/28R	1964	Ex London Buses, 1992
RM1919	ALD919B	AEC Routemaster 5RM	Park Royal		O36/28R	1964	Ex London Buses, 1992
2391	OJD391R	Leyland Fleetline FE30ALR	Park Royal		O44/24D	1977	Ex Wright & Biddell, Rainham, 1997
	THM684M	Daimler Fleetline CRL6	MCW		O44/28D	1974	Ex Wright & Biddell, Rainham, 1997
	GHV40N	Daimler Fleetline CRL6	Park Royal		PO44/27D	1975	Ex Wright & Biddell, Rainham, 1997
	KUC176P	Daimler Fleetline CRL6	Park Royal		O44/27D	1975	Ex Wright & Biddell, Rainham, 1997
	THX271S	Leyland Fleetline FE30ALR	MCW		O44/24D	1977	Ex Wright & Biddell, Rainham, 1997
	GYE351W	MCW Metrobus DR101/12	MCW		H43/28D	1980	Ex London General, 1997
u	MNC494W	MCW Metrobus DR102/10	MCW		H43/30F	1980	Ex Greater Manchester South, 1997
u	MNC497W	MCW Metrobus DR102/10	MCW		H43/30F	1980	Ex Greater Manchester South, 1997

Previous registrations

B238LRA	B903XJO, A3BOB
B240LRA	B901XJO, A5BOB
B241LRA	B904XJO, A4BOB

Special liveries

Madame Tussauds : MB121, MB539/58, MB840, ML5-8.
The Tower is London : BW75/6/88, DM1537, MB123, RCL2241
Allover advertisements : DM1111, RCL2250, RM450, RM752.

LONDON COACHES (KENT)

DK1-13		DAF SB220LC550		Ikarus Citibus				DP42F	1992/94	Route 726 Expresslink livery
1	J801KHD	**4**	J804KHD	**6**	J806KHD	**8**	J808KHD	**10**	J810KHD	**12**	L512KJX
3	J803KHD	**5**	J805KHD	**7**	J807KHD	**9**	J809KHD	**11**	L511KJX	**13**	L513KJX

The coach fleet is listed in the London Coach Handbook

LONDON & COUNTRY LT vehicles

DS10-18		Dennis Dart 9SDL3053		East Lancs EL2000				B30FL	1995				
10	M521MPF	**11**	M522MPF	**12**	M523MPF	**13**	M524MPF	**16**	N528SPA	**17**	N529SPA	**18**	N530SPA

DSL90-96		Dennis Dart SFD322		Plaxton Pointer				B39F	1997				
90	P290FPK	**91**	P291FPK	**92**	P292FPK	**93**	P293FPK	**94**	P294FPK	**95**	P295FPK	**96**	P296FPK

MM473	P473APJ	Mercedes-Benz 711D	Plaxton Beaver	B27F	1996	
MM474	P474APJ	Mercedes-Benz 811D	Plaxton Beaver	B18FL	1996	
MR472	P472APJ	Optare MetroRider	Optare	B29F	1996	
113	G113TND	Mercedes-Benz 811D	Carlyle C16	B20FL	1990	Ex Bee Line Buzz, 1992
189	G689OHE	Mercedes-Benz 811D	Reeve Burgess Beaver	B20FL	1990	Ex Metrowest, Warley, 1992
190	G690OHE	Mercedes-Benz 811D	Reeve Burgess Beaver	B20FL	1990	Ex Metrowest, Warley, 1992
402	K402VPK	Mercedes-Benz 709D	Dormobile	B25FL	1992	
425	L425CPB	Mercedes-Benz 709D	Dormobile	B25FL	1993	

610-622		Volvo Citybus B10M-50		East Lancs				H49/39F	1989				
610	G610BPH	**612**	G612BPH	**614**	G614BPH	**616**	G616BPH	**618**	G618BPH	**620**	G620BPH	**622**	G622BPH
611	G611BPH	**613**	G613BPH	**615**	G615BPH	**617**	G617BPH	**619**	G619BPH	**621**	G621BPH		

The full fleet is listed in the London Country Bus Handbook

LONDON GENERAL

DPL1-16 — Dennis Dart 9SDL3053 — Plaxton Pointer — B35F — 1995

1	M201EGF	4	M204EGF	7	M207EGF	10	M210EGF	13	M213EGF	16	M216EGF
2	M202EGF	5	M205EGF	8	M208EGF	11	M211EGF	14	M214EGF		
3	M203EGF	6	M206EGF	9	M209EGF	12	M212EGF	15	M215EGF		

DR32-153 — Dennis Dart 8.5SDL3003* — Plaxton Pointer — B28F — 1991/92 — Ex London Buses, 1994
* DRL149-53 are 8.5SDL3015

32	WLT532	36	H536XGK	41	H541XGK	46	46CLT	50	H550XGK	150	K150LGO
33	H533XGK	37	H537XGK	43	H543XGK	47	H547XGK	51	H551XGK	151	K151LGO
34	H534XGK	38	H538XGK	44	H544XGK	48	H548XGK	52	H552XGK	152	K152LGO
35	H835XGK	39	H539XGK	45	H545XGK	49	H549XGK	149	K149LGO	153	K153LGO

DRL53-73 — Dennis Dart 9SDL3016 — Plaxton Pointer — B34F — 1992 — Ex London Buses, 1994

53	K853LGN	56	K856LGN	59	K859LGN	62	K862LGN	65	K865LGN	68	K868LGN	71	K871LGN
54	K854LGN	57	K857LGN	60	K860LGN	63	K863LGN	66	K866LGN	69	K869LGN	72	K872LGN
55	K855LGN	58	K858LGN	61	K861LGN	64	K864LGN	67	K867LGN	70	K870LGN	73	K873LGN

DRL74-95 — Dennis Dart 9SDL3024 — Plaxton Pointer — B32F — 1993 — Ex London Buses, 1994

74	K574MGT	77	K577MGT	80	K580MGT	83	K583MGT	86	K586MGT	90	K590MGT	94	K767OGK
75	K575MGT	78	K578MGT	81	K581MGT	84	K584MGT	87	K587MGT	91	K591MGT	95	WLT395
76	K576MGT	79	K579MGT	82	K582MGT	85	K585MGT	89	K589MGT	93	K593MGT		

DW44-58 — Dennis Dart 8.5SDL3003 — Wright Handybus — B30F — 1990-91 — Ex London Buses, 1994

44	JDZ2344	47	WLT470	50	JDZ2350	53	JDZ2353	56	JDZ2356
45	545CLT	48	WLT548	51	JDZ2351	54	JDZ2354	57	JDZ2357
46	WLT346	49	JDZ2349	52	352CLT	55	JDZ2355	58	JDZ2358

DW66-161 — Dennis Dart 8.5SDL3015* — Wright Handybus — B29F — 1991-93 — Ex London Buses, 1994
* DW66-70 are 8.5SDL3003

66	166CLT	68	H368XGC	70	H370XGC	128	K128LGO	130	K130LGO	132	K132LGO	161	NDZ3161
67	H367XGC	69	H369XGC	127	K127LGO	129	K129LGO	131	K131LGO	160	NDZ3160		

GLS1-506 — Leyland National 2 NL106AL11/2R East Lancs Greenway (1992-4) — B24D* — 1981 — Ex London Buses, 1994
*GLS448/86/91/6/505 are B38D

1	GUW466W	446	GUW446W	459	GUW459W	471	GUW471W	479	GUW479W	490	GUW490W	499	WLT599
438	GUW438W	448	WLT648	460	GUW460W	473	GUW473W	480	VLT180	491	GUW491W	500	GUW500W
439	GUW439W	449	GUW449W	463	GUW463W	474	GUW474W	481	GUW481W	492	GUW492W	501	GUW501W
440	GUW440W	450	GUW450W	467	WLT467	476	GUW476W	483	83CLT	493	GUW493W	502	GUW502W
442	GUW442W	452	GUW452W	468	GUW468W	477	GUW477W	486	186CLT	496	WLT696	505	GUW505W
443	WLT843	455	GUW455W	469	GUW469W	478	GUW478W	487	WLT487	498	WLT598	506	GUW506W

LDP1-17 — Dennis Dart SFD112BR1 — Plaxton Pointer — B32F — 1996

1	P501RYM	4	P504RYM	7	P507RYM	10	P510RYM	13	P513RYM	16	P516RYM
2	P502RYM	5	P505RYM	8	P508RYM	11	P511RYM	14	P514RYM	17	P517RYM
3	P503RYM	6	P506RYM	9	P509RYM	12	P512RYM	15	P515RYM		

LDP18-44 — Dennis Dart SFD212BR1 — Plaxton Pointer — B36F — 1996

18	P718RYL	22	P722RYL	26	P726RYL	30	P730RYL	34	P734RYL	38	P738RYL	42	P742RYL
19	P719RYL	23	P723RYL	27	P727RYL	31	P731RYL	35	P735RYL	39	P739RYL	43	P743RYL
20	P720RYL	24	P724RYL	28	P728RYL	32	P732RYL	36	P736RYL	40	P740RYL	44	P744RYL
21	P721RYL	25	P725RYL	29	P729RYL	33	P733RYL	37	P737RYL	41	P741RYL		

M11-202 — MCW Metrobus DR101/9* — MCW — H43/28D* — 1978-79 — Ex London Buses, 1994
* M11-55 are DR101/8; M171 is O43/28F

11	WYW11T	61	WYW61T	158	BYX158V	174	BYX174V	190	BYX190V	198	SGK374V
45	WYW45T	120	BYX120V	164	BYX164V	176	BYX176V	191	BYX191V	201	BYX201V
47	WYW47T	144	BYX144V	165	BYX165V	177	BYX177V	196	BYX196V	202t	BYX202V
56	WYW56T	156	BYX156V	171	VLT71	188	188CLT	197	197CLT		

M207-502 — MCW Metrobus DR101/12 — MCW — H43/28D* — 1980 — Ex London Buses, 1994 * M241 is O43/28F

207	BYX207V	246	BYX246V	274	BYX274V	302	BYX302V	359	GYE359W	420	GYE420W	477	GYE477W
211	BYX211V	249	BYX249V	275	BYX275V	303	BYX303V	361	GYE361W	423	GYE423W	479	VLT179
212	BYX212V	254	BYX254V	278	78CLT	307	BYX307V	375	GYE375W	430	GYE430W	480	GYE480W
214	BYX214V	257	BYX257V	279	BYX279V	318	EYE318V	379	WLT379	431	GYE431W	483	GYE483W
219	BYX219V	258	BYX258V	284	VLT284	323	EYE323V	386	GYE386W	433	GYE433W	484	GYE484W
224	BYX224V	260	BYX260V	286	BYX286V	325	EYE325V	392	GYE392W	435	GYE435W	488	GYE488W
226	BYX226V	261	BYX261V	287	BYX287V	331	EYE331V	401	GYE401W	457	GYE457W	490	GYE490W
231	BYX231V	265	BYX265V	288	BYX288V	333	EYE333V	404	GYE404W	463	WLT463	502	GYE502W
235	BYX235V	267	BYX267V	289	BYX289V	348	GYE348W	405	GYE405W	466	GYE466W		
237	BYX237V	269	BYX269V	292	BYX292V	350	GYE350W	408	GYE408W	471	GYE471W		
239	BYX239V	270	BYX270V	293t	BYX293V	354	GYE354W	411	GYE411W	472	GYE472W		
241	BYX241V	271t	BYX271V	295	BYX295V	355	GYE355W	412	GYE412W	475	GYE475W		
242	BYX242V	273	BYX273V	297	BYX297V	357	GYE357W	416	GYE416W	476	GYE476W		

M231/42/61/75, 325/86 are on loan to Stanwell Bus. M271/93 are based in Plymouth for driver training work.

M513-794 — MCW Metrobus DR101/14 — MCW — H43/28D — 1981-82 — Ex London Buses, 1994

513	GYE513W	542	542CLT	589	GYE589W	662	KYV662X	690	KYV690X	760	KYV760X	794	KYV794X
514	GYE514W	546	GYE546W	597	GYE597W	667	KYV667X	695	KYV695X	763	KYV763X		
516	GYE516W	556	GYE556W	606	KYO606X	668	KYV668X	706	KYV706X	769	KYV769X		
532	GYE532W	566	GYE566W	607	KYO607X	670	KYV670X	725	KYV725X	779	KYV779X		

M806-953 — MCW Metrobus DR101/16 — MCW — H43/28D — 1983 — Ex London Buses, 1994

806	OJD806Y	820	OJD820Y	837	OJD837Y	853	VLT53	877	OJD877Y	908	A908SUL	933	A933SUL
807	OJD807Y	821	OJD821Y	838	OJD838Y	854	OJD854Y	880	OJD880Y	909	A909SUL	940	A940SUL
808	OJD808Y	822	OJD822Y	842	OJD842Y	855	OJD855Y	888	OJD888Y	913	A913SUL	942	A942SUL
811	OJD811Y	823	OJD823Y	845	OGK708Y	862	OJD862Y	897	A897SUL	914	A914SUL	944	A944SUL
812	OJD812Y	826	OJD826Y	846	OJD846Y	867	OJD867Y	900	A900SUL	918	A918SUL	946	A946SUL
814	OJD814Y	828	OJD828Y	847	OJD847Y	868	OJD868Y	902	A902SUL	922	A922SUL	947	A947SUL
816	OJD816Y	830	OJD830Y	848	OJD848Y	870	OJD870Y	904	A904SUL	923	A923SUL	949	A949SUL
817	OJD817Y	833	OJD833Y	849	OJD849Y	871	OJD871Y	905	A905SUL	926	A926SUL	953	A953SUL
818	OJD818Y	834	OJD834Y	852	OJD852Y	873	OJD873Y	907	A907SUL	931	A931SUL		

M965-1440 — MCW Metrobus DR101/17* — MCW — H43/28D* — 1984-86 — Ex London Buses, 1994 * M1046/55 are DR101/19; M1432/5/40 are DPH43/28D

965	A965SYF	1002	A702THV	1203	B203WUL	1226	B226WUL	1302	B302WUL	1364	C364BUV	1391	C391BUV
970	A970SYF	1005	A705THV	1206	B206WUL	1230	B230WUL	1304	304CLT	1370	C370BUV	1410	C410BUV
975	A975SYF	1046	VLT46	1211	B211WUL	1232	B232WUL	1305	B305WUL	1371	C371BUV	1411	C411BUV
976	A976SYF	1055	A755THV	1215	B215WUL	1235	B235WUL	1306	C306BUV	1372	772DYE	1432	WLT432
977	A977SYF	1107	B107WUL	1220	B220WUL	1237	B237WUL	1311	C311BUV	1373	C373BUV	1433	C433BUV
978t	A978SYF	1108	B108WUL	1222	B222WUL	1241	B241WUL	1315	C109NGH	1386	C386BUV	1434	WLT434
983	A983SYF	1177	B177WUL	1223	B223WUL	1264	B264WUL	1337	C337BUV	1387	C387BUV	1435	435CLT
991	A991SYF	1180	B180WUL	1224	B224WUL	1268	B268WUL	1347	C347BUV	1388	C388BUV	1436	VLT136
992	A992SYF	1196	B196WUL	1225	B225WUL	1301	B301WUL	1357	C357BUV	1389	89CLT	1440	C440BUV

ML1-15 — Marshall Minibus — Marshall — B29F — 1996/7

1	P501HEG	4	P504HEG	7	P407KAV	10	P410KAV	13	P403KAV
2	P502HEG	5	P505HEG	8	P408KAV	11	P401KAV	14	P404KAV
3	P503HEG	6	P506HEG	9	P409KAV	12	P402KAV	15	P405KAV

ML1-6 are on loan to Limebourne

MRL135-223 Optare MetroRider MR03 Optare B26F 1990-93 Ex London Buses, 1994

135	H135TGO	191	J191CGK	195	J695CGK	199	J699CGK	203	J703CGK	207	J707CGK
177	VLT277	192	J692CGK	196	J696CGK	200	J710CGK	204	J704CGK	208	J708CGK
178	H678YGO	193	J693CGK	197	J697CGK	201u	J701CGK	205	J705CGK	209	J709CGK
190	H690YGO	194	J694CGK	198	698DYE	202	J702CGK	206	J706CGK	223	K223MGT

NV101-185 Volvo Olympian Northern Counties Palatine 1* H47/27D 1997/8 *159 onwards are Palatine 2

101	P901RYO	114	P914RYO	127	P927RYO	140	R340LGH	153		166		179
102	P902RYO	115	P915RYO	128	P928RYO	141	R341LGH	154		167		180
103	P903RYO	116	P916RYO	129	P929RYO	142	R342LGH	155		168		181
104	P904RYO	117	P917RYO	130	P930RYO	143	R343LGH	156		169		182
105	P905RYO	118	P918RYO	131	R331LGH	144	R344LGH	157		170		183
106	P906RYO	119	P919RYO	132	R332LGH	145	R345LGH	158		171		184
107	P907RYO	120	P920RYO	133	R433LGH	146	R346LGH	159		172		185
108	P908RYO	121	P921RYO	134	R334LGH	147		160		173		
109	P909RYO	122	P922RYO	135	R335LGH	148		161		174		
110	P910RYO	123	P923RYO	136	R336LGH	149		162		175		
111	P911RYO	124	P924RYO	137	R337LGH	150		163		176		
112	P912RYO	125	P925RYO	138	R338LGH	151		164		177		
113	P913RYO	126	P926RYO	139	R339LGH	152		165		178		

RM994 WLT994 AEC Routemaster 5RM Park Royal H36/28R 1961 Ex London Buses, 1994

RML887-2752 AEC Routemaster 7RM (Iveco) Park Royal H40/32R* 1961-68 Ex London Buses 1994* RML2516 is H40/32RD and carries fleet number DRM2516

887	WLT887	2317	CUV317C	2385	JJD385D	2466	JJD466D	2564	JJD564D	2612	NML612E	2669	SMK669F
889	WLT889	2321	CUV321C	2389	JJD389D	2472	JJD472D	2568	JJD568D	2615	NML615E	2680	SMK680F
894	WLT894	2342	CUV342C	2398	JJD398D	2475	JJD475D	2570	JJD570D	2618	NML618E	2693	SMK693F
899	WLT899	2358	CUV358C	2403	JJD403D	2502	JJD502D	2575	JJD575D	2626	NML626E	2725	SMK725F
2262	CUV262C	2360	CUV360C	2412	JJD412D	2516	WLT516	2576	JJD576D	2631	NML631E	2732	SMK732F
2263	CUV263C	2361	CUV361C	2422	JJD422D	2517	JJD517D	2580	JJD580D	2637	NML637E	2736	SMK736F
2290	CUV290C	2363	CUV363C	2441	JJD441D	2520	JJD520D	2590	JJD590D	2640	NML640E	2745	SMK745F
2297	CUV297C	2364	JJD364D	2453	JJD453D	2535	JJD535D	2593	JJD593D	2644	NML644E	2752	SMK752F
2305	CUV305C	2371	JJD371D	2461	JJD461D	2540	JJD540D	2605	NML605E	2648	NML648E		
2316	CUV316C	2376	JJD376D	2465	JJD465D	2543	JJD543D	2606	NML606E	2654	NML654E		

SC1t D585OOV Freight Rover Sherpa Carlyle Citybus B6F 1987 Ex London Buses, 1994
TPL10 C377PCD Leyland Tiger TRCTL11/3RH Plaxton Paramount 3500 2 C49FT 1986 Ex London Central, 1997; on loan to Nostalgiabus

VC1-39 Volvo B10M-50 Northern Counties H47/35D* 1989-91 *VC1/3 are CH45/35D, VC4-6 are H45/35D
Ex London Buses, 1994

1	101CLT	8	G108NGN	14	614DYE	20	WLT920	26	G126NGN	32	G132PGK	38	G138PGK
3	WLT803	9	G109NGN	15	G115NGN	21	621DYE	27	G127NGN	33	G133PGK	39	839DYE
4	WLT474	10	G110NGN	16	G116NGN	22	G122NGN	28	528CLT	34	G134PGK		
5	G105NGN	11	WLT311	17	G117NGN	23	23CLT	29	229CLT	35	G135PGK		
6	VLT60	12	312CLT	18	WLT818	24	G124NGN	30	G130PGK	36	836DYE		
7	G107NGN	13	G113NGN	19	619DYE	25	125CLT	31	G131PGK	37	WLT837		

VWL1 N101HGO Volvo B6LE Wright Crusader B36F 1995 Leased from London Transport Buses

Previous registrations

C109NGH	C315BUV, VLT15	**WLT395**	K595MGT	**WLT837**	G137PGK	**304CLT**	B304WUL
C377PCD	C377PCD, PCN762, VLT71	**WLT432**	C432BUV	**WLT843**	GUW443W	**312CLT**	G112NGN
K767OGK	K594MGT, WLT994	**WLT434**	C434BUV	**WLT920**	G120NGN	**352CLT**	JDZ2352
OGK708Y	OJD845Y, 545CLT	**WLT463**	GYE463W	**WLT994**	WLT994, VLT89	**435CLT**	C435BUV
SGK374V	BYX198V, VLT98	**WLT467**	GUW467W	**23CLT**	G123NGN	**528CLT**	G128PGK
VLT46	A746THV	**WLT470**	JDZ2347	**46CLT**	H546XGK	**542CLT**	GYE542W
VLT53	OJD853Y	**WLT474**	G104NGN	**78CLT**	BYX278W	**545CLT**	JDZ2345
VLT60	G106NGN	**WLT487**	GUW487W	**83CLT**	GUW483W	**614DYE**	G114NGN
VLT71	BYX171V	**WLT516**	JJD516D	**89CLT**	C389BUV	**619DYE**	G119NGN
VLT136	C436BUV	**WLT532**	H532XGK	**101CLT**	G101NGN	**621DYE**	G121NGN
VLT179	GYE479W	**WLT548**	JDZ2348	**125CLT**	G125NGN	**698DYE**	J698CGK
VLT180	GUW480W	**WLT598**	GUW498W	**166CLT**	H366XGC	**772DYE**	C372BUV
VLT277	H677YGO	**WLT599**	GUW499W	**186CLT**	GUW486W	**836DYE**	G136PGK
VLT284	BYX284V	**WLT648**	GUW448W	**188CLT**	BYX188V	**839DYE**	J139DGF
WLT311	G111NGN	**WLT696**	GUW496W	**197CLT**	BYX197V		
WLT346	JDZ2346	**WLT803**	G103NGN	**229CLT**	G129PGK		
WLT379	GYE379W	**WLT818**	G118NGN				

Named vehicles

GLS438 *City of London*, M1440 *The General*

Special liveries

London General livery: M171, M241, M1432/40, RML2516/732.
Overall advertisement : M202, M978, M1389.

AN262	KPJ262W	Leyland Atlantean AN68B/1R	Roe			H43/30F	1981	Ex Maidstone & District, 1995
LR21	TPD121X	Leyland Olympian ONTL11/1R	Roe			H43/29F	1982	Ex London & Country, 1995
LR24	TPD124X	Leyland Olympian ONTL11/1R	Roe			H43/29F	1982	Ex London & Country, 1995

120-151		Dennis Dart 9SDL3034		Northern Counties Paladin		B35F	1994	Ex Kentish Bus, 1997

120	L120YVK	**122**	L122YVK	**124**	L124YVK	**126**	L126YVK
121	L121YVK	**123**	L123YVK	**125**	L125YVK	**151**	L151YVK

160	M160SKR	Dennis Dart 9SDL3053	Plaxton Pointer	B35F	1995		
161	M161SKR	Dennis Dart 9SDL3053	Plaxton Pointer	B35F	1995		
162	M162SKR	Dennis Dart 9SDL3053	Plaxton Pointer	B35F	1995		
163	M163SKR	Dennis Dart 9SDL3053	Plaxton Pointer	B35F	1995		

164-172		Dennis Dart 9SDL3053		Plaxton Pointer		B34F	1995	Ex Leaside, 1997

164	N701GUM	**166**	N703GUM	**168**	N705GUM	**170**	N707GUM	**172**	N709GUM
165	N702GUM	**167**	N704GUM	**169**	N706GUM	**171**	N708GUM		

201-212		Volvo B6		Northern Counties Paladin		B39F	1994	Ex Kentish Bus, 1997

201	L201YCU	**203**	L203YCU	**205**	L205YCU	**207**	L207YCU	**209**	L209YCU	**211**	L211YCU
202	L202YCU	**204**	L204YCU	**206**	L206YCU	**208**	L208YCU	**210**	L210YCU	**212**	L212YCU

311	G311DPA	Leyland Lynx LX2R11G15Z4S	Leyland		B49F	1990	Ex London & Country, 1995
312	G312DPA	Leyland Lynx LX2R11G15Z4S	Leyland		B49F	1990	Ex London & Country, 1995
313	G313DPA	Leyland Lynx LX2R11G15Z4S	Leyland		B49F	1990	Ex London & Country, 1995
314	G314DPA	Leyland Lynx LX2R11G15Z4S	Leyland		B49F	1990	Ex London & Country, 1995
315	G315DPA	Leyland Lynx LX2R11G15Z4S	Leyland		B49F	1990	Ex London & Country, 1995
316	G316DPA	Leyland Lynx LX2R11G15Z4S	Leyland		B49F	1990	Ex London & Country, 1995
331	UPB331S	Leyland National 10351A/1R			B41F	1977	Ex London & Country, 1995
399	D101NDW	Leyland Lynx LX112TL11ZR1	Leyland		B49F	1987	Ex Maidstone & District, 1996
400	D102NDW	Leyland Lynx LX112TL11ZR1	Leyland		B49F	1987	Ex Maidstone & District, 1996
401	G34VME	Leyland Lynx LX2R11C15Z4S	Leyland		B49F	1989	Ex Kentish Bus, 1995
402	G35VME	Leyland Lynx LX2R11C15Z4S	Leyland		B49F	1989	Ex Kentish Bus, 1995
418	D156HML	Leyland Lynx LX112TL11ZR1S	Leyland		B49F	1991	Ex Kentish Bus, 1996
430	L430CPJ	Mercedes-Benz 811D	Plaxton Beaver		B31F	1994	Ex London & Country, 1995
431	L431CPJ	Mercedes-Benz 811D	Plaxton Beaver		B31F	1994	Ex London & Country, 1995
433	L433CPJ	Mercedes-Benz 811D	Plaxton Beaver		B31F	1994	Ex London & Country, 1995
434	L434CPJ	Mercedes-Benz 811D	Plaxton Beaver		B31F	1994	Ex London & Country, 1995
435	L435CPJ	Mercedes-Benz 811D	Plaxton Beaver		B31F	1994	Ex London & Country, 1995
436	L436CPJ	Mercedes-Benz 811D	Plaxton Beaver		B31F	1994	Ex London & Country, 1995
437	L437CPJ	Mercedes-Benz 811D	Plaxton Beaver		B31F	1994	Ex London & Country, 1995
438	P438HKN	Mercedes-Benz 811D	Plaxton Beaver		B31F	1996	

440	M440HPF	Optare MetroRider MR17		Optare				B29F	1994	Ex London & Country, 1995
441	M441HPF	Optare MetroRider MR17		Optare				B29F	1994	Ex London & Country, 1995
442	M442HPF	Optare MetroRider MR17		Optare				B29F	1994	Ex London & Country, 1995
443	M443HPF	Optare MetroRider MR17		Optare				B29F	1994	Ex London & Country, 1995

623-630		Volvo Citybus B10M-50		Northern Counties				H45/31F	1989	Ex London & Country, 1995

623	G623BPH	625	G625BPH	627	G627BPH	629	G629BPH
624	G624BPH	626	G626BPH	628	G628BPH	630	G630BPH

685-700		Volvo Olympian YN2RC16Z4		East Lancs				H44/30F	1994	Ex London & Country, 1995

685	M685HPF	688	M688HPF	691	M691HPF	694	M694HPF	697	M697HPF	700	M700HPF
686	M686HPF	689	M689HPF	692	M692HPF	695	M695HPF	698	M698HPF		
687	M687HPF	690	M690HPF	693	M693HPF	696	M696HPF	699	M699HPF		

701	G640CHF	Volvo Citybus B10M-50	East Lancs	H49/39F	1989	Ex North Western, 1996
704	G643CHF	Volvo Citybus B10M-50	East Lancs	H49/39F	1990	Ex North Western, 1996
705	G647EKA	Volvo Citybus B10M-50	East Lancs	H49/39F	1990	Ex North Western, 1996
710	G661DTJ	Volvo Citybus B10M-50	East Lancs	H49/39F	1990	Ex North Western, 1996
847	E136KYW	MCW Metrorider MF150/38	MCW	B25F	1987	Ex Darlington, 1995
850	E145KYW	MCW Metrorider MF150/38	MCW	B25F	1987	Ex Darlington, 1995
865	F865LCU	MCW Metrorider MF158/15	MCW	B31F	1988	Ex Kentish Bus, 1996
969	J969JNL	Optare MetroRider	Optare	B25F	1991	Ex Kentish Bus, 1997

LONDON PRIDE

RT3232w	KYY961	AEC Regent III 0961	Weymann	H30/26R	1950	Ex Ensign Bus, Purfleet, 1991
RT4169	LYF228	AEC Regent III 0961	Park Royal	O30/26R	1951	Ex London Hop-On, Bermondsey, 1995
103	B103UAT	Dennis Dominator DDA903	Alexander RH	H43/32F	1984	Ex Hull, 1993
105	B105UAT	Dennis Dominator DDA903	Alexander RH	H43/32F	1984	Ex Hull, 1993
106u	SMW57Y	Dennis Dominator DDA164	Northern Counties	H43/31F	1983	Ex Thamesdown, 1995
107	SMW58Y	Dennis Dominator DDA164	Northern Counties	H43/31F	1983	Ex Thamesdown, 1995
110	BOK72V	MCW Metrobus DR102/12	MCW	H43/30F	1980	Ex Stevensons, Uttoxeter, 1997
111	BOK75V	MCW Metrobus DR102/12	MCW	H43/30F	1980	Ex Stevensons, Uttoxeter, 1997
112	GOG223W	MCW Metrobus DR102/18	MCW	H43/30F	1981	Ex Stevensons, Uttoxeter, 1997
114	BOK68V	MCW Metrobus DR102/12	MCW	H43/30F	1980	Ex Stevensons, Uttoxeter, 1996
115	VRG415T	MCW Metrobus DR101/4	MCW	H46/30F	1979	Ex MTL Liverpool, 1996
116	VRG416T	MCW Metrobus DR101/4	MCW	H46/30F	1979	Ex MTL Liverpool, 1996
117	VRG417T	MCW Metrobus DR101/4	MCW	H46/30F	1979	Ex MTL Liverpool, 1996
118	VRG418T	MCW Metrobus DR101/4	MCW	H46/30F	1979	Ex MTL Liverpool, 1996
119	UWW519X	MCW Metrobus DR101/15	Alexander RH	H43/32F	1982	Ex Cardiff Buses, 1996
120	UWW518X	MCW Metrobus DR101/15	Alexander RH	H43/32F	1982	Ex Cardiff Buses, 1996
152u	A502FRS	MCW Metroliner DR130/4	MCW	CH53/16D	1984	Ex McTavish, Hardgate, 1991
182	UJF182	Daimler CSG6-30	Metro-Cammell	H41/31R	1959	Ex London Cityrama, 1994

192	F292NHJ	MCW Metrobus DR102/71		MCW				H46/27F	1988	Ex Capital Citybus, 1994
200	GAJ200V	Dennis Dominator DD121B		Northern Counties				PO43/29F+	1980	Ex Cleveland Transit, 1994
201	GAJ201V	Dennis Dominator DD121B		Northern Counties				PO43/29F+	1980	Ex Cleveland Transit, 1994
202	VVN202Y	Dennis Dominator DDA149		Northern Counties				PO43/29F+	1983	Ex Cleveland Transit, 1994
203	VVN203Y	Dennis Dominator DDA149		Northern Counties				PO43/29F+	1983	Ex Cleveland Transit, 1994
205	GVV205	MCW Metrobus DR101/12		MCW				PO43/28D	1980	Ex London General, 1997
219	BYX219V	MCW Metrobus DR101/12		MCW				PO43/28D	1980	Ex London General, 1997
230	FGE430X	Dennis Dominator DD137B		Alexander RL				PO45/34F	1982	Ex Kelvin Central, 1995
231	FGE439X	Dennis Dominator DD137B		Alexander RL				PO45/34F	1982	Ex Kelvin Central, 1996
232	TYS265W	Dennis Dominator DD137B		Alexander RL				PO45/34F	1981	Ex Kelvin Central, 1996
233	MNS45Y	Dennis Dominator DD162		Alexander RL				PO45/34F	1983	Ex Kelvin Central, 1996
238	MPN138W	Dennis Dominator DD120		East Lancs				PO43/29F+	1981	Ex Eastbourne, 1994
242	FDY142X	Dennis Dominator DDA154		East Lancs				PO43/31F	1982	Ex Eastbourne, 1994
243	FDY143X	Dennis Dominator DDA154		East Lancs				PO43/31F	1982	Ex Eastbourne, 1994
245	FDY145X	Dennis Dominator DDA154		East Lancs				PO43/31F	1982	Ex Eastbourne, 1994

250-265		MCW Metrobus DR102/13		MCW				PO46/27D	1980	Ex Grey-Green, 1995/6
250	EWF450V	253	EWF453V	255	EWF455V	257	EWF457V	265	EWF465V	
252	EWF452V	254	EWF454V	256	EWF456V	260	EWF460V			

266	JWF490W	MCW Metrobus DR102/13		MCW				PO46/30F	1980	Ex Stevensons, Uttoxeter, 1996
270u	WYW26T	MCW Metrobus DR101/8		MCW				PO43/28D	1979	Ex MTL Liverpool, 1997
271	ULS621X	MCW Metrobus DR102/28		Alexander RL				PO45/33F	1982	Ex Cardiff Buses, 1996
281	WYV43T	Leyland Titan TNLXB2RRSp		Park Royal				PO44/26D	1979	Ex Londonlinks, 1997
282	WYV67T	Leyland Titan TNLXB2RRSp		Park Royal				PO44/26D	1980	Ex Londonlinks, 1997
304	A204EHN	Dennis Dominator DDA149		Northern Counties				O43/31F	1983	Ex Cleveland Transit, 1994
305	A205EHN	Dennis Dominator DDA149		Northern Counties				O43/31F	1983	Ex Cleveland Transit, 1994
306	A206EHN	Dennis Dominator DDA149		Northern Counties				O43/31F	1983	Ex Cleveland Transit, 1994
307	A207EHN	Dennis Dominator DDA149		Northern Counties				O43/31F	1983	Ex Cleveland Transit, 1994
317	FKM266V	MCW Metrobus DR101/10		MCW				O46/30F	1980	Ex New Enterprise (Tonbridge), Maidstone, 1997
318	FKM270V	MCW Metrobus DR104/2		MCW				O46/30F	1980	Ex New Enterprise (Tonbridge), Maidstone, 1997
319	KYV804X	MCW Metrobus DR101/14		MCW				O43/30F	1982	Ex MTL London, 1997

320-331		MCW Metrobus DR102/7		MCW				O43/30F	1980	Ex Hull, 1995/6
320	LAT513V	322	LAT502V	324	LAT504V	328	LAT508V	331	LAT511V	
321	LAT501V	323	LAT503V	327	LAT507V	330	LAT510V			

333	EGP33J	Daimler Fleetline CRG6LXB		Park Royal				O45/23F	1970	Ex London Transport, 1985
334	MCD134F	Leyland Titan PD3/4		MCW				O39/30F	1968	Ex London Hop-On, Bermondsey, 1995
336	LUF132F	Leyland Titan PD3/4		MCW				O39/30F	1968	Ex London Hop-On, Bermondsey, 1995
339	MPN139W	Dennis Dominator DD120		East Lancs				O43/31F	1981	Ex Eastbourne, 1994
344	FDY144X	Dennis Dominator DDA154		East Lancs				O43/31F	1982	Ex Eastbourne, 1994
346	FDY146X	Dennis Dominator DDA154		East Lancs				O43/31F	1982	Ex Eastbourne, 1994
348	KUC971P	Leyland Fleetline FE30ALR		MCW				O45/30F+	1976	Ex London Hop-On, Bermondsey, 1995

351	WYV41T	Leyland Titan TNLXB2RRSp	Park Royal	O44/24D	1979	Ex Kinch, Barrow, 1996
352	A860SUL	Leyland Titan TNLXB2RR	Leyland	O44/26D	1983	Ex Stanwell Buses, 1996
353	CUL78V	Leyland Titan TNLXB2RRSp	Park Royal	O44/26D	1979	Ex Londonlinks, 1997
354	CUL167V	Leyland Titan TNLXB2RRSp	Park Royal	O44/26D	1980	Ex Londonlinks, 1997
355u	KYN309X	Leyland Titan TNLXB2RR	Leyland	O44/26D	1981	Ex Londonlinks, 1997
356u	KYV411X	Leyland Titan TNLXB2RR	Leyland	O44/24D	1982	Ex Londonlinks, 1997
359	DHJ301B	Leyland Titan PD3/4	Northern Counties	FCO39/30F	1964	Ex London Hop-On, Bermondsey, 1995
367	JHE137W	MCW Metrobus DR104/6	MCW	O46/31F	1981	Ex Stevenson, Uttoxeter, 1997
368	DTG368V	MCW Metrobus DR102/15	MCW	O47/28F+	1980	Ex Grey-Green, 1996
369	DTG369V	MCW Metrobus DR102/15	MCW	O47/28F+	1980	Ex Grey-Green, 1996
370	DTG370V	MCW Metrobus DR102/15	MCW	O46/31F	1980	Ex Grey-Green, 1996
371	DTG371V	MCW Metrobus DR102/15	MCW	O47/28F+	1980	Ex Grey-Green, 1996
374	A114KFX	MCW Metroliner DR130/3	MCW	O67/20F	1984	Ex North Western, 1990
375	B115ORU	MCW Metroliner DR130/3	MCW	O63/20F	1984	Ex North Western, 1990
378	B824AAT	MCW Metroliner DR130/3	MCW	O63/27F	1984	Ex Pride of the Road, Royston, 1993
379	C906GUD	MCW Metroliner DR130/21	MCW	O63/23F	1986	Ex Taylor, Widnes, 1994
401	B121ORU	MCW Metroliner DR130/3	MCW	O63/20F	1984	Ex Midland Red North, 1990
402	A112KFX	MCW Metroliner DR130/3	MCW	O67/20F	1984	Ex North Western, 1990
403	A113KFX	MCW Metroliner DR130/3	MCW	O67/20F	1984	Ex North Western, 1990
406	B222VHW	MCW Metroliner DR130/3	MCW	O63/16F	1984	Ex Wessex, 1992
407	IIL7269	MCW Metroliner DR130/3	MCW	O63/20F	1984	Ex Midland Red North, 1990
409	B224VHW	MCW Metroliner DR130/3	MCW	O61/18F	1984	Ex Scottish Citylink, 1995
410	B225VHW	MCW Metroliner DR130/3	MCW	O63/22C	1984	Ex Monetgrange, Nottingham, 1995
411	A667XDA	MCW Metroliner DR130/3	MCW	O58/22F	1984	Ex Collins, Castle Goring, 1994
412	SNU122	MCW Metroliner DR130/3	MCW	O62/18D	1984	Ex Leon, Stafford, 1995
413	B825AAT	MCW Metroliner DR130/3	MCW	O63/27F	1984	Ex Prestatyn Coachways, Dyserth, 1995
414	C51VJU	MCW Metroliner DR130/22	MCW	O63/22F	1986	Ex Boyce, Milton of Campsie, 1995
415	C52VJU	MCW Metroliner DR130/22	MCW	O63/22F	1986	Ex McColl, Gartocharn, 1995
417w	C907GUD	MCW Metroliner DR130/21	MCW	O—/23F	1986	Ex Taylor, Widnes, 1994
418	D436OWO	MCW Metroliner DR130/33	MCW	O53/20F	1987	Ex McColl, Gartocharn, 1996
419u	C159UHN	MCW Metroliner DR130/10	MCW	CH55/17F	1985	Ex Stewart, Portsmouth, 1995
421	C593JAT	MCW Metroliner DR130/24	MCW	O63/20F	1986	Ex East Yorkshire, 1996
u	JHE141W	MCW Metrobus DR104/6	MCW	H45/32F	1981	Ex Cardiff Bluebird, Grangetown, 1997
u	JHE143W	MCW Metrobus DR104/6	MCW	H45/32F	1981	Ex Cardiff Bluebird, Grangetown, 1997
u	JHE163W	MCW Metrobus DR104/6	MCW	H45/32F	1981	Ex Cardiff Bluebird, Grangetown, 1997
u	JHE164W	MCW Metrobus DR104/6	MCW	H45/32F	1981	Ex Cardiff Bluebird, Grangetown, 1997
u	B119ORU	MCW Metroliner DR130/3	MCW	CH57/23F	1984	Ex Adkins, Upper Boddington, 1997
u	C133CFB	MCW Metroliner DR130/24	MCW	CH57/22F	1986	Ex Coach Team Pullman, Haddenham, 1996

Previous registrations

B824AAT	B116ORU, 8212RU, A3GNT	D436OWO	D192ESC, A5GJL	IIL7269	B117ORU
B825AAT	B120ORU, 5108VB, A5GNT	DHJ301B	410DCD, PRX207B, BHM288	SNU122	B258AGL
C593JAT	C118FKH, 665EYL	GVV205	BYX255V		

LONDON UNITED/WESTLINK

A112-130 — Volvo Olympian YN3RV18Z4 — Alexander Royale — DPH43/9FL 1995/96

112	N112UHP	115	N115UHP	118	N118UHP	121	N121UHP	124	N124YRW	127	N127YRW	130	N130YRW
113	N113UHP	116	N116UHP	119	N119UHP	122	N122UHP	125	N125YRW	128	N128YRW		
114	N114UHP	117	N117UHP	120	N120UHP	123	N123UHP	126	N126YRW	129	N129YRW		

CD1-8 — Dennis Dart SFD212 — Wright Crusader — B32F 1996

1	VDZ8001	3	VDZ8003	5	VDZ8005	7	VDZ8007
2	VDZ8002	4	VDZ8004	6	VDZ8006	8	VDZ8008

DA1-9 — DAF SB220LC550 — Optare Delta — B49F* 1989-90 — Ex London Buses, 1994 (DA1 ex Gailymatic 1995) * DA1 is DP49F

1	F802NGY	3	G931MYG	5	G933MYG	7	G935MYG	9	G937MYG
2	A5LBR	4	G932MYG	6	G934MYG	8	G936MYG		

DR1-14 — Dennis Dart 8.5SDL3003 — Reeve Burgess Pointer — B28F 1991 — Ex London Buses, 1994

1	H101THE	3	H103THE	5	H105THE	7	H107THE	9	H109THE	11	WLT931	13	H113THE
2	H102THE	4	H104THE	6	H106THE	8	H108THE	10	H110THE	12	H112THE	14	H114THE

DR53-141 — Dennis Dart 8.5SDL3010 — Plaxton Pointer — B24F* 1991-92 — Ex London Buses, 1994 * DR53-57 are B28F

53	J653XHL	64	J364GKH	75	J375GKH	104	J104DUV	115	J115DUV	126	J126DUV	137	J137DUV
54	J654XHL	65	J365GKH	76	J376GKH	105	J105DUV	116	J116DUV	127	J127DUV	138	J138DUV
55	J655XHL	66	J366GKH	77	J377GKH	106	J106DUV	117	J117DUV	128	J128DUV	139	J139DUV
56	J156GAT	67	J367GKH	78	J378GKH	107	J107DUV	118	J118DUV	129	J129DUV	140	J140DUV
57	J157GAT	68	J368GKH	79	J379GKH	108	J108DUV	119	J119DUV	130	J130DUV	141	J141DUV
58	J158GAT	69	J369GKH	80	J380GKH	109	J109DUV	120	J120DUV	131	J131DUV		
59	J159GAT	70	J370GKH	99	J599DUV	110	J110DUV	121	J121DUV	132	J132DUV		
60	J160GAT	71	J371GKH	100	VLT23	111	WLT946	122	J122DUV	133	J133DUV		
61	J161GAT	72	J372GKH	101	J101DUV	112	J112DUV	123	J123DUV	134	J134DUV		
62	J362GKH	73	J373GKH	102	J102DUV	113	J113DUV	124	J124DUV	135	J135DUV		
63	J363GKH	74	J374GKH	103	J103DUV	114	J114DUV	125	J125DUV	136	J136DUV		

DRL96-108 — Dennis Dart 9SDL3024 — Plaxton Pointer — B28F 1993 — Ex London Buses, 1994

96	K96SAG	98	K98SAG	100	ALM2B	102	K102SAG	104	K104SAG	106	K106SAG	108	K108SAG
97	K97SAG	99	K199SAG	101	K101SAG	103	K103SAG	105	K105SAG	107	K107SAG		

DRL159-171				Dennis Dart 9SDL3034		Plaxton Pointer				B28F*		1993/4	Ex London Buses, 1994 * DRL165-9 are B34F
159	L159XRH	161	L161XRH	163	L163XRH	165	L165YAT	167	L167YAT	169	L169YAT	171	L171CKH
160	L160XRH	162	L162XRH	164	L164XRH	166	L166YAT	168	L168YAT	170	L170CKH		

DT1-27				Dennis Dart 8.5SDL3003		Duple Dartline				DP21F		1990	Ex London Buses, 1994
1	G501VYE	5	G505VYE	9	G509VYE	13	G513VYE	17	G517VYE	21	G521VYE	25	G525VYE
2	G502VYE	6	G506VYE	10	G510VYE	14	G514VYE	18	G518VYE	22	G522VYE	26	G526VYE
3	G503VYE	7	G507VYE	11	G511VYE	15	G515VYE	19	G519VYE	23	G523VYE	27	G527VYE
4	G504VYE	8	G508VYE	12	G512VYE	16	G516VYE	20	G520VYE	24	G524VYE		

DT29-167   Dennis Dart 8.5SDL3003   Carlyle Dartline   B28F*   1990-91   * DT29, DT41/3-7 are DP21F; DT73/5/9 are B26F Ex London Buses, 1994

29	G29TGW	48	G48TGW	57	G57TGW	78	H78MOB	86	H86MOB	151	H151MOB	161	H161NON
41	G41TGW	49	G49TGW	71	H71MOB	79	H79MOB	144	H144MOB	152	H152MOB	162	H162NON
42	G42TGW	50	G50TGW	72	H72MOB	80	236CLT	145	H145MOB	153	H153MOB	163	H163NON
43	G43TGW	51	G51TGW	73	H73MOB	81	H81MOB	146	H146MOB	154	H154MOB	164	WLT804
44	G44TGW	52	G52TGW	74	H74MOB	82	H82MOB	147	H147MOB	155	H155MOB	165	H165NON
45	G45TGW	53	G53TGW	75	WLT329	83	H83MOB	148	H148MOB	158	H158NON	166	H166NON
46	G46TGW	54	G54TGW	76	H76MOB	84	H84MOB	149	H149MOB	159	H159NON	167	H167NON
47	G47TGW	56	G56TGW	77	WLT339	85	H85MOB	150	H150MOB	160	H160NON		

DT168	500CLT	Dennis Dart 8.5SDL3003		Duple Dartline			DP21F	1989	Ex London Buses, 1994

DWL1-14				Dennis Dart 9SDL3002		Wright Handybus				B36F		1990	Ex London Buses, 1994
1	JDZ2401	3	JDZ2403	5	JDZ2405	7	JDZ2407	9	JDZ2409	11	JDZ2411	13	JDZ2413
2	JDZ2402	4	JDZ2404	6	JDZ2406	8	JDZ2408	10	JDZ2410	12	JDZ2412	14	JDZ2414

FS29s	C501HOE	Ford Transit 190D		Carlyle			B20F	1985	Ex London Buses, 1994

L292-314   Leyland Olympian ONCL10/1RZ*   Leyland   H47/31F*   1989   * L306-14 are ON2R50C13Z4; L312-4 are DPH43/29F Ex London Buses, 1994

292	G292UYT	296	G296UYT	300	G300UYT	304	G304UYT	308	G308UYT	312	G312UYT
293	G293UYT	297	G297UYT	301	G301UYT	305	G305UYT	309	G309UYT	313	G313UYT
294	G294UYT	298	G298UYT	302	G302UYT	306	G306UYT	310	G310UYT	314	G314UYT
295	G295UYT	299	G299UYT	303	G303UYT	307	G307UYT	311	G311UYT		

LLW1-10				Dennis Lance SLF 11SDA3202		Wright Pathfinder 320				B34D	1993-94	Ex London Buses, 1994
1	ODZ8901	3	ODZ8903	5	ODZ8905	7	ODZ8907	9	ODZ8909			
2	0DZ8902	4	ODZ8904	6	ODZ8906	8	ODZ8908	10	ODZ8910			

LS7	KJD507P	Leyland National 10351A/2R		DP33D	1976	Ex London Buses, 1994
LS13	KJD513P	Leyland National 10351A/2R		B36D	1976	Ex London Buses, 1994
LS24t	KJD524P	Leyland National 10351A/2R		B36D	1976	Ex London Buses, 1994
LS29u	KJD529P	Leyland National 10351A/2R		B36D	1976	Ex London Buses, 1994
LS30	KJD530P	Leyland National 10351A/2R		DP42F	1976	Ex London Buses, 1994
LS35	KJD535P	Leyland National 10351A/2R		DP35D	1976	Ex London Buses, 1994
LS84	OJD884R	Leyland National 10351A/2R	(urban bus)	B38F	1977	Ex West Midlands, 1995
LS88	OJD888R	Leyland National 10351A/2R		DP36F	1977	Ex London Buses, 1994
LS96	OJD896R	Leyland National 10351A/2R	(urban bus)	B38F	1977	Ex London Buses, 1994
LS97	OJD897R	Leyland National 10351A/2R		DP35D	1977	Ex London Buses, 1994
LS98u	OJD898R	Leyland National 10351A/2R		B36D	1977	Ex London Buses, 1994
LS99	OJD899R	Leyland National 10351A/2R	(urban bus)	B38F	1977	Ex London Buses, 1994
LS112	THX112S	Leyland National 10351A/2R		B36F	1977	Ex London Buses, 1994
LS116u	THX116S	Leyland National 10351A/2R		B36D	1977	Ex London Buses, 1994
LS123	THX123S	Leyland National 10351A/2R		DP40F	1977	Ex London Buses, 1994
LS150	THX150S	Leyland National 10351A/2R		B36D	1977	Ex London Buses, 1994
LS153	THX153S	Leyland National 10351A/2R	(urban bus)	B38F	1977	Ex West Midlands, 1995
LS195	THX195S	Leyland National 10351A/2R		B36D	1978	Ex London Buses, 1994
LS227	THX227S	Leyland National 10351A/2R		DP36DL	1978	Ex London Buses, 1994
LS245	THX245S	Leyland National 10351A/2R		DP40F	1978	Ex London Buses, 1994
LS251	THX251S	Leyland National 10351A/2R		B36D	1978	Ex London Buses, 1994
LS259	THX259S	Leyland National 10351A/2R		DP36D	1978	Ex London Buses, 1994
LS268	THX268S	Leyland National 10351A/2R	(urban bus)	B38F	1978	Ex West Midlands, 1995
LS297	YYE297T	Leyland National 10351A/2R	(urban bus)	B38F	1979	Ex London Buses, 1994
LS304	AYR304T	Leyland National 10351A/2R		B36D	1979	Ex London Buses, 1994
LS335	AYR335T	Leyland National 10351A/2R	(urban bus)	B38F	1979	Ex London Buses, 1994
LS337	AYR337T	Leyland National 10351A/2R	(urban bus)	B38F	1979	Ex London Buses, 1995
LS363	BYW363V	Leyland National 10351A/2R		B36D	1979	Ex London Buses, 1994
LS373	BYW373V	Leyland National 10351A/2R	(urban bus)	B38F	1979	Ex West Midlands, 1995
LS381t	BYW381V	Leyland National 10351A/2R		B36D	1979	Ex London Buses, 1994
LS385	BYW385V	Leyland National 10351A/2R	(urban bus)	B38F	1979	Ex London Buses, 1994
LS395	BYW395V	Leyland National 10351A/2R	(urban bus)	B38F	1979	Ex London Buses, 1994
LS405	BYW405V	Leyland National 10351A/2R	(urban bus)	B38F	1979	Ex West Midlands, 1995
LS408u	BYW408V	Leyland National 10351A/2R		B36D	1979	Ex London Buses, 1994
LS411	BYW411V	Leyland National 10351A/2R		DP35D	1979	Ex London Buses, 1994
LS422	BYW422V	Leyland National 10351A/2R		B36D	1979	Ex London Buses, 1994
LS429	BYW429V	Leyland National 10351A/2R		B36D	1979	Ex West Midlands, 1995
LS431	BYW431V	Leyland National 10351A/2R	(urban bus)	B38F	1979	Ex London Buses, 1994
LS434u	BYW434V	Leyland National 10351A/2R		B36D	1979	Ex London Buses, 1994
LX3	G73UYV	Leyland Lynx LX2R11C15Z4S	Leyland	B49F	1989	Ex London Buses, 1994
LX4	G74UYV	Leyland Lynx LX2R11C15Z4S	Leyland	B49F	1989	Ex London Buses, 1994
LX5	G75UYV	Leyland Lynx LX2R11C15Z4S	Leyland	B49F	1989	Ex London Buses, 1994
LX6	G76UYV	Leyland Lynx LX2R11C15Z4S	Leyland	B49F	1989	Ex London Buses, 1994
LX7	G77UYV	Leyland Lynx LX2R11C15Z4S	Leyland	B49F	1989	Ex London Buses, 1994
LX8	G78UYV	Leyland Lynx LX2R11C15Z4S	Leyland	B49F	1989	Ex London Buses, 1994

M8-52

MCW Metrobus DR101/8 — MCW — H43/28D* — 1978-79 — Ex London Buses, 1994 * Trainers are H0/15D

8	WYW8T	17	WYW17T	22t	WYW22T	30t	WYW30T	36t	WYW36T	44	WYW44T
13t	WYW13T	19	WYW19T	28	WYW28T	31t	WYW31T	39	WYW39T	46t	WYW46T
15	WYW15T	21	WYW21T	29	WYW29T	34	WYW34T	43	WYW43T	52	WYW52T

M59-204

MCW Metrobus DR101/9 — MCW — H43/28D* — 1979 — Ex London Buses, 1994 * M147 is H0/15D

59	WYW59T	93	WYW93T	110	BYX110V	134	BYX134V	154	BYX154V	179	BYX179V	193u	BYX193V
68	WYW68T	96	BYX96V	112	BYX112V	138	BYX138V	157	BYX157V	183	BYX183V	195	BYX195V
86	WYW86T	99	BYX99V	122	BYX122V	146	BYX146V	159	BYX159V	186	BYX186V	203	BYX203V
89	WYW89T	100	BYX100V	131	BYX131V	147t	BYX147V	162	BYX162V	187	BYX187V	204	BYX204V

M206-462

MCW Metrobus DR101/12 — MCW — H43/28D* — 1980 — Ex London Buses, 1994* M206/64 are H0/15D

206t	BYX206V	223	BYX223V	264t	BYX264V	363	GYE363W	387	GYE387W	462	GYE462W
221	BYX221V	227	BYX227V	327	EYE327V	366	GYE366W	415	GYE415W		

M506-697

MCW Metrobus DR101/14 — MCW — H43/28D — 1981 — Ex London Buses, 1994

506	GYE506W	554	GYE554W	598	GYE598W	687	KYV687X
526	GYE526W	592	GYE592W	685	KYV685X	697	KYV697X

M813-951

MCW Metrobus DR101/16 — MCW — H43/28D — 1983 — Ex London Buses, 1994

813	OJD813Y	832	OJD832Y	839	OJD839Y	856	OJD856Y	889	OJD889Y	932	A932SUL
815	OJD815Y	835	OJD835Y	841	OJD841Y	864	OJD864Y	906	A906SUL	951	A951SUL
831	OJD831Y	836	OJD836Y	844	OJD844Y	881	OJD881Y	920	A920SUL		

M958-1003

MCW Metrobus DR101/17 — MCW — H43/28D — 1984 — Ex London Buses, 1994 * M1003 is DPH43/28D

958	A958SYF	963	A963SYF	969	A969SYF	981	A981SYF	994	A994SYF	1003	A703THV
960	A960SYF	966	A966SYF	972	A972SYF	985	A985SYF	999	A999SYF		
962	A962SYF	967	A967SYF	980	A980SYF	990	A990SYF	1001	A701THV		

M1006-1029

MCW Metrobus DR101/18 — MCW — DPH41/28D 1984 — Ex London Buses, 1994

1006	A706THV	1010	A710THV	1014	A714THV	1018	A718THV	1022	A722THV	1026	A726THV
1007	A707THV	1011	A711THV	1015	A715THV	1019	A719THV	1023	A723THV	1027	A727THV
1008	A708THV	1012	A712THV	1016	A716THV	1020	A720THV	1024	A724THV	1028	A728THV
1009	A709THV	1013	A713THV	1017	A717THV	1021	A721THV	1025	A725THV	1029	A729THV

M1030-1439 MCW Metrobus DR101/17* MCW H43/28D* 1984-86 * M1048-53 are DR101/19; M1251 is DPH43/28D Ex London Buses, 1994

1030	A730THV	1073	B73WUL	1184	B184WUL	1212	B212WUL	1262	B262WUL	1343	C343BUV	1360	C360BUV
1037	A737THV	1106	B106WUL	1187	B187WUL	1238	B238WUL	1266	B266WUL	1344	C344BUV	1361	C361BUV
1039	A739THV	1110	B110WUL	1188	B188WUL	1240	B240WUL	1269	B269WUL	1345	C345BUV	1363	C363BUV
1048	A748THV	1125	B125WUL	1190	B190WUL	1242	B242WUL	1270	B270WUL	1351	C351BUV	1368	C368BUV
1050	A750THV	1166	B166WUL	1191	B191WUL	1243	B243WUL	1271	B271WUL	1352	C352BUV	1374	C374BUV
1053	A753THV	1171	B171WUL	1194	B194WUL	1251	B251WUL	1272	B272WUL	1353	C353BUV	1381	C381BUV
1064	B64WUL	1172	B172WUL	1200	B200WUL	1257	B257WUL	1336	C336BUV	1356	C356BUV	1439	C439BUV
1069	B69WUL	1178	B178WUL	1207	B207WUL	1261	B261WUL	1341	C341BUV	1358	C358BUV		

MR1u	D461PON	MCW Metrorider MF150/14	MCW	B23F	1987	Ex London Buses, 1994
MR2u	D462PON	MCW Metrorider MF150/14	MCW	B23F	1987	Ex London Buses, 1994
MR4u	D464PON	MCW Metrorider MF150/14	MCW	B23F	1987	Ex London Buses, 1994
MR5u	D465PON	MCW Metrorider MF150/14	MCW	B23F	1987	Ex London Buses, 1994
MR10u	D470PON	MCW Metrorider MF150/14	MCW	B23F	1987	Ex London Buses, 1994
MR30u	E130KYW	MCW Metrorider MF150/38	MCW	B25F	1987	Ex London Buses, 1994
MR42u	E142KYW	MCW Metrorider MF150/38	MCW	B25F	1987	Ex London Buses, 1994
MR134	D482NOX	MCW Metrorider MF150/2	MCW	B25F	1986	Ex London Buses, 1994

MRL81-92 MCW Metrorider MF158/11 MCW B28F 1988 * MRL89-92 are MF158/12 and DP31F
Ex London Buses, 1994

81u	F185YDA	83	F187YDA	85	F189YDA	88	F192YDA	90	F194YDA	92	F196YDA
82u	F186YDA	84u	F188YDA	87	F191YDA	89u	F193YDA	91	F195YDA		

MRW2	A2LBR	MCW Metrorider MF158/11	MCW	B19FL	1988	Ex London Buses, 1994
MRW3	A3LBR	MCW Metrorider MF158/11	MCW	B19FL	1988	Ex London Buses, 1994
MRW4	A4LBR	MCW Metrorider MF158/11	MCW	B19FL	1988	Ex London Buses, 1994

MV1-8 MAN 11.190 Optare Vecta B42F 1995

1	N281DWY	3	N283DWY	5	N285DWY	7	N287DWY
2	N282DWY	4	N284DWY	6	N286DWY	8	N288DWY

RM2033	ALM33B	AEC Routemaster 5RM	Park Royal	H36/28R	1964	Ex London Transport Buses, 1997
RM2078	ALM78B	AEC Routemaster 5RM	Park Royal	H36/28R	1964	Ex London Transport Buses, 1997

RML880-2757 AEC Routemaster 7RM (Cummins) Park Royal H40/32R 1961-68 Ex London Buses, 1994

880	WLT880	2349	CUV349C	2463	JJD463D	2600	NML600E	2662	SMK662F	2720	SMK720F	2744	SMK744F
881	WLT881	2353	CUV353C	2464	JJD464D	2621	NML621E	2697	SMK697F	2721	SMK721F	2751	SMK751F
891	WLT891	2414	JJD414D	2485	JJD485D	2622	NML622E	2700	SMK700F	2722	SMK722F	2757	SMK757F
2269	CUV269C	2432	JJD432D	2489	JJD489D	2645	NML645E	2702	SMK702F	2729	SMK729F		
2293	CUV293C	2447	JJD447D	2500	JJD500D	2646	NML646E	2704	SMK704F	2734	SMK734F		
2298	CUV298C	2455	JJD455D	2519	JJD519D	2650	NML650E	2707	SMK707F	2739	SMK739F		

VA1-10 Volvo Olympian YN2RV18Z4 Alexander Royale H45/29F 1996

1	N131YRW	3	N133YRW	5	N135YRW	7	N137YRW	9	N139YRW
2	N132YRW	4	N134YRW	6	N136YRW	8	N138YRW	10	N140YRW

VA11-31 Volvo Olympian Alexander (Belfast) H47/25D 1997

11	XDZ5911	14	XDZ5914	17	XDZ5917	20	R920WOE	23	R923WOE	26		29
12	XDZ5912	15	XDZ5915	18	R918WOE	21	R921WOE	24	R924WOE	27		30
13	XDZ5913	16	XDZ5916	19	R919WOE	22	R922WOE	25		28		31

XL1	P151BUG	Optare L1100	Optare Excel	B36F	1997
XL2	P152BUG	Optare L1100	Optare Excel	B36F	1997
XL3	P153BUG	Optare L1100	Optare Excel	B36F	1997
XL4	P154BUG	Optare L1100	Optare Excel	B36F	1997
XL6	P156BUG	Optare L1100	Optare Excel	B36F	1997
XL7	P157BUG	Optare L1100	Optare Excel	B36F	1997

Vehicles on loan

M231-386 MCW Metrobus DR101/12 MCW H43/28D 1980 from London General

231	BYX231V	242	BYX242V	261	BYX261V	275	BYX275V	325	EYE325V	386	GYE386W

Previous registrations

A2LBR	F182YDA	VLT23	J610DUV	WLT946	J611DUV
A3LBR	F183YDA	WLT329	H575MOC	236CLT	H880LOX
A4LBR	F184YDA	WLT339	H577MOC	500CLT	G349GCK
ALM2B	K210SAG	WLT804	H264NON		
F802NGY	F54CWY, WLT400	WLT931	H611TKU		

Special liveries

Airbus livery: A112-30
Airbus Direct livery: DT1-27/9, DT41/3-7, DT168
London United Tramways livery: RML880
Overall advertisements: LS112
Kingston University livery: DWL1-3, LS227, MR134
Red and cream training bus livery: M13, M22, M30/1/6, M46, M147, M206/64
Heathrow routes 555-557 livery: DR60/5/6/8, DRL165-71

Disposition of fleet

Westlink: DA1-9, DR10-4/53-9/61-4/7/9/117-20/2, DWL1-14, FS29, LS7/13/24/9/30/5/61/88/97/8/112/6/23/50/95/227/45/51/9/304/63/408/11/22/9/34, M21/9/89/157/9/204/31/42/61/75/325/86/506/813/64/81/1006/352, MR1/2/4/5/10/30/42/134, MRL81-5/7-92, MRW2-4, MV1-8, VA11-31, XL1-4/6/7
London United: All other vehicles

MAIDSTONE & DISTRICT (LT vehicles)

5901	G901SKR	Leyland Olympian ON2R50G13Z4	Northern Counties	H45/30F	1990	Route 402 livery
5902	G902SKR	Leyland Olympian ON2R50C13Z4	Northern Counties	H45/30F	1990	Route 402 livery
5903	G903SKR	Leyland Olympian ON2R50G13Z4	Northern Counties	H45/30F	1990	Route 402 livery
5904	G904SKR	Leyland Olympian ON2R50C13Z4	Northern Counties	H45/30F	1990	Route 402 livery
5905	G905SKR	Leyland Olympian ON2R50G13Z4	Northern Counties	H45/30F	1990	Route 402 livery

METROBUS

80	F80SMC	Leyland Lynx LX112L10ZR1R	Leyland	DP49F	1988	
101	K101JMV	Leyland Lynx 2 LX2R11C15Z4S	Leyland	B51F	1992	Volvo engine
103	D103NDW	Leyland Lynx LX112TL11ZR1R	Leyland	B51F	1987	Ex Merthyr Tydfil, 1989
104	D104NDW	Leyland Lynx LX112TL11ZR1R	Leyland	B51F	1987	Ex Merthyr Tydfil, 1989
110	D110NDW	Leyland Lynx LX112TL11ZR1R	Leyland	B51F	1987	Ex Merthyr Tydfil, 1989
165	F165SMT	Leyland Lynx LX112L10ZR1S	Leyland	B51F	1989	Ex Miller, Foxton, 1991
166	F166SMT	Leyland Lynx LX112L10ZR1S	Leyland	B51F	1989	Ex Miller, Foxton, 1991

223-229 — Dennis Dart 9SDL3011 — Plaxton Pointer — B35F — 1992 — Ex Kentish Bus, 1996

223	J223HGY	224	J224HGY	225	J225HGY	226	J226HGY	227	J227HGY	228	J228HGY	229	J229HGY

501-510 — Optare L1070 — Optare Excel — B35F — 1996

501	P501OUG	503	P503OUG	505	P505OUG	507	P507OUG	509	P509OUG
502	P502OUG	504	P504OUG	506	P506OUG	508	P508OUG	510	P510OUG

575 — E575FTW — Ford Transit VE6 — Ford — B11F — 1988 — Ex private owner, 1990

701-707 — Dennis Dart 8.5SDL3010 — Plaxton Pointer — B32F* — 1991 — * 701 is DP32F

701	J701EMX	702	J702EMX	703	J703EMX	704	J704EMX	705	J705EMX	706	J706EMX	707	J707EMX

708-716 — Dennis Dart 9SDL3011 — Plaxton Pointer — B35F — 1992

708	K708KGU	710	K710KGU	712	K712KGU	714	K714KGU	716	K716KGU
709	K709KGU	711	K711KGU	713	K713KGU	715	K715KGU		

717	L717OMV	Dennis Dart 9.8SDL3032	Plaxton Pointer	B35F	1994
718	L718OMV	Dennis Dart 9.8SDL3032	Plaxton Pointer	B35F	1994
719	L719OMV	Dennis Dart 9.8SDL3032	Plaxton Pointer	B35F	1994
720	L720OMV	Dennis Dart 9.8SDL3032	Plaxton Pointer	B35F	1994
721	M721CGO	Dennis Dart 9.8SDL3054	Plaxton Pointer	B35F	1994
722	M722CGO	Dennis Dart 9.8SDL3054	Plaxton Pointer	B35F	1995
723	M723CGO	Dennis Dart 9.8SDL3054	Plaxton Pointer	B35F	1995

724	M724CGO		Dennis Dart 9.8SDL3054		Plaxton Pointer			B35F	1995				
725	N725KGF		Dennis Dart 9.8SDL3054		Plaxton Pointer			B35F	1995				
726	N726KGF		Dennis Dart 9.8SDL3054		Plaxton Pointer			B35F	1995				
802	F802NGU		Leyland Olympian ONCL10/1RZ		Leyland			H47/31F	1989				
803	F803NGU		Leyland Olympian ONCL10/1RZ		Leyland			H47/31F	1989				

804-816			Leyland Olympian ON2R50C13Z4		Leyland			H47/31F	1990-92				
804	G804SMV	806	G806TMX	808	H808AGX	810	H810AGX	812	J812GGW	814	K814HMV	816	K816HMV
805	G805SMV	807	H807XMY	809	H809AGX	811	H811AGX	813	J813GGW	815	K815HMV		

817-829			Volvo Olympian		Northern Counties Palatine 1			H47/29F	1996				
817	P817SGP	819	P819SGP	822	P822SGP	824	P824SGP	826	P826SGP	829	P829SGP		
818	P818SGP	821	P821SGP	823	P823SGP	825	P825SGP	828	P828SGP				

830-845			Volvo Olympian		East Lancs Pyoneer			H47/25D	1997				
830	R830MFR	833	R833MFR	835	R835MFR	837	R837MFR	839	R839MFR	842	R842MFR	844	R844MFR
831	R831MFR	834	R834MFR	836	R836MFR	838	R838MFR	841	R841MFR	843	R843MFR	845	R845MFR
832	R832MFR												

901	N901HWY		Optare MetroRider MR13		Optare			B26F	1996				
902	N902HWY		Optare MetroRider MR13		Optare			B26F	1996				
903	N903HWY		Optare MetroRider MR13		Optare			B26F	1996				
904	N904HWY		Optare MetroRider MR13		Optare			B26F	1996				
905	N905HWY		Optare MetroRider MR13		Optare			B26F	1996				
906	N906HWY		Optare MetroRider MR13		Optare			B26F	1996				

The coach fleet is listed in the London Coach Handbook.

METROLINE

AV1-22			Volvo Olympian		Alexander RH			H43/25D	1996		
1	585CLT	5	P485MBY	9	P489MBY	13	P493MBY	17	P477MBY	21	P474MBY
2	P482MBY	6	P486MBY	10	P490MBY	14	P494MBY	18	P478MBY	22	P475MBY
3	P483MBY	7	P487MBY	11	P491MBY	15	P495MBY	19	P479MBY		
4	P484MBY	8	P488MBY	12	P492MBY	16	P476MBY	20	P480MBY		

DL1-21			Dennis Dart SFD212BR1		Plaxton Pointer			B36F	1997				
1	P201OLX	4	P204OLX	7	P207OLX	10	P210OLX	13	R113RLY	16	R116RLY	19	R119RLY
2	P202OLX	5	P205OLX	8	P208OLX	11	P211OLX	14	R114RLY	17	R117RLY	20	R120RLY
3	P203OLX	6	P206OLX	9	P209OLX	12	R112RLY	15	R115RLY	18	R118RLY	21	R121RLY

DLD22-53 — Dennis Dart SFD212BR1 — Plaxton Pointer — B30D — 1997

22	R122RLY	27	R127RLY	32	R132RLY	37	R137RLY	42	R142RLY	47	R147RLY	52	R152RLY
23	R123RLY	28	R128RLY	33	R133RLY	38	R138RLY	43	R143RLY	48	R148RLY	53	R153RLY
24	R124RLY	29	R129RLY	34	R134RLY	39	R139RLY	44	R144RLY	49	R149RLY		
25	R125RLY	30	R130RLY	35	R135RLY	40	R140RLY	45	R145RLY	50	R150RLY		
26	R126RLY	31	R131RLY	36	R136RLY	41	R141RLY	46	R146RLY	51	R151RLY		

DLS1-7 — Dennis Dart SFD112BR1 — Plaxton Pointer — B32F — 1997

1	P101OLX	2	P102OLX	3	P103OLX	4	P104OLX	5	P105OLX	6	P106OLX	7	P107OLX

DR15-42 — Dennis Dart 8.5SDL3003 — Reeve Burgess Pointer — B28F* — 1991 — Ex London Buses, 1994
*DR40/2 are Plaxton Pointer B28F

15	H115THE	16	H116THE	17	H117THE	18	H118THE	19	H119THE	40	H540XGK	42	H542XGK

DR81-148 — Dennis Dart 8.5SDL3010 — Plaxton Pointer — B28F — 1992 — Ex London Buses, 1994

81	J381GKH	85	J385GKH	89	J389GKH	93	J393GKH	97	J397GKH	144	K244PAG	148	K248PAG
82	J382GKH	86	J386GKH	90	J390GKH	94	J394GKH	98	J398GKH	145	K245PAG		
83	J383GKH	87	J387GKH	91	J391GKH	95	J395GKH	142	K242PAG	146	K246PAG		
84	J384GKH	88	J388GKH	92	J392GKH	96	J396GKH	143	K243PAG	147	K247PAG		

DT88-157 — Dennis Dart 8.5SDL3003 — Carlyle Dartline — B28F — 1990-91 — Ex London Buses, 1994

88	H588MOC	103	H103MOB	114w	H114MOB	123w	H123MOB	134	H134MOB	140	H140MOB
89	H89MOB	107	H107MOB	115	H115MOB	124	H124MOB	135	H135MOB	141	H141MOB
90	H890LOX	108	H108MOB	116	H116MOB	125	H125MOB	136	H136MOB	142	H142MOB
92	H92MOB	110	H110MOB	118	H118MOB	126	H126MOB	138	H138MOB	156	H156MOB
93	H93MOB	113	H113MOB	122	H122MOB	133	H133MOB	139	H139MOB	157	H157NON

EDR1-9 — Dennis Dart 9.8SDL3040 — Plaxton Pointer — B39F — 1994

1	M101BLE	3	M103BLE	5	M105BLE	7	M107BLE	9	M109BLE
2	M102BLE	4	M104BLE	6	M106BLE	8	M108BLE		

EDR10-44 — Dennis Dart SFD412BR5 — Plaxton Pointer — B39F — 1996

10	P285MLD	15	P290MLD	20	P295MLD	25	P301MLD	30	P306MLD	35	P311MLD	40	P316MLD
11	P286MLD	16	P291MLD	21	P296MLD	26	P302MLD	31	P307MLD	36	P312MLD	41	P317MLD
12	P287MLD	17	P292MLD	22	P297MLD	27	P303MLD	32	P308MLD	37	P313MLD	42	P318MLD
13	P288MLD	18	P293MLD	23	P298MLD	28	P304MLD	33	P309MLD	38	P314MLD	43	P319MLD
14	P289MLD	19	P294MLD	24	P299MLD	29	P305MLD	34	P310MLD	39	P315MLD	44	P320MLD

LLW25-38 — Dennis Lance SLF 11SDA3202 — Wright Pathfinder 320 — B34D — 1993-94 — Ex London Buses, 1994

25	L25WLH	27	L27WLH	29	L29WLH	31	L31WLH	33	L39WLH	35	L35WLH	37	L37WLH
26	L26WLH	28	L28WLH	30	L21WLH	32	L32WLH	34	L34WLH	36	L36WLH	38	L38WLH

LN1-31 Dennis Lance 11SDA3108 Northern Counties Paladin B37D 1993 Ex London Buses, 1994

1u	K301YJA	6u	K306YJA	11u	K311YJA	16u	K316YJA	21t	K321YJA	26u	K326YJA	31t	K331YJA
2u	K302YJA	7u	K307YJA	12u	K312YJA	17u	K317YJA	22u	K322YJA	27u	K327YJA		
3u	K303YJA	8u	K308YJA	13u	K313YJA	18u	K318YJA	23u	K323YJA	28u	K328YJA		
4u	K304YJA	9u	K309YJA	14u	K315YJA	19u	K319YJA	24u	K324YJA	29u	K329YJA		
5u	K305YJA	10u	K310YJA	15u	K315YJA	20u	K320YJA	25u	K325YJA	30u	K330YJA		

M1t	THX101S	MCW Metrobus DR101/3	MCW	H43/28F	1978	Ex London Buses, 1994
M2t	THX102S	MCW Metrobus DR101/3	MCW	H43/28F	1978	Ex London Buses, 1994
M3t	THX103S	MCW Metrobus DR101/3	MCW	H43/28F	1978	Ex London Buses, 1994
M4t	THX104S	MCW Metrobus DR101/3	MCW	H43/28F	1978	Ex London Buses, 1994
M5t	THX105S	MCW Metrobus DR101/3	MCW	H43/28F	1978	Ex London Buses, 1994
M18	WYW18T	MCW Metrobus DR101/8	MCW	H43/28D	1979	Ex London Buses, 1994
M20	WYW20T	MCW Metrobus DR101/8	MCW	H43/28D	1979	Ex London Buses, 1994
M41	WYW41T	MCW Metrobus DR101/8	MCW	H43/28D	1979	Ex London Buses, 1994
M48	WYW48T	MCW Metrobus DR101/8	MCW	H43/28D	1979	Ex London Buses, 1994
M54	WYW54T	MCW Metrobus DR101/8	MCW	H43/28D	1979	Ex London Buses, 1994

M57-192 MCW Metrobus DR101/9 MCW H43/28D 1979 Ex London Buses, 1994 (M135/7/50/92 ex Atlas Bus, 1996)

57	WYW57T	83	WYW83T	91	WYW91T	111t	BYX111V	135	BYX135V	151	BYX151V	172	BYX172V
58	WYW58T	84	WYW84T	94	WYW94T	113	BYX113V	136	BYX136V	155	BYX155V	178	BYX178V
62	WYW62T	85	WYW85T	97	BYX97V	119	BYX119V	137	BYX137V	163	BYX163V	180	BYX180V
70	WYW70T	87	WYW87T	102	BYX102V	125	BYX125V	140	BYX140V	166	BYX166V	184	BYX184V
73	WYW73T	88	WYW88T	107	BYX107V	127	BYX127V	142	BYX142V	167	BYX167V	192	BYX192V
77	WYW77T	90	WYW90T	109	BYX109V	128	BYX128V	150	BYX150V	169	BYX169V		

M222-482 MCW Metrobus DR101/12 MCW H43/28D 1980 Ex London Buses, 1994 (M222/324/52/73 ex London General, 1995; M272/6, M407 ex Atlas Bus, 1996)

222	BYX222V	313	BYX313V	352	GYE352W	403	GYE403W	436	GYE436W	448	GYE448W	467	GYE467W
238	BYX238V	315	BYX315V	367t	GYE367W	407	GYE407W	437	GYE437W	449	GYE449W	468	GYE468W
272	BYX272V	324	EYE324V	373	GYE373W	409t	GYE409W	438	GYE438W	453	GYE453W	473	GYE473W
276	BYX276V	326	EYE326V	376	GYE376W	424	GYE424W	440	GYE440W	455	GYE455W	482	GYE482W
300	BYX300V	335	EYE335V	380	GYE380W	428	GYE428W	443	GYE443W	459	GYE459W		
306	BYX306V	342	EYE342V	391	GYE391W	429	GYE429W	444	GYE444W	460	GYE460W		
309	BYX309V	344	EYE344V	394	GYE394W	432	GYE432W	446t	GYE446W	461	GYE461W		

M524-696 MCW Metrobus DR101/14 MCW H43/28D 1981 Ex London Buses, 1994

524	GYE524W	595	GYE595W	621	KYO621X	683	KYV683X
550	GYE550W	618	KYO618X	655	KYV655X	696	KYV696X

M810-955   MCW Metrobus DR101/16   MCW   H43/28D   1983   Ex London Buses, 1994

810	OJD810Y	**910**	A910SUL	**924**	A924SUL	**937**	A937SUL	**950**	A950SUL
819t	WLT342	**911**	A911SUL	**935**	A935SUL	**945**	A945SUL	**955**	A955SUL

M956-1431   MCW Metrobus DR101/17*   MCW   H43/28D*   1984-86   * M1047 is DR101/19; M1185/236 are DPH43/28D Ex London Buses, 1994

956	A956SYF	**1034**	A734THV	**1167**	B167WUL	**1192**	B192WUL	**1208**	B208WUL	**1348**	C348BUV	**1423**	C423BUV
968	A968SYF	**1035**	A735THV	**1168**	B168WUL	**1193**	B193WUL	**1218u**	B218WUL	**1349**	C349BUV	**1425**	C425BUV
974	A974SYF	**1043**	A743THV	**1174**	B174WUL	**1195**	B195WUL	**1236**	WLT646	**1350**	C350BUV	**1426**	C426BUV
982	A982SYF	**1047**	A747THV	**1181**	B181WUL	**1197**	B197WUL	**1273**	WLT902	**1366**	C366BUV	**1427**	C427BUV
993	A993SYF	**1056**	B56WUL	**1183**	B183WUL	**1198**	B198WUL	**1274**	A274WUL	**1383**	C383BUV	**1428**	C428BUV
995	A995SYF	**1057**	B57WUL	**1185**	WLT893	**1202**	B202WUL	**1339**	C339BUV	**1408**	C408BUV	**1429**	WLT826
1004	A704THV	**1068**	B68WUL	**1186**	B186WUL	**1204**	B204WUL	**1342**	C342BUV	**1409**	C409BUV	**1430**	C430BUV
1031	A731THV	**1071**	B71WUL	**1189**	B189WUL	**1205**	B205WUL	**1346**	C346BUV	**1416**	C416BUV	**1431**	C431BUV

RM70	VLT70	AEC Routemaster 5RM	Park Royal	H36/28R	1959	Ex London Buses, 1994; on loan to Barclays Bank
RM644	WLT644	AEC Routemaster 5RM	Park Royal	O36/28RD	1961	Ex London Buses, 1994
RMC1513tu	513CLT	AEC Routemaster 6RM	Park Royal	H32/25RD	1962	Ex London Buses, 1994

RML893-2755   AEC Routemaster 7RM (Cummins)   Park Royal   H40/32R   1961-68   Ex London Buses, 1994

893	KFF276	**2308**	CUV308C	**2430**	JJD430D	**2509**	JJD509D	**2585**	JJD585D	**2681**	SMK681F	**2706**	SMK706F
902	ALC464A	**2312**	CUV312C	**2431**	JJD431D	**2532**	JJD532D	**2594**	JJD594D	**2689**	SMK689F	**2710**	SMK710F
2274	CUV274C	**2331**	CUV331C	**2439**	JJD439D	**2537**	JJD537D	**2599**	NML599E	**2690**	SMK690F	**2713**	SMK713F
2285	CUV285C	**2348**	CUV348C	**2446**	JJD446D	**2547**	JJD547D	**2634**	NML634E	**2695**	SMK695F	**2727**	SMK727F
2288	CUV288C	**2368**	JJD368D	**2471**	JJD471D	**2558**	JJD558D	**2649**	NML649E	**2698**	SMK698F	**2728**	SMK728F
2289	CUV289C	**2377**	JJD377D	**2478**	JJD478D	**2566**	JJD566D	**2651**	NML651E	**2701**	SMK701F	**2737**	SMK737F
2299	CUV299C	**2384**	JJD384D	**2508**	JJD508D	**2579**	JJD579D	**2652**	NML652E	**2703**	SMK703F	**2755**	SMK755F

T287-481   Leyland Titan TNLXB2RR   Leyland   H44/24D*   1981-82   * T287, T321 are H44/26D Ex Atlas Bus, 1996

287	KYN287X	**321**	KYV321X	**390**	KYV390X	**435**	KYV435X	**481**	KYV481X
302	KYN302X	**375**	KYV375X	**432**	KYV432X	**477**	KYV477X		

Previous registrations

ALC464A	WLT902
KFF276	WLT893
WLT342	OJD819Y
WLT646	B236WUL
WLT826	C429BUV
WLT893	B185WUL
WLT902	B273WUL
585CLT	P481MBY

Special liveries

Tesco livery : DT89/93/103.
Overall advertisements : M367, M409, RM70.

MTL LONDON

DAF539	H539YCX	DAF SB220LC550	Ikarus Citibus	B50F	1991	Ex R&I, 1996
DAF848	F848YJX	DAF SB220LC550	Optare Delta	B49F	1989	Ex Merseybus, 1996
DAF849	F849YJX	DAF SB220LC550	Optare Delta	DP49F	1989	Ex R&I, 1996
DC216	G216LGK	Dennis Dart 9SDL3002	Duple/Carlyle Dartline	B36F	1990	Ex R&I, 1996
DC219	G219LGK	Dennis Dart 9SDL3002	Duple/Carlyle Dartline	B36F	1990	Ex R&I, 1996
DC220	G220LGK	Dennis Dart 9SDL3002	Duple/Carlyle Dartline	B36F	1990	Ex R&I, 1996
DC221	G121RGT	Dennis Dart 9SDL3002	Duple/Carlyle Dartline	B36F	1990	Ex R&I, 1996
DC224	G124RGT	Dennis Dart 9SDL3002	Duple/Carlyle Dartline	B36F	1990	Ex R&I, 1996
DC229	G129RGT	Dennis Dart 9SDL3002	Duple/Carlyle Dartline	B36F	1990	Ex R&I, 1996
DC232	RIB7002	Dennis Dart 9SDL3002	Carlyle Dartline	B36F	1990	Ex R&I, 1996
DM242	RIB8341	Dennis Dart 9.8SDL3035	Marshall C37	B40F	1994	Ex R&I, 1996

DNL101-120		Dennis Dart 9SDL3034	Northern Counties Paladin	B34F	1994	Ex London Buses, 1994

101	L101HHV	104	L104HHV	107	L107HHV	110	L110HHV	114	L114HHV	117	L117HHV	120	L120HHV
102	L102HHV	105	L105HHV	108	L108HHV	112	L112HHV	115	L115HHV	118	L118HHV		
103	L103HHV	106	L106HHV	109	L109HHV	113	L113HHV	116	L116HHV	119	L119HHV		

DP233	33LUG	Dennis Dart 9.8SDL3017	Plaxton Pointer	B40F	1992	Ex R&I, 1996
DP234	K414MGN	Dennis Dart 9SDL3011	Plaxton Pointer	B35F	1993	Ex R&I, 1996
DP235	RIB5085	Dennis Dart 9SDL3011	Plaxton Pointer	B35F	1993	Ex R&I, 1996
DP236	K416MGN	Dennis Dart 9SDL3011	Plaxton Pointer	B35F	1993	Ex R&I, 1996
DP237	K417MGN	Dennis Dart 9SDL3011	Plaxton Pointer	B35F	1993	Ex R&I, 1996
DP238	K418MGN	Dennis Dart 9SDL3011	Plaxton Pointer	B35F	1993	Ex R&I, 1996
DP239	K419MGN	Dennis Dart 9SDL3011	Plaxton Pointer	B35F	1993	Ex R&I, 1996
DP240	M498ALP	Dennis Dart 9SDL3031	Plaxton Pointer	B35F	1994	Ex R&I, 1996
DP241	M499ALP	Dennis Dart 9SDL3031	Plaxton Pointer	B35F	1994	Ex R&I, 1996
DP245	M503ALP	Dennis Dart 9.8SDL3054	Plaxton Pointer	B40F	1995	Ex R&I, 1996
DP246	M504ALP	Dennis Dart 9.8SDL3054	Plaxton Pointer	B40F	1995	Ex R&I, 1996
DP247	M505ALP	Dennis Dart 9.8SDL3054	Plaxton Pointer	B40F	1995	Ex R&I, 1996
DP248	M506ALP	Dennis Dart 9.8SDL3054	Plaxton Pointer	B40F	1995	Ex R&I, 1996
DP273	P673MLE	Dennis Dart SFD212	Plaxton Pointer	B34F	1997	
DP274	P674MLE	Dennis Dart SFD212	Plaxton Pointer	B34F	1997	
DP275	P675MLE	Dennis Dart SFD212	Plaxton Pointer	B34F	1997	
DP276	P676MLE	Dennis Dart SFD212	Plaxton Pointer	B34F	1997	

DRL18-37		Dennis Dart 9SDL3016	Plaxton Pointer	B34F	1992	Ex London Buses, 1994 (DRL30/5/6 ex R&I, 1996)

18	K818NKH	21	K821NKH	24	K824NKH	27	K827NKH	30	K430OKH	33	K433OKH	36	K436OKH
19	K819NKH	22	K822NKH	25	K825NKH	28	K828NKH	31	K431OKH	34	K434OKH	37	K437OKH
20	K820NKH	23	K823NKH	26	K826NKH	29	K429OKH	32	K432OKH	35	K435OKH		

DT87	H87MOB	Dennis Dart 8.5SDL3003	Carlyle Dartline	B28F	1990	Ex Metroline, 1996
DT91	H91MOB	Dennis Dart 8.5SDL3003	Carlyle Dartline	B28F	1990	Ex Metroline, 1996
DT95	H95MOB	Dennis Dart 8.5SDL3003	Carlyle Dartline	B28F	1990	Ex Metroline, 1996
DT96	H96MOB	Dennis Dart 8.5SDL3003	Carlyle Dartline	B28F	1990	Ex Metroline, 1996
DT97	H97MOB	Dennis Dart 8.5SDL3003	Carlyle Dartline	B28F	1990	Ex Metroline, 1996
DT99	H899LOX	Dennis Dart 8.5SDL3003	Carlyle Dartline	B28F	1990	Ex Metroline, 1996
IL208s	RIB7004	Iveco Daily 49.10	LHE	B23F	1989	Ex R&I, 1996
IR202s	RIB5082	Iveco Daily 49.10	Robin Hood City Nippy	B23F	1989	Ex R&I, 1996
IR210	G122CLD	Iveco Daily 49.10	Robin Hood City Nippy	B19F	1989	Ex R&I, 1996

M9-199 MCW Metrobus DR101/9* MCW H43/28D 1978-79 * M9-42 are DR101/8 Ex London Buses, 1994 (M16, M37, M106/8 ex Merseybus, 1995 M117/39 ex London Suburban Bus, 1995)

9	WYW9T	33	WYW33T	75	WYW75T	92	WYW92T	108	BYX108V	126	BYX126V	160	BYX160V
12	WYW12T	35	WYW35T	78	WYW78T	95	WYW95T	114	BYX114V	130	BYX130V	161	BYX161V
16	WYW16T	37	WYW37T	79	WYW79T	98	BYX98V	115	BYX115V	133	BYX133V	181	BYX181V
25	WYW25T	42	WYW42T	80	WYW80T	101	BYX101V	117	BYX117V	139	BYX139V	189	BYX189V
27	WYW27T	67	WYW67T	81	WYW81T	103	BYX103V	118	BYX118V	145	BYX145V	194	BYX194V
32	WYW32T	72	WYW72T	82	WYW82T	106	BYX106V	124	BYX124V	148w	BYX148V	199	BYX199V

M213-501 MCW Metrobus DR101/12 MCW H43/28D 1980 Ex London Buses, 1994 (M229 ex London Suburban Bus, 1995; M377, M501 ex Merseybus, 1995)

213	BYX213V	243	BYX243V	322	EYE322V	341	EYE341V	377	GYE377W	501	GYE501W
229	BYX229V	294	BYX294V	328	EYE328V	356	GYE356W	481	GYE481W		

M512-802 MCW Metrobus DR101/14 MCW H43/28D* 1981-82 Ex London Buses, 1994

512	GYE512W	565	GYE565W	576	GYE576W	608	KYO608X	640	KYV640X	693	KYV693X	800	KYV800X
560	GYE560W	570	GYE570W	578	GYE578W	616	KYO616X	656	KYV656X	739	KYV739X	801	KYV801X
561	GYE561W	571	GYE571W	579	GYE579W	620	KYO620X	674	KYV674X	755	KYV755X	802	KYV802X
563	GYE563W	572	GYE572W	588	GYE588W	623	KYO623X	677	KYV677X	764	KYV764X		
564	GYE564W	574	GYE574W	594	GYE594W	639	KYV639X	678	KYV678X	797	KYV797X		

M824-934 MCW Metrobus DR101/16 MCW H43/28D 1983 Ex London Buses, 1994

824	OJD824Y	878	OJD878Y	896	A896SUL	915	A915SUL	921	A921SUL	934	A934SUL
829	OJD829Y	879	OJD879Y	899	A899SUL	916	A916SUL	925	A925SUL		
876	OJD876Y	890	OJD890Y	912	A912SUL	917	A917SUL	928	A928SUL		

M957-1414 MCW Metrobus DR101/17 MCW H43/28D* 1984-86 * M1045/52 are DR101/19; M1045 is DPH43/28D; M1080 is H43/30F; M1393/6 are DPH38/28F Ex London Buses, 1994

957	A957SYF	1042	A742THV	1076	B76WUL	1117	B117WUL	1150	B150WUL	1277	B277WUL	1369	C369BUV
961t	A961SYF	1045t	A745THV	1077	B77WUL	1118	B118WUL	1151	B151WUL	1284	B284WUL	1385	C385BUV
964	A964SYF	1052	A752THV	1078	B78WUL	1119	B119WUL	1153	B153WUL	1287	B287WUL	1390	C390BUV
971	A971SYF	1058	B58WUL	1079	B79WUL	1120	B120WUL	1156	B156WUL	1292	B292WUL	1392	C392BUV
987	A987SYF	1059	B59WUL	1080t	B80WUL	1141	B141WUL	1157	B157WUL	1325	C325BUV	1393	C393BUV
989	A989SYF	1060	B60WUL	1081	B81WUL	1142	B142WUL	1158	B158WUL	1329	C329BUV	1394	C394BUV
997	A997SYF	1061	B61WUL	1082	B82WUL	1143	B143WUL	1159	B159WUL	1330	C330BUV	1395	C395BUV
1032	A732THV	1063	B63WUL	1083	B83WUL	1145	B145WUL	1160	B160WUL	1331	C331BUV	1396	C396BUV
1033	A733THV	1065	B65WUL	1111	B111WUL	1146	B146WUL	1161	B161WUL	1333	C333BUV	1397	C397BUV
1038	A738THV	1066	B66WUL	1113	B113WUL	1147	B147WUL	1163	B163WUL	1334	C334BUV	1403	C403BUV
1040	A740THV	1067t	B67WUL	1114	B114WUL	1148	B148WUL	1234	B234WUL	1355	C355BUV	1414	C414BUV
1041	A741THV	1072	B72WUL	1115	B115WUL	1149	B149WUL	1250	B250WUL	1365	C365BUV		

MC1 P481HEG Marshall Midibus Marshall B29F 1996

MM254-278 MAN 11.220 Marshall B38F 1996 MM254-68 ex R&I, 1996

254	N121XEG	258	N125XEG	262	N129XEG	266	N133XEG	271	P471JEG	275	P475JEG
255	N122XEG	259	N126XEG	263	N130XEG	267	N134XEG	272	P472JEG	276	P476JEG
256	N123XEG	260	N127XEG	264	N131XEG	268	N135XEG	273	P473JEG	277	P477JEG
257	N124XEG	261	N128XEG	265	N132XEG	270	P470JEG	274	P474JEG	278	P478JEG

MMS269 N161YEG Mercedes-Benz 811D Marshall B26F 1996
MR87 F89GGC Mercedes-Benz 811D Robin Hood C29F 1989 Ex R&I, 1996
MR90 F90GGC Mercedes-Benz 811D Robin Hood C29F 1989 Ex R&I, 1996

MRL210-222 Optare MetroRider MR03 Optare B26F 1991-93 Ex London Buses, 1994

210	J210BWU	213	J213BWU	216	J216BWU	219	J219BWU	222	K422HWY
211	J211BWU	214	J214BWU	217	J217BWU	220	J220BWU		
212	J212BWU	215	J215BWU	218	J218BWU	221	J221BWU		

MRL223 P448SWX Optare MetroRider Optare B29F 1997
MRL224 P449SWX Optare MetroRider Optare B29F 1997
MV249 M507ALP MAN 11.190 Optare Vecta B42F 1995 Ex R&I, 1996
MV250 M508ALP MAN 11.190 Optare Vecta B42F 1995 Ex R&I, 1996
MV251 N701FLN MAN 11.190 Optare Vecta B42F 1995 Ex R&I, 1996
MV252 N702FLN MAN 11.190 Optare Vecta B42F 1995 Ex R&I, 1996
MV253 N703FLN MAN 11.190 Optare Vecta B42F 1995 Ex R&I, 1996

MW18-37 — Mercedes-Benz 811D — Wright — B26F — 1993 — Ex London Buses, 1994

18	NDZ7918	21	NDZ7921	24	NDZ7924	27	NDZ7927	30	NDZ7930	33	NDZ7933	36	K510FYN
19	NDZ7919	22	NDZ7922	25	NDZ7925	28	NDZ7928	31	NDZ7931	34	NDZ7934	37	K476FYN
20	NDZ7920	23	NDZ7923	26	NDZ7926	29	NDZ7927	32	NDZ7932	35	NDZ7935		

OM243	M501ALP	Optare MetroRider MR33	Optare	B25F	1995	Ex R&I, 1996
OM244	M502ALP	Optare MetroRider MR33	Optare	B25F	1995	Ex R&I, 1996
OM279	P509NWU	Optare MetroRider	Optare	B25F	1996	

RM29-2186 — AEC Routemaster 5RM — Park Royal — H36/28R — 1959-65 — Ex London Buses, 1994 (RM1081, 2097 ex London Transport Buses, 1997)
† Fitted with plain upper deck front windows

29	OYM453A	765	WLT765	1171	171CLT	1348	348CLT	1799	799DYE	1979	ALD979B	2136	CUV136C
268	VLT268	912	WLT912	1185	XYJ427	1568	568CLT	1804	EYY327B	2023	ALM23B	2153	CUV153C
446	WLT446	1081w	81CLT	1218	218CLT	1700	KGJ167A	1840	840DYE	2041	ALM41B	2186	CUV186C
646†	KFF257	1158	158CLT	1283	283CLT	1758	758DYE	1971	ALD971B	2097w	ALM97B		

RML903-2731 — AEC Routemaster 7RM (Cummins)* — Park Royal — H40/32R — 1961-67 — Ex London Buses, 1994 (RML2443, RML2633/59 ex London Transport Buses, 1997)
*RML903 retains its AEC engine

903	WLT903	2296	CUV296C	2395	JJD395D	2479	JJD479D	2620	NML620E	2699	SMK699F
2282	CUV282C	2310	CUV310C	2413	JJD413D	2511	JJD511D	2633u	NML633E	2731	SMK731F
2284	CUV284C	2367	JJD367D	2419	JJD419D	2561	JJD561D	2659u	SMK659F	
2295	CUV295C	2393	JJD393D	2443u	JJD443D	2603	NML603E	2679	SMK679F	

S11-20 — Scania N113DRB — Alexander RH — H47/31F — 1991 — Ex London Buses, 1994

11	J811HMC	13	J813HMC	15	J815HMC	17	J817HMC	19	J819HMC
12	J812HMC	14	J814HMC	16	J816HMC	18	J818HMC	20	J820HMC

SR108-121 — Mercedes-Benz 811D — Optare StarRider — B26F — 1989 — Ex London Buses, 1994

108	G108KUB	110	G110KUB	112	G112KUB	114	G114KUB	116	G116KUB	120	G120KUB
109	G109KUB	111	G111KUB	113	G113KUB	115	G115KUB	117	G117KUB	121	G121KUB

V201-217 — Volvo Olympian YN2RV18Z4 — Northern Counties Palatine 2 — H47/25D — 1993-94 — Ex London Suburban Bus, 1995

201	L201SKD	204	L204SKD	207	L207SKD	210	L210SKD	214	L214TWM	217	L217TWM
202	L202SKD	205	L205SKD	208	L208SKD	212	L212TWM	215	L215TWM		
203	L203SKD	206	L206SKD	209	L209SKD	213	L213TWM	216	L216TWM		

Previous registrations

EYY327B	804DYE	KFF257	WLT646
G122CLD	G210LGK, RIB5087	KGJ167A	700DYE
K476FYN	NDZ7937	OYM453A	VLT29
K510FYN	NDZ7936	RIB5082	F202HGN

RIB5085	K415MGN
RIB7002	CWN12A, H403HOY
RIB7004	G208LGK
XYJ427	185CLT
33LUG	J823GGF

Special liveries

SightseerS livery: M1045/67, M1393/6
X43 Express : S11/3-20
Contract liveries : MR87/90

NETWORK WATFORD Route 142 and 340 buses

5069	A149FPG	Leyland Olympian ONTL11/1R	Roe	H43/29F	1984	Ex London Country North West, 1990
5071	A151FPG	Leyland Olympian ONTL11/1R	Roe	H43/29F	1984	Ex London Country North West, 1990
5072	A152FPG	Leyland Olympian ONTL11/1R	Roe	H43/29F	1984	Ex London Country North West, 1990
5073	A153FPG	Leyland Olympian ONTL11/1R	Roe	H43/29F	1984	Ex London Country North West, 1990
5074	A154FPG	Leyland Olympian ONTL11/1R	Roe	H43/29F	1984	Ex London Country North West, 1990
5075	A155FPG	Leyland Olympian ONTL11/1R	Roe	H43/29F	1984	Ex London Country North West, 1990
5080	B270LPH	Leyland Olympian ONTL11/1R	Eastern Coach Works	H43/29F	1985	Ex London Country North West, 1990
5081	B271LPH	Leyland Olympian ONTL11/1R	Eastern Coach Works	H43/29F	1985	Ex London Country North West, 1990
5082	B272LPH	Leyland Olympian ONTL11/1R	Eastern Coach Works	H43/29F	1985	Ex London Country North West, 1990
5083	B273LPH	Leyland Olympian ONTL11/1R	Eastern Coach Works	H43/29F	1985	Ex London Country North West, 1990

5111-25 Leyland Olympian ONCL10/1RZ Leyland H47/31F 1989/90 Ex London Country North West, 1990

5111	G281UMJ	5114	G284UMJ	5117	G287UMJ	5120	G290UMJ	5123	G293UMJ
5112	G282UMJ	5115	G285UMJ	5118	G288UMJ	5121	G291UMJ	5124	G294UMJ
5113	G283UMJ	5116	G286UMJ	5119	G289UMJ	5122	G292UMJ	5125	G295UMJ

5126-5132 Leyland Olympian ON2R50C13Z4 Leyland H47/29F 1991

5126	H196GRO	5127	H197GRO	5128	H198GRO	5129	H199GRO	5130w	H201GRO	5131	H202GRO	5132	H203GRO

NOSTALGIABUS

	KYE905	Bedford OB	Duple	C29F	1949	Ex preservation, 1997
RF136	MLL523	AEC Regal IV 9821LT	Metro-Cammell	B39F	1952	Ex preservation, 1991
7	MXX367	Guy Special NLLVP	Eastern Coach Works	B26F	1954	Ex preservation, 1991
RM357	YVS288	AEC Routemaster 5RM	Park Royal	H36/28R	1960	Ex Watford & District, Watford, 1997
RM378	WFO410	AEC Routemaster 5RM	Park Royal	H36/24R	1961	Ex Watford & District, Watford, 1997
RM1183	183CLT	AEC Routemaster 5RM	Park Royal	H36/28R	1962	Ex London & Country, 1996
RM1394	394CLT	AEC Routemaster 5RM	Park Royal	H36/24R	1963	Ex Watford & District, Watford, 1997
RMC1462	462CLT	AEC Routemaster 6RM	Park Royal	H32/25RD	1962	Ex preservation, 1991
RM1571	571CLT	AEC Routemaster 5RM	Park Royal	H36/24R	1963	Ex Watford & District, Watford, 1997
RM2156	CUV156C	AEC Routemaster 5RM	Park Royal	H36/24R	1965	Ex Watford & District, Watford, 1997
RM2180	CUV180C	AEC Routemaster 5RM	Park Royal	H36/24R	1965	Ex Watford & District, Watford, 1997
	RHC51S	AEC Reliance 6U2R	Plaxton Supreme III	C53F	1977	Ex Thomas, West Ewell, 1992
DMS2333	THX333S	Leyland Fleetline FE30ALR	MCW	H44/24D	1978	Ex Hodge, South Mimms, 1996
LL64	A316GLV	Leyland Olympian ONTL11/2R	Alexander RH	CH43/25F	1983	Ex MTL Liverpool, 1997
LL65	A317GLV	Leyland Olympian ONTL11/2R	Alexander RH	CH43/25F	1983	Ex MTL Liverpool, 1997
	B102SED	Leyland Olympian ONLXB/2R	East Lancs	DP47/31F	1985	Ex Warrington, 1996

Previous registrations

YVS288	WLT357, EDS278A	WFO410	WLT378

SOUTH LONDON

DIB1	J929CYL	DAF SB220LC550	Ikarus Citibus			B48F	1992	Ex County, 1997
DIB2	J930CYL	DAF SB220LC550	Ikarus Citibus			B48F	1992	Ex Grey-Green, 1997
DIB3	J931CYL	DAF SB220LC550	Ikarus Citibus			B48F	1992	Ex Grey-Green, 1997
DIB4	J413NCP	DAF SB220LC550	Ikarus Citibus			B48F	1992	Ex Birmingham Omnibus, Tividale, 1997
DIB5	J414NCP	DAF SB220LC550	Ikarus Citibus			B48F	1992	Ex Birmingham Omnibus, Tividale, 1997

DR20-31		Dennis Dart 8.5SDL3003	Plaxton Pointer			B28F	1991	Ex London Buses, 1994

20	H120THE	22	H122THE	24	H124THE	26	H126THE	28	H128THE	30	H130THE
21	H621TKU	23	H123THE	25	H125THE	27	H127THE	29	H129THE	31	H131THE

DRL38-48		Dennis Dart 9SDL3016	Plaxton Pointer			B34F	1992	Ex Leaside, 1996 (DRL47/8 ex County, 1997)

38	K538ORH	40	K540ORH	42	K542ORH	44	K544ORH	48	K548ORH
39	K539ORH	41	K541ORH	43	K543ORH	47	K547ORH		

DRL147-158		Dennis Dart 9SDL3024	Plaxton Pointer			B34F	1993	Ex London Buses, 1994

147	L247WAG	149	L149WAG	151	L151WAG	153	L153WAG	155	L155WAG	157	L157WAG
148	L148WAG	150	L150WAG	152	L152WAG	154	L154WAG	156	L156WAG	158	L158WAG

DRL210	N710GUM	Dennis Dart 9SDL3053	Plaxton Pointer	B34F	1995	
DRL211	N711GUM	Dennis Dart 9SDL3053	Plaxton Pointer	B34F	1995	
DRL212	N712GUM	Dennis Dart 9SDL3053	Plaxton Pointer	B34F	1995	
DRL213	P913PWW	Dennis Dart SFD112	Plaxton Pointer	B34F	1996	
DRL214	P914PWW	Dennis Dart SFD112	Plaxton Pointer	B34F	1996	
DRL215	P915PWW	Dennis Dart SFD112	Plaxton Pointer	B34F	1996	
DRL216	P916PWW	Dennis Dart SFD112	Plaxton Pointer	B34F	1996	
DRL217	P917PWW	Dennis Dart SFD112	Plaxton Pointer	B34F	1996	
DRL218	P918PWW	Dennis Dart SFD112	Plaxton Pointer	B34F	1996	
DT65	H465UGO	Dennis Dart 8.5SDL3003	Carlyle Dartline	B28F	1990	Ex London Buses, 1994
DT66	H466UGO	Dennis Dart 8.5SDL3003	Carlyle Dartline	B28F	1990	Ex London Buses, 1994
DT67	H467UGO	Dennis Dart 8.5SDL3003	Carlyle Dartline	B28F	1990	Ex London Buses, 1994
DT68	H468UGO	Dennis Dart 8.5SDL3003	Carlyle Dartline	B28F	1990	Ex London Buses, 1994
DT69	H469UGO	Dennis Dart 8.5SDL3003	Carlyle Dartline	B28F	1990	Ex London Buses, 1994
DT70	H470UGO	Dennis Dart 8.5SDL3003	Carlyle Dartline	B28F	1990	Ex London Buses, 1994
DT132	H132MOB	Dennis Dart 8.5SDL3003	Carlyle Dartline	B28F	1991	Ex Metroline, 1997
DT143	H143MOB	Dennis Dart 8.5SDL3003	Carlyle Dartline	B28F	1991	Ex Metroline, 1997
L1	A101SYE	Leyland Olympian ONTL11/1R	Eastern Coach Works	H47/28D	1984	Ex London Buses, 1994
L2	A102SYE	Leyland Olympian ONLXB/1R	Eastern Coach Works	H47/28D	1984	Ex London Buses, 1994
L3	A103SYE	Leyland Olympian ONLXB/1R	Eastern Coach Works	H47/28D	1984	Ex London Buses, 1994

L4-259 Leyland Olympian ONLXB/1RH Eastern Coach Works H42/26D* 1986-87 * L166-71 are DPH42/26D Ex London Buses, 1994

4	C804BYY	45	C45CHM	148	D148FYM	171	D171FYM	194	D194FYM	217	217CLT	240	D240FYM
5	C805BYY	46	C46CHM	149	D149FYM	172	WLT372	195	D195FYM	218	D218FYM	241	D241FYM
6	C806BYY	47	VLT47	150	D150FYM	173	VLT173	196	D196FYM	219	519CLT	242	D242FYM
8	WLT807	49	C49CHM	151	WLT751	174	D174FYM	197	D197FYM	220	D220FYM	243	D243FYM
13	VLT13	50	C50CHM	152	D152FYM	175	D175FYM	198	D198FYM	221	D221FYM	244	VLT244
14	C814BYY	52	C52CHM	153	D153FYM	176	D176FYM	199	D199FYM	222	D222FYM	245	D245FYM
16	WLT916	56	C56CHM	154	WLT554	177	D177FYM	200	D200FYM	223	D223FYM	246	D246FYM
17	C817BYY	58	C58CHM	155	D155FYM	178	D178FYM	201	D201FYM	224	D224FYM	247	D247FYM
20	C820BYY	59	C59CHM	156	656DYE	179	D179FYM	202	D202FYM	225	D225FYM	248	D248FYM
21	C21CHM	63	C63CHM	157	D157FYM	180	480CLT	203	D203FYM	226	D226FYM	249	D249FYM
22	C22CHM	65	C65CHM	158	D158FYM	181	D181FYM	204	D204FYM	227	D227FYM	250	D250FYM
24	C24CHM	66	C66CHM	159	D159FYM	182	D182FYM	205	D205FYM	228	D228FYM	251	D251FYM
25	C25CHM	78	C78CHM	160	D160FYM	183	D183FYM	206	D206FYM	229	D229FYM	252	D252FYM
26	C26CHM	79	C79CHM	161	D161FYM	184	D184FYM	207	D207FYM	230	D230FYM	253	D253FYM
27	VLT27	99	C99CHM	162	D162FYM	185	D185FYM	208	D208FYM	231	D231FYM	254	D254FYM
31	C31CHM	102	C102CHM	163	D163FYM	186	D186FYM	209	D209FYM	232	D232FYM	255	D255FYM
32	C32CHM	113	C113CHM	164	D164FYM	187	D187FYM	210	D210FYM	233	D233FYM	256	D256FYM
33	330CLT	135	D135FYM	165	D165FYM	188	D188FYM	211	D211FYM	234	D234FYM	257	D257FYM
35	C35CHM	139	D139FYM	166	D166FYM	189	D189FYM	212	D212FYM	235	D235FYM	258	D258FYM
36	C36CHM	140	D140FYM	167	D167FYM	190	319CLT	213	TD213FYM	236	D236FYM	259	D259FYM
37	C37CHM	143	D143FYM	168	D168FYM	191	D191FYM	214	D214FYM	237	D237FYM		
38	C38CHM	146	D146FYM	169	D169FYM	192	D192FYM	215	815DYE	238	D238FYM		
41	C41CHM	147	D147FYM	170	7CLT	193	D193FYM	216	D216FYM	239	D239FYM		

LDR22-39 Dennis Dart SFD412 Plaxton Pointer B40F 1996

22	P822RWU	25	P825RWU	28	P828RWU	31	P831RWU	34	P834RWU	37	P837RWU
23	P823RWU	26	P826RWU	29	P829RWU	32	P832RWU	35	P835RWU	38	P838RWU
24	P824RWU	27	P827RWU	30	P830RWU	33	P833RWU	36	P836RWU	39	P839RWU

M7t	WYW7T	MCW Metrobus DR101/8	MCW	H43/28D	1978	Ex London Buses, 1994
M10t	WYW10T	MCW Metrobus DR101/8	MCW	H43/28D	1978	Ex London Buses, 1994
M38	WYW38T	MCW Metrobus DR101/8	MCW	H43/28D	1979	Ex London Buses, 1994
M40	WYW40T	MCW Metrobus DR101/8	MCW	H43/28D	1979	Ex London Buses, 1994
M49	WYW49T	MCW Metrobus DR101/8	MCW	H43/28D	1979	Ex London Buses, 1994

M60-200 MCW Metrobus DR101/9 MCW H43/28D 1979 Ex London Buses, 1994 (M64, M74 ex Leaside, 1997)

60	WYW60T	64	WYW64T	66	WYW66T	74	WYW74T	132	BYX132V	168	BYX168V	182	BYX182V
63	WYW63T	65t	WYW65T	69	WYW69T	129	BYX129V	149	BYX149V	173	BYX173V	200	BYX200V

M208-503 MCW Metrobus DR101/12 MCW H43/28D 1980 Ex London Buses, 1994 (M290 ex Leaside, 1996; M474 ex Leaside via County, 1997; M464, M500 ex Leaside, 1997)

208	BYX208V	248	BYX248V	296	BYX296V	378	GYE378W	400	GYE400W	458	GYE458W
210	BYX210V	251	BYX251V	298	BYX298V	384	GYE384W	402	GYE402W	464	GYE464W
225	BYX225V	263	BYX263V	299	BYX299V	388	GYE388W	410	GYE410W	474	GYE474W
230	BYX230V	277u	BYX277V	314	BYX314V	395	GYE395W	417	GYE417W	492	GYE492W
232	BYX232V	280	BYX280V	346	GYE346W	396	GYE396W	439	GYE439W	496	GYE496W
233	BYX233V	283	BYX283V	365	GYE365W	398	398CLT	454	GYE454W	500	GYE500W
240	BYX240V	290	BYX290V	372	GYE372W	399	GYE399W	456	GYE456W	503u	GYE503W

M507-805 MCW Metrobus DR101/14 MCW H43/28D 1981-82 Ex London Buses, 1994 (M507/8/15/8/9/22/5/8/34 ex Leaside, 1997)

507	GYE507W	518	GYE518W	525	GYE525W	555	GYE555W	601	GYE601W	671	KYV671X	724	KYV724X
508	GYE508W	519	GYE519W	528	GYE528W	568	GYE568W	629	KYO629X	680	KYV680X	741	KYV741X
511	GYE511W	520	GYE520W	534	GYE534W	577	GYE577W	633	KYV633X	682	KYV682X	799	KYV799X
515	GYE515W	521	GYE521W	541	GYE541W	580	GYE580W	634	KYV634X	691	KYV691X	803	KYV803X
517	GYE517W	522	GYE522W	552	GYE552W	584	GYE584W	654	KYV654X	722	KYV722X	805	KYV805X

M809-954 MCW Metrobus DR101/16 MCW H43/28D 1983 Ex London Buses, 1994 (M927 ex Leaside, 1997)

809	OJD809Y	827	OJD827Y	858	OJD858Y	865	OJD865Y	894	A894SUL	927	A927SUL	948	A948SUL
825	OJD825Y	850	OJD850Y	863	OJD863Y	869	OJD869Y	895	A895SUL	930	A930SUL	954	WLT954

M959	A959SYF	MCW Metrobus DR101/17	MCW		H43/28D	1984	Ex London Buses, 1994
M973	A973SYF	MCW Metrobus DR101/17	MCW		H43/28D	1984	Ex London Buses, 1994
M984	A984SYF	MCW Metrobus DR101/17	MCW		H43/28D	1984	Ex London Buses, 1994
M998	A988SYF	MCW Metrobus DR101/17	MCW		H43/28D	1984	Ex London Buses, 1994
M1036	A736THV	MCW Metrobus DR101/17	MCW		H43/28D	1984	Ex Leaside, 1997
M1062	B62WUL	MCW Metrobus DR101/17	MCW		H43/28D	1984	Ex London Buses, 1994

M1084-1105 MCW Metrobus DR134/1 MCW H43/28D 1984 Ex London Buses, 1994

1084	B84WUL	1088	B88WUL	1092	B92WUL	1096	B96WUL	1100	B100WUL	1104	B104WUL
1085	B85WUL	1089	B89WUL	1093	B93WUL	1097	B97WUL	1101	B101WUL	1105	B105WUL
1086	B86WUL	1090	B90WUL	1094	B94WUL	1098	B98WUL	1102	B102WUL		
1087	B87WUL	1091	B91WUL	1095	B95WUL	1099	B99WUL	1103	B103WUL		

M1116	B116WUL	MCW Metrobus DR101/17	MCW		H43/28D	1984	Ex London Buses, 1994
M1354	C354BUV	MCW Metrobus DR101/17	MCW		H43/28D	1985	Ex London Buses, 1994
M1359	C359BUV	MCW Metrobus DR101/17	MCW		DPH43/28D	1985	Ex London Buses, 1994
M1407	C407BUV	MCW Metrobus DR101/17	MCW		H43/28D	1985	Ex London Buses, 1994
M1441	A441UUV	MCW Metrobus DR102/45	MCW		H43/28D	1984	Ex London Buses, 1994
M1442	A442UUV	MCW Metrobus DR132/5	MCW		H43/28D	1984	Ex London Buses, 1994
MR93u	E873NJD	MCW Metrorider MF150/96	MCW		B25F	1988	Ex East London, 1995

MRL107-133 MCW Metrorider MF158/16* MCW B28F* 1988 * MRL133 is MF158/17 and DP28F
Ex London Buses, 1994

107	F107YVP	122	F122YVP	123	F123YVP	124	F124YVP	127	F127YVP	129	F129YVP	133	F133YVP

RM6-2217 AEC Routemaster 5RM (Iveco) Park Royal H36/28R 1959-65 Ex London Buses, 1994
(RM385 ex London Transport Buses, 1997)
† Fitted with plain upper deck front windows

6†	VLT6	385	WLT385	664	WLT664	997	WLT997	1361	VYJ808	1801	801DYE	1978	ALD978B
25	VLT25	432	SVS617	676	WLT676	1003	3CLT	1398	KGJ118A	1811	EGF220B	2179	CUV179C
275†	VLT275	467	XVS851	719	WLT719	1124	VYJ806	1593	593CLT	1822	822DYE	2217	CUV217C
348	WLT348	531	WLT531	970	WLT970	1324	324CLT	1734	734DYE	1872	ALD872B		

RML892-2759 AEC Routemaster 7RM (Iveco) Park Royal H40/32R 1961-68 Ex London Buses, 1994 (* Ex Kentish Bus, 1997)
† Fitted with plain upper deck front windows

892	WLT892	2343*	CUV343C	2407	JJD407D	2521	JJD521D	2549	JJD549D	2619*	NML619E	2741	SMK741F
895	WLT895	2347*	CUV347C	2410*	JJD410D	2523*	JJD523D	2572	JJD572D	2636	NML636E	2753	SMK753F
2264	CUV264C	2351	CUV351C	2452*	JJD452D	2524*	JJD524D	2573	JJD573D	2653	NML653E	2759	SMK759F
2266*	CUV266C	2366	JJD366D	2477	JJD477D	2531*†	JJD531D	2574*	JJD574D	2692	SMK692F		
2301*	CUV301C	2375	JJD375D	2491	JJD491D	2533*	JJD533D	2577*	JJD577D	2715*	SMK715F		
2307	CUV307C	2382*	JJD382D	2505*	JJD505D	2536*	JJD536D	2586*	JJD586D	2718	SMK718F		
2324	CUV324C	2383*	JJD383D	2512*	JJD512D	2545	JJD545D	2591*	JJD591D	2726	SMK726F		
2333	CUV333C	2387*	JJD387D	2514*	JJD514D	2548*	JJD548D	2608	NML608E	2730	SMK730F		

VE648-684 Volvo B10M-50 East Lancs H45/31D 1990/1 Ex Londonlinks, 1997

648	H648GPF	654	H654GPF	660	H660GPF	667	H667GPF	673	H673GPF	679	H679GPF
649	H649GPF	655	H655GPF	661	H661GPF	668	H668GPF	674	H674GPF	680	H680GPF
650	H650GPF	656	H656GPF	662	H662GPF	669	H669GPF	675	H675GPF	681	H681GPF
651	H651GPF	657	H657GPF	663	H663GPF	670	H670GPF	676	H676GPF	682	H682GPF
652	H652GPF	658	H658GPF	664	H664GPF	671	H671GPF	677	H677GPF	683	H683GPF
653	H653GPF	659	H659GPF	665	H665GPF	672	H672GPF	678	H678GPF	684	H684GPF

Previous registrations

EGF220B	811DYE	VLT244	D244FYM	WLT916	C816BYY	330CLT	C30CHM
KGJ118A	398CLT	VYJ806	124CLT	WLT954	A954SUL	398CLT	GYE398W
SVS617	WLT432	VYJ808	361CLT	XVS851	WLT467	480CLT	D180FYM
VLT13	C813BYY	WLT372	D172FYM	7CLT	D170FYM	519CLT	D219FYM
VLT27	C27CHM	WLT554	D154FYM	217CLT	D217FYM	656DYE	D156FYM
VLT47	C47CHM	WLT751	D151FYM	319CLT	D190FYM	815DYE	D215FYM
VLT173	D173FYM	WLT807	C807BYY	324CLT	324CLT, VYJ807		

Special liveries

Overall advertisement : M149

LONDON SOVEREIGN

RML2265-2756		AEC Routemaster 7RM (Cummins)		Park Royal				H40/32R	1965-68	Leased from London Buses		
2265	CUV265C	2404	JJD404D	2538	JJD538D	2582	JJD582D	2663	SMK663F	2686	SMK686F	2756	SMK756F
2322	CUV322C	2487	JJD487D	2563	JJD563D	2598	JJD598D	2668	SMK668F	2694	SMK694F		
2341	CUV341C	2527	JJD527D	2569	JJD569D	2627	NML627E	2674	SMK674F	2719	SMK719F		

29-52		Leyland Olympian ON2R50C13Z4		Northern Counties				H47/30F	1991			
29	H139GGS	41	H141GGS	43	H143GGS	45	H145GGS	47	H147GGS	49	H149GGS	51	H151GGS
30	H140GGS	42	H142GGS	44	H144GGS	46	H146GGS	48	H148GGS	50	H150GGS	52	H152GGS

57	WYV57T	Leyland Titan TNLXB2RRSp	Park Royal	H44/28F	1979	Ex London Buses, 1994
620	NUW620Y	Leyland Titan TNLXB2RR	Leyland	H44/28F	1982	Ex London Buses, 1993
706	OHV706Y	Leyland Titan TNLXB2RR	Leyland	H44/28F	1983	Ex London Buses, 1993

SOVEREIGN (Harrow)

410-424		Mercedes-Benz 811D		Reeve Burgess Beaver				B31F	1990-91		
410	H410FGS	413	H413FGS	417	H417FGS	419	H419FGS	422	H422FGS	424	H424FGS
411	H411FGS	415	H415FGS	418	H418FGS	421	H421FGS	423	H423FGS		

435	K5SBC	Mercedes-Benz 811D	Plaxton Beaver	B31F	1993

453-461		Mercedes-Benz 811D		Plaxton Beaver				B31F	1994/95		
453	L953MBH	455	M455UUR	457	M457UUR	458	M458UUR	459	M459UUR	460	M460UUR	461	M461UUR
454	L954MBH	456	M456UUR										

907-931		Mercedes-Benz 709D		Reeve Burgess Beaver				B23F	1989/90		
907	G907UPP	921	H921FGS	923	H923FGS	926	H926FGS	929	H929FGS	931	H931FGS
909	G909UPP	922	H922FGS	925	H925FGS	927	H927FGS	930	H930FGS		

STAGECOACH EAST LONDON

DA10-35   DAF SB220LC550   Optare Delta   B40D   1989-93   * DA10 is DP36D   Ex London Buses, 1994

10	G684KNW	14	J714CYG	18	J718CYG	22	J722CYG	26	J726CYG	30	K630HWX	34	K634HWX
11	J711CYG	15	YLJ332	19	J719CYG	23	J723CYG	27	J727CYG	31	K631HWX	35	K635HWX
12	J712CYG	16	J716CYG	20	J720CYG	24	J724CYG	28	J728CYG	32	K632HWX		
13	472YMF	17	J717CYG	21	J721CYG	25	J725CYG	29	J729CYG	33	K633HWX		

DA13/5 are on extended loan to Stagecoach South (Hampshire Bus)

DAL1-27   Dennis Dart 9.8SDL3054   Alexander Dash   B36F   1995

1	N301AMC	5	N305AMC	9	N309AMC	13	N313AMC	17	N317AMC	21	N321AMC	25	N325AMC
2	N302AMC	6	N306AMC	10	N310AMC	14	N314AMC	18	N318AMC	22	N322AMC	26	N326AMC
3	N303AMC	7	N307AMC	11	N311AMC	15	N315AMC	19	N319AMC	23	N323AMC	27	N327AMC
4	N304AMC	8	N308AMC	12	N312AMC	16	N316AMC	20	N320AMC	24	N324AMC		

DRL109-146   Dennis Dart 9SDL3024   Plaxton Pointer   B34F   1993   * DRL139-146 are 9SDL3034
Ex London Buses, 1994

109	K109SRH	116	K116SRH	125	K125SRH	131	K131SRH	136	L136VRH	141	L141VRH	146	L146VRH
111	K211SRH	119	K119SRH	126	K126SRH	132	K132SRH	137	L137VRH	142	L142VRH		
113	K113SRH	121	K121SRH	128	K128SRH	133	K133SRH	138	L138VRH	143	L143VRH		
114	K114SRH	122	K122SRH	129	K129SRH	134	K134SRH	139	L139VRH	144	L144VRH		
115	K115SRH	124	K124SRH	130	K130SRH	135	K135SRH	140	L140VRH	145	L145VRH		

DW133-159   Dennis Dart 8.5SDL3015   Wright Handybus   B29F   1993   Ex London Buses, 1994

133	NDZ3133	137	NDZ3137	141	NDZ3141	145	NDZ3145	149	NDZ3149	153	NDZ3153	157	NDZ3157
134	NDZ3134	138	NDZ3138	142	NDZ3142	146	NDZ3146	150	NDZ3150	154	NDZ3154	158	NDZ3158
135	NDZ3135	139	NDZ3139	143	NDZ3143	147	NDZ3147	151	NDZ3151	155	NDZ3155	159	NDZ3159
136	NDZ3136	140	NDZ3140	144	NDZ3144	148	NDZ3148	152	NDZ3152	156	NDZ3156		

DT36   G36TGW   Dennis Dart 8.5SDL3003   Carlyle Dartline   B28F   1990   Ex Docklands Transit, 1997

DWL15-26   Dennis Dart 9SDL3016   Wright Handybus   B35F   1993   Ex London Buses, 1994

15	NDZ3015	17	NDZ3017	19	NDZ3019	21	NDZ3021	23	NDZ3023	25	NDZ3025
16	NDZ3016	18	NDZ3018	20	NDZ3020	22	NDZ3022	24	NDZ3024	26	NDZ3026

LCY1-9   Dennis Dart SFD212BR1   Alexander ALX200   B29DL   1997   London City Airport blue livery

1	P101NJN	3	P103NJN	5	P105NJN	7	P107NJN	9	R209XNO
2	P102NJN	4	P104NJN	6	P106NJN	8	R208XNO		

| MR16 | D476PON | MCW Metrorider MF150/14 | | MCW | | | B23F | 1987 | Ex London Buses, 1994 |
| MRL144 | H144UUA | Optare MetroRider MR03 | | Optare | | | B26F | 1990 | Ex Selkent, 1996 |

PD1-18		Dennis Dart SFD412BR5		Plaxton Pointer			B37D	1997	
1	R701YWC	4	R704YWC	7	R707YWC	10	R710YWC	13	R713YWC	16	R716YWC
2	R702YWC	5	R705YWC	8	R708YWC	11	R711YWC	14	R714YWC	17	R717YWC
3	R703YWC	6	R706YWC	9	R709YWC	12	R712YWC	15	R715YWC	18	R718YWC

PD410-427		Dennis Dart 9.8SDL3054		Plaxton Pointer			B40F	1996	Ex Docklands Transit, 1997
410	N410MBW	413	N413MBW	416	N416MBW	419	N419MBW	422	N422MBW	425	N425MBW
411	N411MBW	414	N414MBW	417	N417MBW	420	N420MBW	423	N423MBW	426	N426MBW
412	N412MBW	415	N415MBW	418	N418MBW	421	N421MBW	424	N424MBW	427	N427MBW

RM613	WLT613	AEC Routemaster 5RM	Park Royal	H36/28R	1960	Ex London Buses, 1994
RM980	USK625	AEC Routemaster 5RM	Park Royal	H36/28R	1961	Ex Bluebird Buses, 1997
RM1289u	XLS596A	AEC Routemaster 5RM	Park Royal	H36/28R	1962	Ex Bluebird Buses, 1997
RM1527	527CLT	AEC Routemaster 5RM	Park Royal	H36/28R	1963	Ex London Buses, 1994
RM1599	YTS820A	AEC Routemaster 5RM	Park Royal	H36/28R	1963	Ex Bluebird Buses, 1997
RMA5	NMY635E	AEC Routemaster 9RM	Park Royal	H35/25F	1967	Ex London Buses, 1994
RMA8	NMY640E	AEC Routemaster 9RM	Park Royal	H32/24F	1967	Ex London Buses, 1994
RMC1456	LFF875	AEC Routemaster 6RM	Park Royal	H32/25RD	1962	Ex London Buses, 1994
RMC1461	461CLT	AEC Routemaster 6RM	Park Royal	H32/25RD	1962	Ex London Buses, 1994
RMC1485	485CLT	AEC Routemaster 6RM	Park Royal	H32/25RD	1962	Ex London Buses, 1994

RML886-2760		AEC Routemaster 7RM		Park Royal			H40/32R	1961-68	Ex London Buses, 1994

Iveco engines except a AEC and c Cummins

886c	WLT886	2392	JJD392D	2445c	JJD445D	2493	JJD493D	2592	JJD592D	2657	NML657E	2723c	SMK723F
890c	XFF814	2399	JJD399D	2450	JJD450D	2495c	JJD495D	2607	NML607E	2661c	SMK661F	2738	SMK738F
898	XFF813	2402	JJD402D	2451	JJD451D	2496c	JJD496D	2610c	NML610E	2665	SMK665F	2743c	SMK743F
2272c	CUV272C	2415	JJD415D	2456c	JJD456D	2497c	JJD497D	2616c	NML616E	2670c	SMK670F	2748c	SMK748F
2286c	CUV286C	2429	JJD429D	2462	JJD462D	2541c	JJD541D	2624	NML624E	2671c	SMK671F	2749	SMK749F
2300	CUV300C	2435	JJD435D	2470	JJD470D	2550c	JJD550D	2639c	NML639E	2696c	SMK696F	2760a	SMK760F
2303	CUV303C	2437	JJD437D	2481	JJD481D	2565c	JJD565D	2641c	NML641E	2705c	SMK705F		
2311c	CUV311C	2444	JJD444D	2488	JJD488D	2581c	JJD581D	2642c	NML642E	2709	SMK709F		

S22-29		Scania N113DRB		Alexander RH			H47/31F	1991	Ex London Buses, 1994
22	J822HMC	24	J824HMC	26	J826HMC	28	J828HMC
23	J823HMC	25	J825HMC	27	J827HMC	29	J829HMC

S30-71 — Scania N113DRB — Northern Counties Palatine — H44/25D — 1991/92 — Ex London Buses, 1994 * S30/1 are H47/33F

30	J230XKY	36	J136HMT	42	J142HMT	48	K848LMK	54	K854LMK	60	K860LMK	66	K866LMK
31	J231XKY	37	J137HMT	43	J143HMT	49	K849LMK	55	K855LMK	61	K861LMK	67	K867LMK
32	J132HMT	38	J138HMT	44	J144HMT	50	K850LMK	56	K856LMK	62	K862LMK	68	K868LMK
33	J133HMT	39	J139HMT	45	J145HMT	51	K851LMK	57	K857LMK	63	K863LMK	69	K869LMK
34	J134HMT	40	J140HMT	46	K846LMK	52	K852LMK	58	K858LMK	64	K864LMK	70	K870LMK
35	J135HMT	41	J141HMT	47	K847LMK	53	K853LMK	59	K859LMK	65	K865LMK	71	K871LMK

SLD1-19 — Dennis Dart SFD212 — Alexander ALX200 — B36F — 1996/97

1	P21HMF	4	P24HMF	7	P27HMF	10	P610SEV	13	R713XAR	16	R716VPU	19	R719VPU
2	P31HMF	5	P25HMF	8	P28HMF	11	P611SEV	14	R714VPU	17	R717VPU		
3	P23HMF	6	P26HMF	9	P29HMF	12	R712XAR	15	R715VPU	18	R718VPU		

SLW15-30 — Scania N113CRL — Wright Pathfinder 320 — B37D — 1994 — SLW15 ex London Buses, 1994

15	RDZ6115	18	RDZ6118	21	RDZ6121	24	RDZ6124	27	RDZ6127	30	RDZ6130
16	RDZ6116	19	RDZ6119	22	RDZ6122	25	RDZ6125	28	RDZ6128		
17	RDZ6117	20	RDZ6120	23	RDZ6123	26	RDZ6126	29	RDZ6129		

SR1-119 — Mercedes-Benz 811D — Optare StarRider — B26F — 1988-89 — Ex London Buses, 1994

1	E155CGJ	32	F32CWY	65	F165FWY	72	F172FWY	76	F176FWY	105	G105KUB
2	E712LYU	50	F50CWY	66	F166FWY	73	F173FWY	78	F178FWY	106	G106KUB
12	F912YWY	56	F156FWY	70	F170FWY	74	F174FWY	79	F179FWY	107	G107KUB
13	F913YWY	60	F160FWY	71	F171FWY	75	F175FWY	91	G91KUB	119	G119KUB

T1-163 — Leyland Titan TNLXB2RRSp — Park Royal — H44/22D — 1978-80 — a DPH44/26F b H44/26D E — Ex London Buses, 1994 (T163 Selkent, 1995)

1	THX401S	7	WYV7T	14	WYV14T	22b	WYV22T	30b	WYV30T	35	WYV35T	163b	CUL163V
2b	THX402S	8	WYV8T	15	WYV15T	23	WYV23T	31	WYV31T	36b	WYV36T		
3b	WYV3T	11b	WYV11T	16	WYV16T	24	WYV24T	32	WYV32T	39b	WYV39T		
4	WYV4T	12b	WYV12T	18	WYV18T	25b	WYV25T	33b	WYV33T	63a	WLT890		
6	WYV6T	13	WYV13T	21	WYV21T	28	WYV28T	34	WYV34T	80a	WLT898		

T261 — GYE261W — Leyland Titan TNTL112RR — Park Royal/Leyland — H44/26D — 1981 — Ex London Buses, 1994

T264-789 — Leyland Titan TNLXB2RR — Leyland — H44/24D — 1981-83 — a H44/26D b O44/24D c H44/27F — Ex London Buses, 1994

264	GYE264W	298	KYN298X	331a	KYV331X	379	KYV379X	406	KYV406X	445	KYV445X	458	KYV458X
266a	GYE266W	306	KYN306X	334	KYV334X	380	KYV380X	428	KYV428X	446	KYV446X	460	KYV460X
268	GYE268W	311a	KYN311X	340	KYV340X	386	KYV386X	434	KYV434X	448	KYV448X	461	KYV461X
272	GYE272W	318	KYV318X	360	KYV360X	387	KYV387X	437	KYV437X	453	KYV453X	462	KYV462X
285a	KYN285X	320a	KYV320X	366	KYV366X	394	KYV394X	441	KYV441X	454	KYV454X	465	KYV465X
286	KYN286X	326	KYV326X	378	KYV378X	395	KYV395X	444	KYV444X	456	KYV456X	466	KYV466X

467	KYV467X	514	KYV514X	544	KYV544X	571	NUW571Y	595	NUW595Y	624	NUW624Y	653	NUW653Y
469	KYV469X	515	KYV515X	545	KYV545X	572	NUW572Y	597	NUW597Y	625	NUW625Y	654c	NUW654Y
470	KYV470X	517	KYV517X	546	KYV546X	573	NUW573Y	598	NUW598Y	627	NUW627Y	657	NUW657Y
473	KYV473X	521	KYV521X	548	KYV548X	574	NUW574Y	600	NUW600Y	629	NUW629Y	658	NUW658Y
476	KYV476X	522	KYV522X	549	KYV549X	576	NUW576Y	601c	NUW601Y	630	NUW630Y	660	NUW660Y
480	KYV480X	525	KYV525X	550	NUW550Y	578	NUW578Y	602	NUW602Y	631	NUW631Y	662	NUW662Y
486	KYV486X	526	KYV526X	551	NUW551Y	579	NUW579Y	603	NUW603Y	632	NUW632Y	664cu	NUW664Y
488	KYV488X	527	KYV527X	552	NUW552Y	580	NUW580Y	605	NUW605Y	633	NUW633Y	665	NUW665Y
490	KYV490X	529	KYV529X	553	NUW553Y	581	NUW581Y	606	NUW606Y	634	NUW634Y	666u	NUW666Y
492	KYV492X	531	KYV531X	554	NUW554Y	582	NUW582Y	608	NUW608Y	636	NUW636Y	668	NUW668Y
495	KYV495X	532	KYV532X	555	NUW555Y	583	NUW583Y	609	NUW609Y	637	NUW637Y	669	NUW669Y
496	KYV496X	533	KYV533X	556	NUW556Y	584	NUW584Y	610	NUW610Y	639	NUW639Y	675	NUW675Y
497	KYV497X	535	KYV535X	557	NUW557Y	585	NUW585Y	613	NUW613Y	640	NUW640Y	686	OHV686Y
500	KYV500X	536	KYV536X	559	NUW559Y	586	NUW586Y	614	NUW614Y	641	NUW641Y	691	OHV691Y
503	KYV503X	537	KYV537X	562	NUW562Y	588	NUW588Y	615	NUW615Y	644	NUW644Y	702	OHV702Y
505	KYV505X	539	KYV539X	563	NUW563Y	589	NUW589Y	617	NUW617Y	646	NUW646Y	749	OHV749Y
506	KYV506X	540	KYV540X	564	NUW564Y	590	NUW590Y	619	NUW619Y	648u	NUW648Y	751	OHV751Y
508	KYV508X	541	KYV541X	565	NUW565Y	591	NUW591Y	621	NUW621Y	650	NUW650Y	789	OHV789Y
512bt	KYV512X	542	KYV542X	568	NUW568Y	592	NUW592Y	622	NUW622Y	651u	NUW651Y		
513	KYV513X	543	KYV543X	569	NUW569Y	593u	NUW593Y	623	NUW623Y	652	NUW652Y		

T802-1050			Leyland Titan TNLXB2RR		Leyland				H44/26D	1983-84	Ex London Buses, 1994		
802	OHV802Y	840u	A840SUL	902	A902SYE	922	A922SYE	945	A945SYE	960t	A960SYE	1050	A650THV
819	RYK819Y	867	A867SUL	905	A905SYE	935	A935SYE	949t	A949SYE	965t	A965SYE		
832	A832SUL	873	A873SUL	921	A921SYE	944	A944SYE	953t	A953SYE	971t	A971SYE		

T1128	486CLT		Leyland Titan TNLXB1RF		Park Royal			DPH43/29F	1979	Ex London Buses, 1994

VA44-81			Volvo Olympian		Alexander			H51/28D	1997	
44	P644SEV	50	R150VPU	56	R156VPU	62	R162VPU	68	R168VPU	74	R174VPU	80	R180VPU
45	P645SEV	51	R151VPU	57	R157VPU	63	R163VPU	69	R169VPU	75	R175VPU	81	R181VPU
46	P646SEV	52	R152VPU	58	R158VPU	64	R164VPU	70	R170VPU	76	R176VPU		
47	R747XAR	53	R153VPU	59	R159VPU	65	R165VPU	71	R171VPU	77	R177VPU		
48	R148VPU	54	R154VPU	60	R160VPU	66	R166VPU	72	R172VPU	78	R178VPU		
49	R149VPU	55	R155VPU	61	R161VPU	67	R167VPU	73	R173VPU	79	R179VPU		

VN1-43					Volvo Olympian			Northern Counties Palatine 1			H49/31F*		1996		*VN27-43 are H49/25D	
1	P801GMU	8	P808GMU	15	P815GMU	22	P822GMU	29	P529HMP	36	P536HMP	43	P543HMP
2	P802GMU	9	P809GMU	16	P816GMU	23	P823GMU	30	P530HMP	37	P537HMP
3	P803GMU	10	P810GMU	17	P817GMU	24	P824GMU	31	P531HMP	38	P538HMP
4	P804GMU	11	P811GMU	18	P818GMU	25	P825GMU	32	P532HMP	39	P539HMP
5	P805GMU	12	P812GMU	19	P819GMU	26	P826GMU	33	P533HMP	40	P540HMP
6	P806GMU	13	P813GMU	20	P820GMU	27	P527HMP	34	P534HMP	41	P541HMP
7	P807GMU	14	P814GMU	21	P821GMU	28	P528HMP	35	P535HMP	42	P542HMP

VN111-121					Volvo Olympian			Northern Counties Palatine 1			H45/23D		1997	
111	R211XNO	113	R113XNO	115	R115XNO	117	R117XNO	119	R119XNO	121	R121XNO
112	R112XNO	114	R114XNO	116	R116XNO	118	R118XNO	120	R120XNO

VP4	H654UWR	Volvo B10M-60	Plaxton Paramount 3500 3	C49FT	1991	Ex Willetts, Yorkley, 1995
VP5	H655UWR	Volvo B10M-60	Plaxton Paramount 3500 3	C49FT	1991	Ex Wallace Arnold, 1995
VP7	H657UWR	Volvo B10M-60	Plaxton Paramount 3500 3	C49FT	1991	Ex Metrobus, Orpington, 1995
1716	NFX667	Dennis Dart 9.8SDL3017	Alexander AM	DP32F	1992	Ex Busways, 1996; on extended loan to Stagecoach South (Hampshire Bus)
1719	XYK976	Dennis Dart 9.8SDL3017	Alexander AM	DP32F	1992	Ex Busways, 1996; on extended loan to Stagecoach South (Hants & Surrey)

Previous registrations

E155CGJ	E711LYU, WLT461	NFX667	K716PCN	XFF814	WLT890	630DYE	WDA3T, 486CLT
H654UWR	H659UWR	USK625	WLT980	XLS596A	289CLT	472YMF	J713CYG
H655UWR	H660UWR	WLT890	WYV63T	XYK976	K719PCN		
H657UWR	H655UWR	WLT898	CUL80V	YLJ332	J715CYG		
LFF875	456CLT	XFF813	WLT898	YTS820A	599CLT		

On order

21 Dennis Dart SLF - Alexander
57 Volvo Olympian double-deckers (30 bodied by Northern Counties, 27 bodied by Alexander)

Named vehicles

RMA5 King Charles, RMC 1456 Prince Albert, RMC 1461 Sir Christopher Wren, RMC1485 King William I, T512 Phoenix, T1128 The Ranger

Special liveries

East London Line livery: MRL144, SR12/3/32/50/6/60/70/2-6/91/105-7/19.
Green Line livery: RMC1461.
Stagecoach livery: T3.
Tesco livery: DW159.
South West Trains livery: DA13/5, 1716/9.
London City Airport livery : DRL125/6, LCY1-9.

STAGECOACH SELKENT

DRL110-127		Dennis Dart 9SDL3024		Plaxton Pointer				B34F	1993	Ex East London, 1997			
110	K110SRH	**112**	K112SRH	**117**	K117SRH	**118**	K118SRH	**120**	K120SRH	**123**	K123SRH	**127**	K127SRH

DT30-55		Dennis Dart 8.5SDL3003		Carlyle Dartline				B28F*	1990	*DT30/1/55 are DP28F			
										Ex London Buses, 1994			
30	G30TGW	**31**	G31TGW	**33**	G33TGW	**38**	G38TGW	**39**	G39TGW	**40**	G40TGW	**55**	WLT575

DW59-71		Dennis Dart 8.5SDL3003		Wright Handybus				B28F	1991	Ex London Buses, 1994	
59	JDZ2359	**61**	JDZ2361	**63**	JDZ2363	**65**	JDZ2365				
60	JDZ2360	**62**	JDZ2362	**64**	JDZ2364	**71**	JDZ2371				

L7-263		Leyland Olympian ONLXB/1RH		Eastern Coach Works				H42/26D*	1986-87	* L260 is DPH42/30F, L261-3 are DPH42/26D	
										Ex London Buses, 1994	
7	C807BYY	**43**	C43CHM	**68**	C68CHM	**83**	C83CHM	**108**	C108CHM	**122**	C122CHM	**136**	D136FYM
9	C809BYY	**44**	C44CHM	**69**	C69CHM	**86**	C86CHM	**109**	C109CHM	**123**	C123FYM	**137**	D137FYM
10	C810BYY	**48**	C48CHM	**70**	C70CHM	**87**	C87CHM	**110**	C110CHM	**124**	D124FYM	**141**	D141FYM
11	C811BYY	**51**	C51CHM	**71**	C71CHM	**91**	WLT491	**111**	C111CHM	**125**	D125FYM	**142**	D142FYM
12	C812BYY	**53**	C53CHM	**72**	C72CHM	**92**	C92CHM	**112**	C112CHM	**126**	D126FYM	**144**	D144FYM
15	C815BYY	**54**	C54CHM	**73**	C73CHM	**94**	C94CHM	**114**	C114CHM	**127**	D127FYM	**145**	D145FYM
18	C818BYY	**55**	C55CHM	**74**	C74CHM	**97**	C97CHM	**115**	C115CHM	**128**	D128FYM	**260**	VLT20
19	C819BYY	**57**	C57CHM	**75**	C75CHM	**98**	C98CHM	**116**	C116CHM	**129**	D129FYM	**262**	VLT14
23	C23CHM	**60**	C60CHM	**76**	C76CHM	**103**	C103CHM	**117**	C117CHM	**130**	D130FYM	**263**	D367JJD
28	C28CHM	**61**	C61CHM	**77**	C77CHM	**104**	C104CHM	**118**	C118CHM	**131**	D131FYM		
29	C29CHM	**62**	C62CHM	**80**	C80CHM	**105**	C105CHM	**119**	C119CHM	**132**	D132FYM		
30	C30CHM	**64**	C64CHM	**81**	C81CHM	**106**	C106CHM	**120**	C120CHM	**133**	D133FYM		
42	C42CHM	**67**	C67CHM	**82**	C82CHM	**107**	C107CHM	**121**	C121CHM	**134**	D134FYM		

LV1-12		Dennis Lance 11SDA3108		Plaxton Verde				B42D	1994	Ex London Buses, 1994	
1	L201YAG	**3**	L203YAG	**5**	L205YAG	**7**	L207YAG	**9**	L209YAG	**11**	L211YAG
2	L202YAG	**4**	L204YAG	**6**	L206YAG	**8**	L208YAG	**10**	L210YAG	**12**	WLT461

MB1-18		Mercedes-Benz 0814D		Plaxton Beaver 2				B29F	1997		
1	R501YWC	**4**	R504YWC	**7**	R507YWC	**10**	R510YWC	**13**	R513YWC	**16**	R516YWC
2	R502YWC	**5**	R505YWC	**8**	R508YWC	**11**	R511YWC	**14**	R514YWC	**17**	R517YWC
3	R503YWC	**6**	R506YWC	**9**	R509YWC	**12**	R512YWC	**15**	R515YWC	**18**	R518YWC

MRL142-176 Optare MetroRider MR03 Optare B26F 1990-91 Ex London Buses, 1994

142	H142UUA	148	H148UUA	152	H152UUA	161u	H161WWT	165u	H165WWT	169	H169WWT	173	H173WWT
143	H143UUA	149	H149UUA	153	H153UUA	162	H162WWT	166u	H166WWT	170	H170WWT	174	H174WWT
145	H145UUA	150	H150UUA	154	H154UUA	163u	H163WWT	167u	H167WWT	171u	H171WWT	175u	H175WWT
147	H147UUA	151	H151UUA	160u	H160WWT	164	H564WWR	168u	H168WWT	172	H172WWT	176u	H176WWT

MT4w F394DHL Mercedes-Benz 709D Reeve Burgess Beaver B20FL 1988 Ex London Buses, 1994

SLD20-29 Dennis Dart SLF Plaxton Pointer B33F 1997

20	R120VPU	22	R122VPU	24	R124VPU	26	R126VPU	28	R128VPU
21	R121VPU	23	R123VPU	25	R125VPU	27	R127VPU	29	R129VPU

T9	WYV9T	Leyland Titan TNLXB2RRSp	Park Royal	H44/26D	1979	Ex East London, 1996
T10	WYV10T	Leyland Titan TNLXB2RRSp	Park Royal	H44/26D	1979	Ex East London, 1996
T17	WYV17T	Leyland Titan TNLXB2RRSp	Park Royal	H44/26D	1979	Ex East London, 1996
T19	WYV19T	Leyland Titan TNLXB2RRSp	Park Royal	H44/26D	1979	Ex East London, 1996
T20	WYV20T	Leyland Titan TNLXB2RRSp	Park Royal	H44/26D	1979	Ex East London, 1996
T26	WYV26T	Leyland Titan TNLXB2RRSp	Park Royal	H44/26D	1979	Ex East London, 1996
T37	WYV37T	Leyland Titan TNLXB2RRSp	Park Royal	H44/22D	1979	Ex East London, 1996
T38	WYV38T	Leyland Titan TNLXB2RRSp	Park Royal	H44/22D	1979	Ex East London, 1996
T40	WYV40T	Leyland Titan TNLXB2RRSp	Park Royal	H44/26D	1979	Ex East London, 1996
T66	WYV66T	Leyland Titan TNLXB2RRSp	Park Royal	H44/26D	1979	Ex East London, 1996
T86t	CUL86V	Leyland Titan TNLXB2RRSp	Park Royal	H44/26D	1979	Ex London Buses, 1994
T98t	CUL98V	Leyland Titan TNLXB2RRSp	Park Royal	H44/26D	1979	Ex London Buses, 1994
T114t	CUL114V	Leyland Titan TNLXB2RRSp	Park Royal	H44/24D	1979	Ex London Buses, 1994
T120t	CUL120V	Leyland Titan TNLXB2RRSp	Park Royal	H44/24D	1979	Ex London Buses, 1994
T130t	CUL130V	Leyland Titan TNLXB2RRSp	Park Royal	H44/26D	1980	Ex London Buses, 1994
T137t	CUL137V	Leyland Titan TNLXB2RRSp	Park Royal	H44/24D	1980	Ex London Buses, 1994
T140	CUL140V	Leyland Titan TNLXB2RRSp	Park Royal	H44/26D	1980	Ex East London, 1996
T142t	CUL142V	Leyland Titan TNLXB2RRSp	Park Royal	H44/26D	1980	Ex London Buses, 1994
T175	CUL175V	Leyland Titan TNLXB2RRSp	Park Royal	H44/26D	1980	Ex East London, 1996
T193	CUL193V	Leyland Titan TNLXB2RRSp	Park Royal	H44/26D	1980	Ex East London, 1996
T214	CUL214V	Leyland Titan TNLXB2RRSp	Park Royal	H44/26D	1980	Ex East London, 1996
T222	CUL222V	Leyland Titan TNLXB2RRSp	Park Royal	H44/26D	1980	Ex East London, 1996
T223	CUL223V	Leyland Titan TNLXB2RRSp	Park Royal	H44/26D	1980	Ex East London, 1996
T224t	CUL224V	Leyland Titan TNLXB2RRSp	Park Royal	H44/24D	1980	Ex London Buses, 1994
T230	EYE230V	Leyland Titan TNLXB2RRSp	Park Royal	H44/24D	1980	Ex East London, 1996
T260	GYE260W	Leyland Titan TNLXB2RR	Park Royal/Leyland	H44/26D	1981	Ex East London, 1996
T262	GYE262W	Leyland Titan TNLXB2RR	Park Royal/Leyland	H44/26D	1981	Ex East London, 1996
T263	GYE263W	Leyland Titan TNLXB2RR	Park Royal/Leyland	H44/26D	1981	Ex East London, 1996

T267-785 — Leyland Titan TNLXB2RR — Leyland — H44/24D* — 1981-83

* T267 is H44/26D Ex London Buses, 1994 (T439/71/98, 501/2/4/58/60 ex East London, 1997)

No	Reg	No	Reg	No	Reg	No	Reg	No	Reg	No	Reg	No	Reg
267	GYE267W	447	KYV447X	501	KYV501X	558	NUW558Y	680	OHV680Y	748	OHV748Y	772	OHV772Y
368	KYV368X	471	KYV471X	502	KYV502X	560	NUW560Y	721	OHV721Y	770	OHV770Y	785	OHV785Y
439u	KYV439X	498	KYV498X	504	KYV504X	616	NUW616Y	740	OHV740Y	771	OHV771Y		

T804-1122 — Leyland Titan TNLXB2RR* — Leyland — H44/26D* — 1983-84

* T877/80 are TNTL112RR, T881-3/5 are TNL112RR, T1079/81/3/91-3/100/6/10/4 are O44/29F Ex London Buses, 1994

No	Reg	No	Reg	No	Reg	No	Reg	No	Reg	No	Reg	No	Reg
804	OHV804Y	830	A830SUL	855	A855SUL	918	A918SYE	1027	A627THV	1067	A67THX	1103	B103WUV
805	OHV805Y	834	A834SUL	856	A856SUL	925	A925SYE	1028	A628THV	1077	A77THX	1106	B106WUV
810	OHV810Y	836	A836SUL	857	A857SUL	926	A926SYE	1029	A629THV	1079	B79WUV	1108	B108WUV
812	OHV812Y	837	A837SUL	859	A859SUL	950	A950SYE	1030	A630THV	1081	B81WUV	1110	B110WUV
813	OHV813Y	838	A838SUL	866	A866SUL	951	A951SYE	1031	A631THV	1083	B83WUV	1112	B112WUV
814	OHV814Y	841	A841SUL	868	A868SUL	961	A961SYE	1032	A632THV	1089	B89WUV	1113	B113WUV
815	OHV815Y	842	A842SUL	874	A874SUL	976	A976SYE	1034	A634THV	1091	B91WUV	1114	B114WUV
816	RYK816Y	843	A843SUL	877	A877SUL	978	A978SYE	1035	A635THV	1092	B92WUV	1115	B115WUV
818	RYK818Y	845	A845SUL	880	A880SUL	988	A988SYE	1036	A636THV	1093	B93WUV	1116	B116WUV
821	RYK821Y	847	A847SUL	881	A881SUL	996	A996SYE	1045	A645THV	1096	B96WUV	1117	B117WUV
822	RYK822Y	848	A848SUL	882	A882SUL	999	A999SYE	1048	A648THV	1099	B99WUV	1118	B118WUV
828	A828SUL	850	A850SUL	883	A883SUL	1003	A603THV	1052	A652THV	1100	B100WUV	1121	B121WUV
829	A829SUL	854	A854SUL	885	A885SUL	1025	A625THV	1065	A65THX	1101	B101WUV	1122u	B122WUV

VN82-110 — Volvo Olympian — Northern Counties Palatine 1 — H45/23D — 1997

No	Reg	No	Reg	No	Reg	No	Reg	No	Reg	No	Reg	No	Reg
82	R82XNO	87	R87XNO	91	R91XNO	95	R95XNO	99	R207XNO	103	R103XNO	107	R107XNO
83	R83XNO	88	R188XNO	92	R92XNO	96	R96XNO	100	R210XNO	104	R104XNO	108	R108XNO
84	R84XNO	89	R89XNO	93	R93XNO	97	R97XNO	101	R101XNO	105	R105XNO	109	R109XNO
85	R85XNO	90	R190XNO	94	R94XNO	98	R98XNO	102	R102XNO	106	R206XNO	110	R110XNO
86	R86XNO												

301-352 — Volvo Olympian YN2RC16V3 — Northern Counties Palatine 1 — H45/23D — 1995

No	Reg	No	Reg	No	Reg	No	Reg	No	Reg	No	Reg	No	Reg
301	M301DGP	309	M309DGP	317	M317DGP	325	N325HGK	333	N353HGK	341	N341HGK	349	N349HGK
302	M302DGP	310	M310DGP	318	M318DGP	326	N326HGK	334	N334HGK	342	N342HGK	350	N350HGK
303	M303DGP	311	M311DGP	319	M319DGP	327	N327HGK	335	N335HGK	343	N343HGK	351	N351HGK
304	M304DGP	312	M312DGP	320	M320DGP	328	N328HGK	336	N336HGK	344	N344HGK	352	N352HGK
305	M305DGP	313	M313DGP	321	N321HGK	329	N329HGK	337	N337HGK	345	N345HGK		
306	M306DGP	314	M314DGP	322	N322HGK	330	N330HGK	338	N338HGK	346	N346HGK		
307	M307DGP	315	M315DGP	323	N323HGK	331	N331HGK	339	N339HGK	347	N347HGK		
308	M308DGP	316	M316DGP	324	N324HGK	332	N332HGK	340	N340HGK	348	N348HGK		

601-614			Dennis Dart 9.8SDL3054			Alexander Dash			B36F		1995/96			
601	N601KGF	**603**	N603KGF	**605**	N605KGF	**607**	N607KGF	**609**	N609KGF	**611**	N611LGC	**613**	N613LGC
602	N602KGF	**604**	N604KGF	**606**	N606KGF	**608**	N608KGF	**610**	N610KGF	**612**	N612LGC	**614**	N614LGC

615-640			Dennis Dart SFD412BR5			Alexander Dash			B36F		1996			
615	P615PGP	**619**	P619PGP	**623**	P623PGP	**627**	P627PGP	**631**	P631PGP	**636**	P636PGP	**640**	P640PGP
616	P616PGP	**620**	P620PGP	**624**	P624PGP	**628**	P628PGP	**632**	P632PGP	**637**	P637PGP		
617	P617PGP	**621**	P621PGP	**625**	P625PGP	**629**	P629PGP	**633**	P633PGP	**638**	P638PGP		
618	P618PGP	**622**	P622PGP	**626**	P626PGP	**630**	P630PGP	**634**	P634PGP	**639**	P639PGP		

Previous registrations

D367JJD	D263FUL, VLT9
VLT14	D262FUL
VLT20	D260FYM
WLT461	L212YAG
WLT491	C91CHM
WLT575	G55 TGW

Special liveries

Stagecoach livery : T86, T98, T114/20/30/7/42, T224

TELLINGS-GOLDEN MILLER Bus Fleet

B731YUD	Ford Transit 190D	Carlyle	B20F	1985	Ex Buslink, Stubwood, 1995
B731YUD	Ford Transit 190D	Carlyle	B20F	1985	Ex Stevensons, Uttoxeter, 1995
D141TMR	Mercedes-Benz L307D	Whittaker	12	1987	Ex Stone, Wilton, 1997
E224PWY	MCW Metrorider MF150/34	MCW	DP23F	1987	Ex Stevensons, Uttoxeter, 1994
E232PWY	MCW Metrorider MF150/41	MCW	B23F	1987	Ex Cardiff Bluebird, Grangetown, 1995
E804UDT	MCW Metrorider MF150/15	MCW	B23F	1987	Ex Stevensons, Uttoxeter, 1994
E808UDT	MCW Metrorider MF150/15	MCW	B23F	1987	Ex Cardiff Bluebird, Grangetown, 1994
E604VKC	MCW Metrorider MF150/40	MCW	B23F	1987	Ex Cardiff Bluebird, Grangetown, 1995
E460ANC	Mercedes-Benz L507D	Made-to-Measure	B16F	1988	Ex Spirit of London, Hounslow, 1996
E834EUT	Mercedes-Benz L307D	Yeates	8	1987	Ex Capital, West Drayton, 1997
F101YVP	MCW Metrorider MF150/115	MCW	B25F	1988	Ex Cardiff Bluebird, Grangetown, 1995
F34CWY	Mercedes-Benz 811D	Optare StarRider	B26F	1989	Ex Bridge, Paisley, 1997
F46CWY	Mercedes-Benz 811D	Optare StarRider	B26F	1989	Ex Bridge, Paisley, 1997
M70TGM	Mercedes-Benz 709D	Plaxton Beaver	B23F	1995	
M80TGM	Mercedes-Benz 709D	Plaxton Beaver	B23F	1995	
M90TGM	Mercedes-Benz 709D	Plaxton Beaver	B23F	1995	
N70TGM	Mercedes-Benz 609D	Plaxton Beaver	B23F	1996	
P701LCF	Mercedes-Benz 0814D	Plaxton Beaver II	B31F	1997	
P702LCF	Mercedes-Benz 0814D	Plaxton Beaver II	B31F	1997	
P703LCF	Mercedes-Benz 0814D	Plaxton Beaver II	B31F	1997	
P704LCF	Mercedes-Benz 0814D	Plaxton Beaver II	B31F	1997	
R705MJH	Mercedes-Benz 0814D	Plaxton Beaver II	B31F	1997	
R706MJH	Mercedes-Benz 0814D	Plaxton Beaver II	B31F	1997	

	Dennis Dart SLF	Plaxton Pointer		B39F	1997	
R501SJM	R503SJM	R505SJM	R507SJM	R509SJM	R511SJM	R513SJM
R502SJM	R504SJM	R506SJM	R508SJM	R510SJM	R512SJM	R514SJM

The coach fleet is listed in the London Coach Handbook.

THAMESWAY

No.	Reg	Chassis	Body	Seating	Year	Notes
230	D230PPU	Mercedes-Benz L608D	Reeve Burgess	B20F	1986	Ex Eastern National, 1990
231	D231PPU	Mercedes-Benz L608D	Reeve Burgess	B20F	1986	Ex Eastern National, 1990
233	D233PPU	Mercedes-Benz L608D	Reeve Burgess	B20F	1986	Ex Eastern National, 1990
234	D234PPU	Mercedes-Benz L608D	Reeve Burgess	B20F	1986	Ex Eastern National, 1990

| 245-260 | | Mercedes-Benz 709D | Reeve Burgess Beaver | B23F | 1989/90 | |

245	F245MVW	247	F247NJN	250	F250NJN	252	F252NJN	255	F255RHK	257	F257RHK	260	F260RHK
246	F246MVW	248	F248NJN	251	F251NJN	253	F253RHK	256	F256RHK	259	F259RHK		

No.	Reg	Chassis	Body	Seating	Year	Notes
301	H301LPU	Mercedes-Benz 709D	Reeve Burgess Beaver	B23F	1990	
302	H302LPU	Mercedes-Benz 709D	Reeve Burgess Beaver	B23F	1990	
303	H303LPU	Mercedes-Benz 709D	Reeve Burgess Beaver	B23F	1990	
304	H304LPU	Mercedes-Benz 709D	Reeve Burgess Beaver	B23F	1990	
305	H305LPU	Mercedes-Benz 709D	Reeve Burgess Beaver	B23F	1990	
306	H306LPU	Mercedes-Benz 709D	Reeve Burgess Beaver	B23F	1990	

| 389-395 | | Mercedes-Benz 709D | Reeve Burgess Beaver | B23F | 1991 | Ex Eastern National, 1992 |

389	H389MAR	390	H390MAR	391	H391MAR	392	H392MAR	393	H393MAR	394	H394MAR	395	H395MAR

No.	Reg	Chassis	Body	Seating	Year	Notes
396	K396GHJ	Mercedes-Benz 709D	Plaxton Beaver	B23F	1993	
397	K397GHJ	Mercedes-Benz 709D	Plaxton Beaver	B23F	1993	
398	K398GHJ	Mercedes-Benz 709D	Plaxton Beaver	B23F	1993	

| 411-419 | | Mercedes-Benz 0814D | Marshall | B27F | 1997 | |

411	R411VPU	413	R413VPU	415	R415VPU	417	R417VPU	419	R419VPU
412	R412VPU	414	R414VPU	416	R416VPU	418	R418VPU		

No.	Reg	Chassis	Body	Seating	Year	Notes
800	F800RHK	Mercedes-Benz 811D	Reeve Burgess Beaver	B31F	1989	
801	F801RHK	Mercedes-Benz 811D	Reeve Burgess Beaver	B31F	1989	
802	F802RHK	Mercedes-Benz 811D	Reeve Burgess Beaver	B31F	1989	
803	F803RHK	Mercedes-Benz 811D	Reeve Burgess Beaver	B31F	1989	
804	F804RHK	Mercedes-Benz 811D	Reeve Burgess Beaver	B31F	1989	

| 805-811 | | Mercedes-Benz 811D | Plaxton Beaver | B31F | 1992 | |

805	K805DJN	806	K806DJN	807	K807DJN	808	K808DJN	809	K809DJN	810	K810DJN	811	K811DJN

No.	Reg	Chassis	Body	Seating	Year	Notes
851	N851CPU	Dennis Dart 9SDL3053	Marshall C36	B17FL	1995	
852	N852CPU	Dennis Dart 9SDL3053	Marshall C36	B17FL	1995	
853	N853CPU	Dennis Dart 9SDL3053	Marshall C36	B17FL	1995	
854	N854CPU	Dennis Dart 9SDL3053	Marshall C36	B17FL	1995	

901-917		Dennis Dart 9SDL3016		Plaxton Pointer				B35F		1992		
901	K901CVW	**904**	K904CVW	**907**	K907CVW	**910**	K910CVW	**913**	K913CVW	**916**	K916CVW
902	K902CVW	**905**	K905CVW	**908**	K908CVW	**911**	K911CVW	**914**	K914CVW	**917**	K917CVW
903	K903CVW	**906**	K906CVW	**909**	K909CVW	**912**	K912CVW	**915**	K915CVW		

973-987		Dennis Dart SFD412		Plaxton Pointer				B40F		1996
973	N973EHJ	**976**	N976EHJ	**979**	N979EHJ	**982**	N982EHJ	**985**	N985EHJ
974	N974EHJ	**977**	N977EHJ	**980**	N980EHJ	**983**	N983EHJ	**986**	N986EHJ
975	N975EHJ	**978**	N978EHJ	**981**	N981EHJ	**984**	N984EHJ	**987**	N987EHJ

THORPES

D480PON	MCW Metrorider MF150/18	MCW	DP19F	1987	Ex Metroline, 1997
E930KYR	MCW Metrorider MF150/46	MCW	B25F	1987	Ex Rhondda, 1995
E134SNY	MCW Metrorider MF150/52	MCW	B23F	1988	Ex Cardiff, 1995
E135SNY	MCW Metrorider MF150/52	MCW	B23F	1988	Ex Cardiff, 1995
E137SNY	MCW Metrorider MF150/52	MCW	B23F	1988	Ex Cardiff, 1995
J514WTW	Mercedes-Benz 709D	Wadham Stringer Wessex	B19FL	1991	Ex Javelin, Wandsworth, 1997
J520WTW	Mercedes-Benz 709D	Wadham Stringer Wessex	B20FL	1991	Ex Javelin, Wandsworth, 1997
J529WTW	Mercedes-Benz 709D	Wadham Stringer Wessex	B23FL	1991	Ex Javelin, Wandsworth, 1997
J530WTW	Mercedes-Benz 709D	Wadham Stringer Wessex	B15FL	1991	Ex Javelin, Wandsworth, 1997
K2FET	Mercedes-Benz 709D	Alexander (Belfast) AM	B16FL	1993	
K3FET	Mercedes-Benz 709D	Alexander (Belfast) AM	B16FL	1993	
M190TEV	Mercedes-Benz 709D	WSC Wessex	B20FL	1994	Ex Javelin, Wandsworth, 1997
M191TEV	Mercedes-Benz 709D	WSC Wessex	B20FL	1994	Ex Javelin, Wandsworth, 1997
N100FET	Optare L970	Optare Excel	B27FL	1996	
N200FET	Optare L970	Optare Excel	B27FL	1996	
N300FET	Optare L970	Optare Excel	B27FL	1996	
N400FET	Optare L970	Optare Excel	B27FL	1996	

Special liveries

LT Stationlink : N100-400FET

The coach fleet is listed in London Coach Handbook

NOTES

NOTES